Mackinder

Frontispiece:
Mackinder at the age of 72

The original, by Sir William Rothenstein, hangs in the London School of Economics

MACKINDER

Geography as an
Aid to Statecraft

W. H. PARKER
M.A., M.Sc., D.Phil. (Oxon)

CLARENDON PRESS · OXFORD
1982

Oxford University Press, Walton Street, Oxford OX2 6DP
London Glasgow New York Toronto
Delhi Bombay Calcutta Madras Karachi
Kuala Lumpur Singapore Hong Kong Tokyo
Nairobi Dar es Salaam Cape Town
Melbourne Auckland
and associates in
Beirut Berlin Ibadan Mexico City Nicosia

Published in the United States by
Oxford University Press, New York

British Library Cataloguing in Publication Data
Parker, W. H.
Mackinder: geography as an aid to statecraft.
1. Mackinder, Sir Halford John
2. Geopolitics
I. Title
327.1'01'1   JC319
ISBN 0-19-823235-7

Library of Congress Cataloging in Publication Data
Parker, W. H. (William Henry), 1912–
Mackinder—geography as an aid to statecraft.
Bibliography: p.
Includes index.
1. Geopolitics. 2. Mackinder, Halford John,
Sir, 1861–1947. I. Title.
JC319.P28   327.1'01'10924   82-3623

ISBN 0-19-823235-7   AACR2

Printed and bound in Great Britain
by Butler & Tanner Ltd, Frome and London

Preface

This book is concerned with the ideas and ideals of a great
Englishman and is biographical only in so far as is necessary to
give the essential personal background to the intellectual causes
he strove to promote (Chapters 1, 2). Such causes were many
but chief among them were the establishment of geography in
Britain as a respectable academic discipline, and the promotion
of imperial unity. These two missions were related, for his intuitive perception of the true principles of applied geography
enabled him to see that Britain, unless integrated with her
imperial possessions into a single power, would rapidly decline,
while large continental states such as America, China, Russia
– and Germany too if successful in her territorial ambitions –
would become the great powers of the future. His 'heartland
theory', a by-product of this applied geography, has made him
one of the most influential thinkers of modern times. Terms he
coined, such as Heartland and World Island, found their way
into the minds and mouths of statesmen who may never have
read his books or heard his name. British Foreign Secretary
Ernest Bevin told the Cabinet in 1948 that 'physical control of
the whole World Island is what the Politburo is aiming at', and
American President Nixon wrote of Russia as the Heartland
power in his book *The Real War*. A. L. Rowse tells how, at a
meeting with the ex-president, 'our own Mackinder's concept
of geopolitics' was mentioned, adding that this is 'how Nixon
sees things from the summit of his experience' (*Daily Telegraph*,
25 April 1981).

However, Mackinder never intended to provide arguments
for anti-Russian or anti-Soviet policies. He would have been
happier to have been listened to when advocating the conser-
vation of British primacy, power, and prestige through the
adoption of his enlightened imperialism, his reformed capitalism, and his educated democracy, or when advocating the
preservation of the freedom of men and nations through his
balanced regionalism and his protected nationalism. Such
themes are discussed in Chapters 3 and 4. Chapter 5 looks at

Mackinder as a geographer, while Chapters 6, 7, and 8 are geopolitical.

I am indebted to all who have written on Mackinder before me, and in particular to Professor L. M. Cantor, Dr Brian Blouet, and the late Professor E. W. Gilbert. Professor Cantor very kindly lent me a copy of his unpublished thesis on Mackinder. I would like also to thank Dr Blouet, Professor Cantor, Mrs J. C. Malin, Dr D. I. Scargill, and Dr D. R. Stoddart for presenting me with offprints or reprints of relevant articles, and Mr P. C. Masters for help with photography. The Librarians and Staffs of the Bodleian Library, the Oxford School of Geography, Christ Church, the Royal Geographical Society, the Staff College, and the College of Preceptors have all rendered me valuable assistance. I am especially grateful to Dr Paul Coones for putting his remarkable bibliographical knowledge at my disposal, and for helping me in a thousand ways; and also to Mr W. A. Parker for his careful and critical reading of the manuscript.

Contents

MAPS

PLATES
Frontispiece. Mackinder at the age of 72

Chapter 1

Life and Work 1861–1905:
Oxford and Reading

Halford John Mackinder was born at Elswitha Hall, Caskgate Street, Gainsborough, in the county of Lincolnshire, on 15 February 1861. His father was Draper Mackinder, MD, FRCS, a doctor and the local medical officer of health; his mother, Fanny Anne, was the daughter of Halford Wootton Hewitt, twice mayor of Lichfield, and after whom he was named. Mackinder is thought to be a corruption of Mackindoe, and the family was Scottish in origin, having migrated to England after the 1745 rebellion. Perhaps because of his name Mackinder has occasionally been described as Scottish (e.g. de Blij 1967, p. 106; Cantor 1960, p. 17),* though he regarded himself as an Englishman.

Once, when urging that 'the study of the solid should come before that of the flat' in geographical teaching, he looked back to his nursery days for this illustration:

Among the memories of my childhood I have one so vividly to the point, that I am going to set it on record. In my nursery we used to 'play at cubes' as we said. I knew *practically* what a cube was before I knew what a square was. Our 'cubes' were bricks for building houses and railways, and all the other constructions of the nursery. They were none of your soft bricklets of pinewood, with rounded and dented edges, and with pictures painted over them. They were blocks of hard oak, a good three inches across, cut truly, so that each face was a square, each edge a line, and each angle a point. There was no trace of picture upon them. All the wall paintings and paperings in our houses were added by our telling to one another. (Mackinder 1914, p. 9)

The young Halford proved to be an intelligent, imaginative, inquiring, and active boy with a strong curiosity about natural

---

* The Harvard system of references has been used in this book. The author's name and date of publication are given in the text, with further particulars of the work quoted or referred to, given in the Bibliography.

phenomena; to this was soon added a love of the history of travel and exploration, an interest in international affairs, and a passion for making maps. The Trent eagre aroused his interest, and he made maps from explorations of the environs of Gainsborough. In September 1870 he started at Gainsborough Grammar School, and later recalled taking home the telegraphed news of the Prussian victory at Sedan which he had seen displayed outside the post office on his way from school. He remembered too writing a military history of the Franco-Prussian war at about the same time. While still at the grammar school he read the voyages of Captain Cook. He was, he recalled (1931a), 'rather a lonely boy'; he had two brothers (Augustus and Lionel), but they were younger by four and eight years. He also remembered (1930, p. 266) that 'when a boy' he 'travelled in a ship'; he does not say where or when, but it called at 'foreign ports'.

In 1874 (*aet.* 13) he was sent to Epsom College, a public school founded in 1854 for doctors' sons. His continuing curiosity as to the nature of things is illustrated by an anecdote:

When a boy I was once stranded at School during the Easter holidays because of measles at home, and happened to see in a newspaper that Professor Tyndall was to lecture at the Royal Institution. In my form we had been reading his pellucid lectures on 'Heat as a mode of Motion', so I wrote to him and explained that I was a schoolboy and short of pocket money, but that he was my hero. By the next post I received a ticket *gratis*. I went to the Head, got leave for Town, and heard Tyndall lecture on 'Fluorescence' and saw some wonderful experiments.[1]

He continued to read books on travel and history, and to make maps, claiming later (1928, p. 3) to have been 'caned for drawing maps' in Latin lessons. Already he felt an 'intuitive' love of geography, although school had nothing worthy of the name to offer; it suggested a unifying philosophy instead of 'chaos in the multiplicity of phenomena' (ibid.).

At Epsom he played rugby and was a member of the debating and dramatic societies; he won three essay prizes and contributed a remarkable article on 'Geological Epsom' to the school

[1] Autobiographical fragment in Mackinder Papers at School of Geography, Oxford. John Tyndall (1820–93) was Professor of Natural Philosophy at the Royal Institution from 1853 to 1887.

magazine. This 'shows him, though still quite young, the possessor of clear, incisive and astonishingly mature ideas on the study of geology, and of an admirable prose style' (Cantor 1960, p. 5). In 1878 (*aet.* 17) he was awarded the Gilchrist scholarship at St Bartholomew's Hospital. This, had he wished to follow his father in medicine, would have given him free training, but he preferred to work for entry to Oxford. In 1879 he failed narrowly to win scholarships at Exeter and Merton Colleges, and was offered an exhibition at Merton; but in 1880 he accepted a Christ Church junior studentship in Physical Science of £85 a year[2] for five years.

Had there been in 1880 an Honour School of Geography at Oxford there is little doubt that Mackinder would have read it. Actually he read Physical Science (*Scientia Naturalis*), concentrating on biology. From 1881 his studies were directed by H. N. Moseley, Linacre Professor of Comparative Anatomy, and he 'spent two happy years at the Museum under his influence'.[3] This influence was in the Darwin–Huxley tradition—Moseley had been the naturalist on the *Challenger*.[4]

In June 1883 (*aet.* 22) Mackinder took the examination for the Honour School of Physical Science and was placed in the first class, even though he had devoted much of his time and energy to political and military activities. He spoke in the second Oxford Union debate of his first term, and by the end of that term was taking part 'robustly' in debates. In his second term he moved a motion, and in his third (Trinity 1881) became Secretary. He was elected Treasurer in Trinity term 1882, and President in Trinity term 1883.[5] By then he must have suspected 'that he was at least as good as the best of his generation in the Union' (Blouet 1975, p. 8). His other great interest was the Army. He joined the OU Army Volunteer Reserve and was a captain in the University Rifle Corps. His interest in military

[2] Raised to £100 in 1882.
[3] Autobiographical fragment.
[4] The vessel circumnavigated the earth in 1872–6 in a scientific expedition jointly organized by the Royal Society and the Admiralty.
[5] 'The minute books convey the impression not only that Mackinder was constantly in the fray of the debates but that he was displaying considerable organizational ability' (Blouet 1975, p. 8); 'his gift of clear, incisive and forceful speech, possibly aided by the ability to show a combative spirit when occasion seemed to require, was a factor in his election as President of the Union' (Unstead 1949, p. 52).

history and strategy led him to join the Kriegspiel Club, which included many senior members of the University, notably H. B. George, the military historian.

Mackinder divided his fourth year at Oxford (1883-4) between history and geology. He sat the Final Honour School of Modern History in 1884 and was placed in the second class, no mean achievement for one who had spent a mere few months reading for this exacting school.[6] His concurrent geological labours were crowned with success when he won the Burdett-Coutts scholarship worth £115 a year for two years. He had probably by now worked out his philosophy of geography: it would consider human communities in their mutual relationships with physical environments, and so bridge the gap between physical science and the humanities. Formal study and training in geology and history would fit him to make the synthesis.

There was, however, no living to be made in geography—or so it seemed in the summer of 1884. He must embrace a profession, and in Michaelmas term he came up for a fifth year and began to read Law. His Oxford Union successes had probably convinced him that he might do well as a barrister, and he may have seen law as preliminary to politics. In the summer of 1885, however, he abandoned the Oxford law course and went to London[7] to join the chambers of a shipping lawyer specializing in international law, which, he said, was the most geographical aspect of law. Within a year he had passed his finals and was called to the Bar at the Inner Temple in the summer of 1886 (*aet.* 25).

Meanwhile, in 1885, an opportunity had presented itself which was to change the course of his life, and to lead to the rebirth of English geography and its establishment as a university subject. A close friend of his undergraduate days, Michael Sadler,[8] had become secretary to the Oxford University Extension which, since 1878, had been giving courses in various parts

[6] The distribution of candidates among the classes in 1884 was: I-8, II-14, III-27, IV-22 (*Oxford Univ. Calendar 1885*, p. 202).

[7] Lodging at 8 Old Quebec St., Portman Square (M. 1885).

[8] Sir Michael Ernest Sadler (1861-1943). Promoted education in the Oxford Univ. Extension 1885-95 and in the Board of Education 1895-1903. Vice-Chancellor of Leeds University 1911-23. Master of University College, Oxford 1923-34.

of the country. Sadler invited Mackinder to participate, and the impecunious law student gladly accepted; for not only would it help pay the expense of living in London, but it would give him a chance to work out and expound his ideas on the nature of geography. 'After all,' he remarked many years later (1921, p. 377), 'one of the best ways of learning a subject is to set to work to teach it!'

University Extension worked thus: 'lecturers were sent to give systematic courses in large towns, and the courses were followed by classes for the more earnest students. At the end of each course, examinations were held for those wishing to enter for them, and the papers were assessed by someone other than the lecturer' (Cantor 1960, p. 70). The work was organized by local committees who had to guarantee the expenses. They therefore sought popular subjects, and at first took some convincing that geographical courses would provide the necessary appeal. Audiences were drawn mainly from the lower-middle and working classes, and had a large proportion of elementary school teachers. Mackinder and Sadler (1891, p. 70) wrote that a gratifying characteristic of Extension work was 'the way in which it brings together students of very different ranks ... In an examination recently ... among those to whom were awarded certificates of distinction were a national school-mistress, a young lawyer, a plumber, and a railway signalman.' They had, moreover, 'been told several times by shrewd observers, of a change for the better in the conversation and social tone of some suburb of a manufacturing town as the result of the delivery of courses of Extension lectures' (ibid., p. 69). They set down the requirements for an Extension lecturer in terms that probably describe Mackinder himself and reflect his experience. He

must be strong enough to bear considerable fatigue. His occupation entails long and frequent journeys ... Moreover, the task of repeatedly lecturing to large audiences involves strain and excitement. The very intensity of the interest which the good lecturer takes in his work carries with it the danger of over-stimulation and consequent reaction.

He must also

possess some University distinction as evidence that he is competent to teach the subject or group of subjects on which he proposes to lecture. It is, however, the man of sound knowledge and many interests, rather than the learned specialist, who is needed ... The lecturer does not deal with children, but with grown men and women. He must therefore make their practical experience of life tell on the subject which he commends to their attention.

He must ... have some of the powers which go to make a good platform speaker. He cannot afford to weary his hearers, for they are not compelled to come to listen to him again. It is his difficult task to combine the lucidity and force of good platform-speaking with the accuracy and precision which characterize the scholar. (ibid., pp. 103–5)

Mackinder's first Extension lecture was given in the Rotherham Mechanics' Institute, where he lectured on physical geography[9] to about four hundred workmen, on 17 November 1885 (*aet.* 24). In the first months of 1886 he lectured at Bath, Gainsborough, and Lincoln, and soon enthusiastic reports were coming in. In May he was formally appointed University Extension Lecturer in Natural Science and Economic History (Cantor 1960, pp. 70–3). He did not lecture only on geography: among his earliest courses was one on 'Wealth and Wages'; the understanding of economics gained while preparing these lectures was used to good effect in his later political activities and in his writings. It was no easy task for a law student striving to pass his Bar examinations in the minimum time, to take on the preparation and delivery of so many lectures, to conduct the classes which followed, and to mark the essays of the more conscientious students, especially as extensive travel was involved.

The year 1886 was also momentous for British geography, which had decayed into a lamentable state. With minor exceptions it had no place in secondary and university education; where it was practised, it involved the memory principally and gave little stimulus to the brain. It had no unity of theme or purpose. But in 1886 two fresh but swelling streams merged to flow on into the twentieth century as a new academic river. The first had its source in Mackinder's 'intuitive' sympathy for geography and the passionate energy and missionary zeal with which

---

[9] M. also lectured at Rotherham on 14 Dec., 11 Jan. and 9 Feb. 1886. The subject matter he later would have called Physiography rather than Physical Geography, e.g. 'Glaciers and volcanoes', 'How we foretell tomorrow's weather'. He was 'frequently applauded' (Garnett 1967, pp. 21–2).

he was prepared to propagate it; the other sprang from the efforts of the Royal Geographical Society to redeem it from its lowly plight. How the Society, contributing financial help as well as its prestige, and Mackinder, bringing rare ability as well as fervour, together achieved the establishment of university geography at Oxford has already been well told (Unstead 1949, Scargill 1976), and need only be summarized here.

For some years an influential group within the Council of the RGS had believed the Society should do something for geographical education in Britain, although others thought it should confine itself to the furtherance of travel and exploration as heretofore. The 'educationalists' decided to 'strengthen their case by obtaining evidence of what was being done on the Continent and particularly in Germany.' Accordingly the Council, in 1884, appointed J. S. Keltie[10] as an 'inspector' of the situation abroad, and in 1885 he presented his report. 'The facts with their clear implications could not be disputed; the British neglect of Geography stood condemned' (Unstead 1949, pp. 49–50).[11]

Keltie had brought back an impressive collection of material used in the teaching of geography in Germany and elsewhere. The Society decided to put this on public display in the winter of 1885–6, and it was at this exhibition that Mackinder met Keltie, whose views on geography coincided with and reinforced his own. He promptly joined the RGS and, although continuing his law career for a while, started to lecture in University Extension on what he now significantly called 'the New Geography'. The enthusiastic reports which came back to Oxford about these lectures reached the ear of Galton[12], one of the more influential members of the RGS Council. As a result, the Society decided to make a grant towards Mackinder's lectures, and asked H. W. Bates, the naturalist of Amazon fame who was then

[10] Sir John Scott Keltie (1840–1927); editor of the *Statesman's Yearbook* 1884–1927, and of the *Geogrl J.* 1893–1917; served the RGS first as Librarian and then as Secretary.

[11] Compared with an almost total neglect in British secondary and university education, Keltie (1886, p. 37) found that 'in those [countries] concerning which I have obtained information—Belgium, Holland, Germany, Austria, France, Sweden, and Norway, and even Spain . . . It has the same treatment as history, as natural science, as physics and chemistry.'

[12] Sir Francis Galton (1822–1911), FRS, traveller, meteorologist, psychologist, founder of the school of eugenics.

Assistant Secretary of the Society, to send for the young man and get him to write down what he meant by this 'new' geography. This he did, and so impressed were the Council that he was asked to read a paper on it. Accordingly, on 31 January 1887, he spoke to a crowded meeting of the Society on 'The Scope and Methods of Geography'.

Mackinder later recalled (1931, p. 3) that his address was given to the accompaniment of an '*obligato* of seafaring language which came *sotto voce* from a worthy admiral ... who sat in the front row', and the young lecturer (*aet.* 25) was subjected to repeated interjections of 'damned cheek' from the same source (1931, p. 3).[13] The case for a geographical synthesis to replace a physiography taught by geologists and a political geography consisting of facts to be memorized, was generally well received. The paper was considered so important that the next meeting, on 14 February 1887, was allocated wholly to a discussion of it. *The Times* commented thus on the proceedings:

The last two meetings have been regular field-nights at the Royal Geographical Society. The Society has been virtually asked to say whether it will commit itself to the New Geography or remain behind the age and all other similar societies of the first rank. Hitherto, as everyone knows, the meetings of this most popular of societies have been a favourite resort of those who wish to be amused for an hour or two by listening to red-hot tales of exploration and adventure. (18 Feb. 1887)

Mackinder's paper was 'a classic document in the history of the development of British geography' (Unstead 1949, p. 53).[14] For long it was seen as the starting-point of modern geography in Britain and is so regarded abroad (e.g. Troll 1952, Isachenko 1971). It is now recognized that not all its ideas were new— there had been voices crying in the wilderness. The difference now was that a man had arrived who was not merely content with 'crying', but followed it up by energetically cultivating the wilderness with every means possible—lobbying, speaking, lecturing, writing, examining, travelling, and then populating it with a growing host of teachers and disciples who went forth

---

[13] Blouet (1975) identifies the 'worthy admiral' as 'Admiral Erasmus Ommanney (1814-1904), a highly distinguished commander and explorer.'

[14] For further discussion of 'The scope and methods of geography' see below, pp. 107-9.

from his lectures imbued with the ideas and trained in the methods of what was, in every practical respect, in the British educational context, a new geography. Mackinder himself used a somewhat similar analogy: geography had been 'a no-man's land, encumbered with weeds and dry bones . . . it was necessary to reannex the garden and to clear and cultivate the waste' (1921, p. 377).

A beginning was made at Oxford where well-disposed historians had told the RGS that what was wanted to help things forward 'was a representative of Geography who would secure a hearing by his wide knowledge and power of making the subject attractive' (Unstead 1949, p. 52). Now that both University and Society knew that such a person had been found, formal negotiations between them re-opened in July 1886 and made real progress: on 28 February 1887 the Vice-Chancellor informed the Society of the University's proposal to appoint a Reader in Geography for five years with a stipend of £300, and the Society undertook to pay half (Scargill 1976, p. 443).[15] In June 1887 Mackinder (*aet.* 26) was appointed the first Reader in Geography at Oxford since Richard Hakluyt in the sixteenth century.

During his initial quinquennium (1887–92) Mackinder lectured on an average twice a week during term time. When he was 70 years old he recalled (1931, p. 2) how in his first lecture he 'had an audience of three, one man and two women. The man was a don who told me he knew the geography of Switzerland, for he had just read Baedeker from cover to cover. The two ladies brought their knitting.' His memory was slightly at fault, as in October 1887 he had written to Bates that his audience consisted of '2 undergraduates, 1 BA, 1 MA, 1 DD, and 2 ladies'; for his second lecture 'the whole of Monday's audience returned except the MA, and 2 more arrived, 1 more undergraduate and 1 more lady . . . They were evidently interested, indeed the BA quite enthusiastic.'[16] He insisted on devoting half his time to physical geography, undeterred by the

---

[15] To help him fit himself for his new post the RGS also voted him £50, which he used in the summer of 1887 to visit the Brenner Pass and make 'a careful study of the Brenner section of the great trade route between the Adriatic and Flanders' (Cantor 1960, p. 14).

[16] Letter in the RGS archives, dated 28 Oct. 1887, qu. by Cantor (1960, pp. 113–14).

negligible demand. At the end of his first year he wrote (1888d, p. 532): 'I have never been without an audience, a fate not altogether unknown just now to Oxford Professors and Readers and I shall continue to devote one course of lectures to such subjects until that fate befalls me.' But even after his fifth year he had to report (1892a, p. 399) that 'on the physical side, my instruction has been required by only two undergraduates'. This was because physical geography 'fits in even partially with no recognized course of study in the University'.

On the human side the new Reader was far more successful; there was a potential audience in the large numbers reading Modern History, for they were required to know some geography. An audience of fifty became common for these lectures; numbers never fell below twenty and on occasion reached eighty. When he first took up the Readership, Mackinder had hoped to teach a regional geography 'consisting of a complex of patterns', but 'in order to enlist a class for a novel subject', he 'had to begin by teaching European history on a geographical background' (Mackinder 1890b, p. 420).

At first the Reader found that 'beyond a blackboard, and a few borrowed maps' he was 'totally without the necessary means of illustration', but in 1889 the University granted him £100 for the purchase of necessary materials; he was able to buy some German wall maps and 'at least the nucleus of a collection of the necessary apparatus' (Mackinder 1888d, p. 532; RGS 1892a, p. 490). He found the means to provide his hearers with copies of his syllabus in a novel way: 'there has been a small and fluctuating attendance of residents in Oxford not connected with the University, and on them I have felt justified in imposing a nominal fee, with the proceeds of which a syllabus of each lecture has been printed and distributed to the class' (Mackinder 1890b, p. 419).

He was always seeking ways of furthering the subject, and in November 1888 he was urging the RGS to help with the institution of a University prize. Eventually he had his way, and in 1891 an annual grant of £100, half from the University and half from the RGS, was introduced for travel and research abroad. He hoped (1891, p. 429) that 'in this way we may induce a few men to spend a postgraduate year in the study of geography, and that we may be able to mark one of them each year as a specialist suited to teach geography'. The Warden of Merton and the Provost of Queen's had supported the proposal, and Mackinder was obviously not backward in making friends in his cause. His position had been strengthened by his appointment as an *ex officio* member of the Board of the Faculty of Modern History, 'the body of the University whose function is to regulate the studies and examinations of the Honour School of Modern History' (Mackinder 1892a). He scarcely mentions the strong prejudice against geography as a university subject at Oxford. But as Cantor (1960, p. 152) writes, 'only those familiar with the difficulties which attend the introduction of a new study into the curriculum of an ancient university can appreciate the labour which this achievement required and the qualities demanded to obtain it.' Many years later, in a letter to Weigert (1942, p. 5), he wrote, 'When I started teaching geography at Oxford in 1887, I was opposed by quite a few liberal thinkers on the ground that the study of geography lent itself to the growth of militarism and imperialism.'

On 3 January 1889 (*aet.* 27) Halford Mackinder was married by the Bishop of Winchester to Emilie Catherine ('Bonnie'), second daughter of Dr C. D. Ginsburg, a leading Old Testament scholar, at Christ Church, Virginia Water. It was perhaps the need to support a wife that led him to increase the number of Extension lectures given in various parts of the country from 102 in 1887-8 to 112 in 1888-9, for his Oxford salary, set against his needs, was, in his words, a mere 'pittance'. His wife may well have objected to so much absence from home, for in 1889-90 he reduced the number of Extension lectures to 66 given in nine different towns, still a formidable task. In his report to the RGS he gave his reason for the drop as the need to devote more time to University work; yet in the next academic year, 1890-1, when he increased his tally of University lectures from 42 to 56, he also gave 102 Extension lectures in fifteen towns. He said later (1921, p. 378) that 'as my stipend was not very large, I threw myself into Extension lecturing, and in three years travelled 30,000 miles and taught several thousand pupils.' And behind the travelling and the lecturing lay untold hours of administration, thought, preparation, marking, and unscheduled consultation and advice.

As if all this was not enough, he was in demand from training colleges, keen to know more about the 'new geography', and he could not deny them, for teachers were the key to the future. Most successful were four lectures on the teaching of geography given at the College of Preceptors in London in November 1889: 'on the occasion of each, the room was packed with an audience of 400 teachers of all grades. Many came considerable distances, several even from Brighton' (Mackinder 1890b). Also in 1889 he gave nine lectures to 700 students at the Extension summer school at Oxford, spoke at Rugby School and University College, London, and travelled up to Edinburgh to deliver a paper to the Scottish Geographical Society in December. He served too as examiner and syllabus-setter for the Oxford and Cambridge Board and the Oxford Local Examinations, realizing the importance of examinations in influencing how a subject is taught. And in 1888 he had joined with Keltie and Ravenstein as editor of a series of books on exploration. Listed among the volumes either 'ready' or 'in an advanced state of preparation', was *Ross and the Antarctic* by H. J. Mackinder. This book never appeared for, as H. R. Mill wrote in his autobiography (1951, p. 76), 'Mackinder found that his other commitments prevented him from writing it, and the task was handed over to me.' It was at this time that an Old Epsomian reported in the school magazine that, 'Mackinder we rarely see, so manifold and engrossing are his duties as Reader in Geography. His lectures are well attended, and if I am to judge from an opinion expressed to me by a student of the fair sex, they are also exceedingly popular' (qu. in Cantor 1960, p. 17).

In the Easter vacation of 1892 he went to Philadelphia to represent Oxford at the American Association for the Extension of University Teaching, and lectured there. He also visited Harvard, Princeton, Johns Hopkins, Washington, and Chicago, lecturing and investigating the state of geography. The President of the University of Chicago asked him to join the faculty. As he was embarking at New York to return to England he received a telegram from Christ Church, Oxford, offering him a studentship (fellowship) if he would do Extension work at Reading. Michael Sadler, himself a Student of Christ Church and the able Secretary of Oxford University Extension, had persuaded the College to sponsor an Extension college at Reading, conveniently close to Oxford, and where there was an active and successful Extension association, and he had convinced them that Mackinder was the man to run it. On 27 May 1892 the Reading University Extension Association accepted Christ Church's offer of Mackinder's services as Principal, and on 29 September, Reading University Extension College was opened by the Dean of Christ Church. As the new college lacked accommodation and funds, the new Principal's task was not easy, especially as this was an additional responsibility imposed upon an already busy man. It was a job, however, that suited Mackinder's combative and determined spirit and drew forth his political talent and organizing ability. He later confessed that in this struggle he had committed 'irregularities which would set the hair of inspectors on end' (Cantor 1960, p. 96), and his principal lieutenant and eventual successor wrote of how he 'ploughed ahead, leaving a wake of troubled waters', and how

this College of ours seemed always to be battling upon all its fronts ... No doubt the College of 1892 might have been moored under the willows in a local backwater. Mackinder decided otherwise. 'I have never known', said the Bishop of Oxford in 1901, 'a more aspiring and restless institution.' When Mackinder left us, there were some who sighed for an interval of quiescence. (Childs 1933, pp. 11, 129)

Cantor (1960, p. 91) has written:

From the beginning Reading broke nearly all the previously established rules. Unlike other civic educational institutions, which have subsequently become universities, it was not in a great industrial city. It was not a 'College of Science', and was financed neither by a single great benefactor nor by a municipal corporation.

Instead, it was 'sustained by the dynamic personality of H. J. Mackinder' (Armytage 1955, p. 227).

His versatility was reflected in the multifarious activities of the College. It provided a variety of courses for students leaving the various grades of school at 13/14, 16, and 18, and for whole-time, part-time, day and evening students:

By 1894, it had also become the pupil-teacher centre for the district, and in this respect was virtually a secondary school. It also ran the early equivalent of refresher courses for teachers, and from its own resources provided peripatetic teachers who visited neighbouring schools giving instruction, especially in history, geography and fine art. Moreover, it was now authorized to grant diplomas in

Agriculture, was in process of building a new Dairy Institute and had agreed on plans for a new Art Department. (Cantor 1960, p. 92)

[Mackinder] was the Principal of Reading College for 11 years, from 1892 to 1903, eleven years of continuous progress. In that time, new departments were gradually added, degree work was developed in the Humanities and in the Sciences, new buildings arose, and corporate life developed through various societies. In 1899, the College was affiliated to the University of Oxford; in 1899 too it established its own scheme of teacher training. In 1902, the Treasury Commissioners examined its work, approved of what they saw, and recommended that it be given a Treasury Grant of £1,000 a year and the rank of a University College. Thus, on Saturday, August 2nd, 1902, at the Court of Governors, the name of the College was officially changed to that of University College, Reading. (ibid., pp. 92–3)

Mackinder continued to give adult education lectures until 1903. Every winter from 1893 to 1898 he lectured in London under the joint auspices of the Royal Geographical Society and the London University Extension Society. A series of ten lectures on the Relations of Geography to History in Europe and Asia was given in the first three months of 1893 to audiences of 'two hundred persons from all parts of London'; these were repeated in 1894 at Gresham College. In the winter of 1894–5 there were twenty-five lectures, and the subject was changed to the History of Geography and Geographical Discovery; there were supplementary classes after the lectures and essays were set for the keener students, mainly teachers. But Mackinder had to report (1895c, p. 26) that 'on three occasions I was absent owing to illness and my place was most kindly and efficiently taken by Dr H. R. Mill[17], who conducted the Easter examination. In 1895–6 there were twenty of these London lectures on the Principles of Geography, and in 1896–7, twenty-five on Europe, Asia and Africa. In 1897–8 the average audience was 220; of these 140 also attended the classes. The London Extension Society was highly pleased, reporting

an exceptional degree of success among the pupil–teachers who have attended his lectures in great numbers and with the most beneficial effects. The Council of the Royal Geographical Society, to whose generous support it is in great measure due that these courses are

[17] H. R. Mill (1861–1950) was the Librarian of the RGS. The examination was undertaken by Sir Clements Markham, its President. For the marking of the essays M. had 'the able assistance of Mr W. G. de Burgh, MA, of Balliol College, Oxford.'

maintained, cannot but be gratified at the continuously satisfactory results of their policy. (qu. in Cantor 1960, pp. 99–100)

He continued to travel the country giving Extension lectures, and among his other speaking engagements in the 1890s were: a speech at the annual conference of the Oxford University Extension at Bournemouth in 1894; a discourse on the teaching of geography to the Sheffield branch of the Teachers' Guild in 1895; five lectures to an audience of 600 teachers at University College, Liverpool, in 1897; and addresses to the Association of Principals and Lecturers of Training Colleges, and to the College of Preceptors in 1898–9. He was also Oxford's representative to education conferences in Paris, Brussels, and Le Havre (Mackinder 1895a, pp. 24–5). His Bournemouth speech was significant because its educational topic was widened into a social and political theme; it certainly impressed its hearers. The chairman of the local committee wrote:

I have never listened to a speech of greater force, or one delivered with more perfect elocution. To describe its effect in sufficiently moderate language seems to need some control of the pen ... its general effect upon the audience (of 150) as seen from the platform was a remarkable testimony to the power of oratory to entrance the listeners. (qu. in Cantor 1960, p. 101)

The *Oxford University Gazette* remarked that the speech would not soon be forgotten by those who heard it.

This period also saw the beginnings of Mackinder's connection with the London School of Economics. The School was founded by Sidney Webb in 1895, using money from the Hutchinson Bequest. Hewins, the first Director, was an Oxford man who had known Mackinder as a colleague in University Extension; he now appointed him to lecture part-time in geography. Webb and Hewins hoped to gather 'a varied group of specialists who would have an approach to the pressing problems of the day quite different from that of the professors of the older universities' whose outlook seemed to them too narrow and abstract (Hayek 1946, p. 5). Mackinder fitted these requirements. In his first session (1886–7) he gave twenty-eight lectures, and his class 'though small, was remarkable for the number of students which it contained from foreign universities, chiefly Russian, Japanese and American' (Mackinder 1897, p. 653).

He remained Reader in Geography at Oxford, the University having renewed his appointment in 1892, with the RGS again agreeing to pay half his salary. There was continued progress. In 1893 he was able to report 'attendances ... considerably larger than any which I have yet been able to record'. In 1896–7 'a tutor and his pupils in one of the colleges asked me to supplement my public teaching by giving to them a short course of private lectures'; in the following year three colleges enlisted his help in this way. In 1898–9 the lecture attendances were 'the largest since the readership was established' and totalled over a hundred during Hilary term (ninety-three men from eighteen colleges and thirteen ladies from three colleges). But physical geography still languished: in one year he 'only had the opportunity of giving a little instruction in that subject to one undergraduate and two or three ladies'.[18]

In 1895 Mackinder began to agitate strongly for the establishment of a London institute or school of geography in which a complete training could be given and a supply of competent teachers produced. His visit to Harvard in 1892 seems to have suggested the idea of a separate department, for he came back full of praise for the geographical institute there; but Reading had then become his immediate preoccupation. It was the great success of his Gresham College lectures that brought the matter again to the fore; it seemed that, just as a permanent adult education college had grown out of Extension lectures at Reading, so a geographical institute might develop in London out of his winter classes there. London seemed the ideal centre for such an institute because of its great population and accessibility, and because a new teaching university was about to be established there in which prejudice against and resistance to a new subject would be small compared with Oxford. He was also becoming politically ambitious and a London base would be more advantageous for him personally.

His argument for an institute was logical: there was little point in further advancing geography at university level until there was a demand from undergraduates who had been taught it well at school; this presupposed the availability of trained geography schoolmasters, and this in turn presupposed facilities

[18] The quotations and information in this paragraph are from his annual reports published in the *Geogrl J.*

for training them. As he believed that geography was essential for the elementary education of an imperial people, he was not only interested in the public schools as suppliers to the universities, but also in the whole educational system:

Of course we look forward to the training of a few specialists, but we must have—forming the lowest layer of the pyramid—a great body of students who obviously affect the community, and who would learn their elementary work in the same school in which the highest work would be done ... Sooner or later a teaching university is going to be organized in London, and this scheme may go in as an entire faculty of geography. We should thus teach the teachers; we should get men from Oxford and Cambridge to take one year's course, who, adding to their history or mathematics or whatever subject they had taken, would then have a greater value when they went back to the schools. (Mackinder 1896b, p. 91)

He had been Reader at Oxford for eight years, and although his work was highly successful, he was but an adjunct to the History School, and further progress did not seem likely. He was convinced that Oxford was 'not the place for planting our educational tree' (Stoddart 1975, p. 11). At the sixth International Geographical Congress, held in London in 1895, he gave his reasons. There were at Oxford seven faculties or subject-groups, and geography could be introduced 'only as a subordinate subject in one of these seven groups, unless indeed, you are ready to take the bold step of demanding an eighth group for that subject alone'. But 'the formation of an eighth group must necessarily involve not simply a single teacher, but a number of teachers, a whole faculty as it were.' There was 'no money available for the erection of such a grand school of geography' for 'the value of university lands has gone down to an unprecedented extent'. In fact, 'if we are to succeed at all in our scheme for the introduction of geography, it is absolutely essential that we should subordinate it to the history faculty' (Mackinder 1896b, 91).

The RGS was also dissatisfied with the progress at Oxford, and looked favourably on Mackinder's project for a London Institute. In 1897 it discontinued its annual grant of £150 towards the Reader's salary:[19]

---

[19] The University decided to continue the Readership, but increased its share (£150) to only £200, so that M. lost a third of his salary.

The Council did not contemplate originally that it would be necessary for them to subsidize the Readership for more than five years. They at least hoped that in ten years the object which they had in view would have been accomplished. It was hoped by that time that the subject would have taken sufficient hold in the University, that it would be accorded a substantial place in examinations and that thereby the great public schools would have been induced to take it up in earnest. (qu. in Scargill 1976, p. 446)

Markham, the Society's President, expressed the hope that such instruction as Mackinder was giving at Gresham College, London, might 'eventually be placed on a permanent basis', and in December 1895 the Secretary, Keltie, wrote to the Director of the London School of Economics asking whether the School would be prepared to co-operate in such a scheme. But the LSE had only been open for three months, and it was too early to give practical consideration to such an idea. However, in May 1897 Markham affirmed that, 'The Council has now resolved to give a large measure of support, out of Society funds, to a London School of Geography, if such an institution be successfully established under Mr Mackinder's auspices' (Cantor 1962, p. 34).

Yet the Society hesitated before committing itself to the necessary financial support, and decided, before proceeding, to try Oxford. Markham wrote to the Vice-Chancellor in June 1898 that they were thinking of founding a School of Geography at London, but giving Oxford a chance of pre-empting this, and offering to go halves in the cost. His letter concluded: 'I may now draw your attention to the fact that at Berlin, Vienna and Harvard Universities there are schools of geography well equipped, and each provided with several teachers. My suggestion is to help to found an equivalent school at Oxford, which would stand alone in this country' (Scargill 1976, p. 447). The University reacted favourably and promptly: proposals for the setting-up of the School were finally approved on 16 May 1899. Mackinder (*aet.* 38) retaining his post as Reader, was appointed Director of the new Department; his salary reverted to £300, and he was to have an assistant and two part-time lecturers. Premises were made available and equipped on the upper floor of the Old Ashmolean Museum. A. J. Herbertson was brought from Edinburgh with the title of 'Assistant to the Reader and

Lecturer in Regional Geography', and the lecturers were to be H. N. Dickson (physical geography) and G. B. Grundy (ancient geography).

Mackinder now held posts concurrently at Oxford, Reading, and London,[20] in each of which he was doing pioneering work of an exacting kind. Each would have been a full-time job in itself for someone without his energy and resourcefulness; but although he was inevitably away from one or other place when some thought he should not have been, his talent and flair were such as to more than compensate for his absence. He was a pluralist of the best kind.

Reading College and the Oxford School of Geography were not the only lasting institutions launched by Mackinder in the 1890s. He also took the lead in the formation of the Geographical Association of Great Britain, the association of British teachers of geography. A public-school master, B. B. Dickinson, wrote in 1892 to the RGS suggesting the exchange of lantern slides among schoolmasters; the Society referred the matter to Mackinder who called a meeting of those interested in the Senior Common Room of Christ Church, his Oxford college, on 20 May 1893. Although those who attended had come to talk about the slide–exchange, 'Mr Mackinder, with his well-known directness, summed up the discussion and proposed the formation of an Association for the improvement of the status and teaching of Geography' (qu. in Unstead 1949, p. 55). The first general meeting of this new society was held in December 1894 when Mackinder spoke on 'geography as a training of the mind'.[21]

Although he had been pressing for a university geography department for years, the rather sudden agreement between the RGS and Oxford to open the School of Geography in October 1899 cannot have been altogether welcome. Apart from the fact that he would have preferred it to have been in London, the new development was unfortunate in its timing; he was planning

[20] The LSE post was part-time until 1900, but M. was also giving the Extension course at Gresham College from 1893 to 1898.

[21] For the foundation of the Geographical Association see Fleure (1953) and Warrington (1947, 1953). There seems some reluctance to accord M. the honour of founding the GA. Even Gilbert (1951, p. 6) writes of Dickinson as 'rightly regarded as the founder of the Geographical Association', but as the idea and the initiative both appear to have come from M., he must at least be regarded as the *primus inter pares* of the co-founders.

an assault upon Mount Kenya for the long vacation of that year, and by the time the institution of the School was approved and he appointed its Director, his preparations were well advanced:

Quietly I worked at surveying with Cole of the R.G.S. in the vacations of 1897 and 1898, and spent some weeks with a good alpine guide around Zermatt and so proved that I was steady of hand and sure of foot. A professional neither in surveying nor climbing to be sure, but fairly useful and safe in good expert company, and not likely to bring a party to disaster, or to make a muddle with theodolite and plane table. (qu. in Blouet 1975, p. 13)

Mackinder was perhaps still conscious of his involvement in the controversy between 'educationalists' and 'explorationists': between what many saw as the 'theoretical' and the 'practical'. He may well not himself have been fully satisfied to be wholly an academic, however successful. Many years later he said that, 'at that time most people would have had no use for a geographer who was not an adventurer and explorer'. The much easier—though higher—peak of Kilimanjaro had recently been climbed by a German, 'and it was likely that the idea of climbing Kenya was in the air'. Mackinder, who was later to appear almost obsessed with the rivalry between Britain and Germany, naturally wished this more difficult task to be achieved by an Englishman. The recent building of the Uganda railway meant that two-thirds of the distance from the coast to the mountain could now be covered expeditiously, and there was no time to be lost if he was not to have competitors.[22]

In 1887 Count Teleki had climbed to 14,000 feet, and in 1893 Gregory had got 2,000 feet higher. Mackinder aimed not merely at reaching the summit but at a 'thorough scientific examination of the mountain and its vicinity'; he therefore took along not only two Alpine mountaineers, but also two naturalists recommended by the Natural History Museum. He was accompanied as well by Campbell Hausburg, his wife's uncle, 'a remarkable shot with a rifle and an expert photographer', who paid most of the expenses; the RGS also helped financially.

[22] It is likely that Mount Kenya was chosen as the scene of M's exploit because of a relationship between his wife and Hilda Hinde, the wife of S. L. Hinde, a British official at Nairobi; Hilda Hinde was living with Lady Mackinder in her last years in Switzerland.

Mackinder left London on 8 June 1899 (*aet.* 38), and his party of six sailed from Marseilles on the 10th; eighteen days later they reached Zanzibar where they recruited sixty-six Swahilis. The Uganda railway took them from Mombasa to Nairobi, where they hired two Masai guides and ninety-six Kikuyu tribesmen. On 26 July the 170-strong expedition left Nairobi and that evening pitched their first camp. The next three weeks were spent in crossing hilly and partly forested country to the foot of the mountain. Difficulties and dangers abounded: smallpox was rampant in the area; on one occasion 'the whole body of Kikuyu porters attempted to desert, and were only checked by a display of firearms'; on 6 August an arrow fell at Mackinder's feet, and the party 'rather nervously climbed some 500 feet under the eyes of spearmen perched on the rocks above us' (Mackinder 1900).

On 17 August the base camp was pitched at the foot of the mountain, some of the Kikuyu porters were paid off and sent home, and a party was sent off under Sulimani, the Swahili headman, in search of food. Mackinder, with the mountain party, then began the ascent; they moved up through the forest zone and on the morrow pitched their half-way camp at 10,300 feet. The next two or three days were spent reconnoitring the mountain. But on 24 August Mackinder had to return to the base camp because of news that Sulimani's party had been ambushed with the loss of two Swahilis, and had not returned with provisions. The situation was critical:

We found ourselves in the midst of the desert, with the only fertile region in our neighbourhood in hostility against us. Nothing remained but to break up our base camp and to send the porters to feed themselves elsewhere; they were accordingly despatched with Saunders [one of the naturalists] over the Saltima range—crossed for the first time by a white man—to the Government station at Naivasha. All the food that could be got together amounted to six days' rations for a ten days' journey, but owing to Saunders's pluck and determination, the detachment reached its destination safely. (Mackinder 1900a, p. 107)

Mackinder then reclimbed the mountain to where César Ollier and Joseph Brocherel, the two Alpine mountaineers, had established the final camp and built a stone hut, and on 30 August the three men made their first attempt on the peak, spending the night at 16,800 feet; but the next day they found their progress cut off by an impassable chasm, and had to return to the top camp. Thence Hausburg, César, and Joseph made a photographic reconnaissance of the peak while Mackinder went down to base for news of the parties who had gone for food. As there was none, he decided that they would all have to make for Naivasha 'lest starvation overtake us', but in the nick of time Sulimani and Saunders arrived back with food and a military escort. A final attempt on the mountain was then decided upon, and so, while Hausburg led the bulk of the expedition to Naivasha, Mackinder with the four remaining white men and 'fifteen picked black men' as porters, again ascended the mountain.

At noon on 12 September Mackinder, César, and Joseph left the top camp and began the difficult climb over the loose stone of moraines, across the ice of glaciers, and up the steep face of rocky arêtes. There was one 'precipitous ascent of perhaps 30 feet' where their 'chief difficulty was with the loose condition of the stone ... the jointing was into blocks, many of them over-hanging, and they often came away in the hand'. They spent the night on a niche in the rock, with 'just room ... to lie side by side, and grew stiff and cold-footed' (1930a, p. 531).

On the 13th they were away again at dawn, having to cut steps in a hanging glacier to make their way across: 'at first we traversed the ice obliquely upward, each step requiring thirty blows with the axe ... The glacier was so steep that our shoulders were close to it. Had we fallen we should have gone over an ice cliff to the Darwin Glacier several hundred feet below.' At noon they reached the summit (17,040 feet), and after spending forty minutes there, made their perilous way down to the top camp, reaching it at 10.20 p.m., 'hungry and weary, but triumphant'.

Before leaving the mountain, Mackinder carried out a plane-table survey of its upper part, crossing the heads of six valleys to which he gave names, including Hausburg's and his own. On 21 September he began the journey home, and arrived in London on 30 October. His return and the success of his mission were reported in *The Times* on 2 November, but the first news of the mountain's conquest to reach Europe appears to have been a telegram read at the Berlin meeting of the Inter-

national Geographical Congress at the beginning of October.
On 22 January 1900 Mackinder described his adventure to the
Royal Geographical Society, summarising the results as follows:

a plane table sketch of the upper part of Kenya, together with rock
specimens, two route surveys along lines not previously traversed, a
series of meteorological and hypsometrical observations, photographs
by the ordinary and by the Ives colour processes, collections of mam-
mals, birds and plants, and a small collection of insects. (1900, p. 475)

Sir Thomas Holdich, Vice-President of the Society, in introducing the paper, threw an interesting sidelight on the history
of colour photography: 'This is the first time, I believe, in which
the art of colour photography has been applied to the illustration of a scientific expedition; at any rate, it is the first time the
results have been shown in this room.'

Thirty years later Mackinder (1930a) gave a more detailed
account of the actual climb to the summit. In it he referred to
'that holiday many years ago', but his feat was described by one
who later attempted the mountain (Dutton 1929, p. 108) as 'no
mere holiday climb, but a long-drawn-out trial of skill and
endurance, gloriously brought to success', and the British Re-
sident at Nairobi told the RGS in 1900:

I think he has said too little of the difficulties he had to overcome. He
came into the country at a time when it was famine-stricken ... as a
consequence, great difficulty was experienced in getting food ...
shortly before Mr Mackinder's expedition started we had been involved in trouble with the natives, whom we know to be very treach-
erous. We lost one officer and a number of men, and for that reason
did not perhaps encourage Mr Mackinder to go to Mount Kenya as
much as we might have done. With famine among primitive natives,
small-pox almost invariably goes hand-in-hand, and an epidemic was
raging from Mombasa to the Uganda border. It was only with the
greatest care and most stringent precautions that Mr Mackinder
succeeded in getting his caravan through the country without contam-
ination. He has laid no stress on these points, but his pluck in dealing
with difficult situations ... had more to do with his success than he
implied in his paper. (*Geogrl J.* xv, pp. 477–8)

And there is no doubt that he had demonstrated organizing
ability, leadership, judgement, resolution, and courage of a
high order. As he acknowledged, success was also due to the
loyalty, bravery, and skill of his companions, especially César

Ollier, 'a fine man both physically and in character'. The mountain was not again climbed to the summit until 1929 (by Shipton and Harris); it succumbed a third time in 1943 to Felice Benuzzi, after his escape from a Kenyan POW camp (Benuzzi 1952).[23] There had been many unsuccessful attempts.

The School of Geography had perforce to open without its Director in October 1899, and as a result serious work did not begin until January 1900. Arriving back late from Africa, Mackinder seems to have got off on the wrong foot. There was resentment at his frequent absences: he had to attend to his duties at Reading and London, and to keep his many other academic engagements, not to mention increasing political interests. To make matters worse, his part-time lectureship at the LSE was elevated in 1902 to a full-time lectureship in Economic Geography.[24] His duties were

to give a course of not less than 60 lectures on Economic and Political Geography, extending over all three terms of the academic year;
to give in every session not less than one course of lectures of such length as may be approved by the Senate on Applications of Geography to definite Economic and Political Problems;
to supervise the work of all students in this department;
to advise in the organisation of the Geography Department of the School of Economics. (qu. in Cantor 1960, p. 160)

Rather a tall order for a man who was at the same time Reader in Geography and Director of the School of Geography at Oxford, and Principal of University College, Reading.[25] In

[23] These were purely mountaineering feats. M. and his party also made a scientific study. This work was resumed by Spink (1945).

[24] 'In 1898, the London University Act changed the University to a teaching one; hitherto it had been merely an examining body. Whereupon the School of Economics applied for admission as a School of the University. This was agreed to the following March and took formal effect from the beginning of the 1900 session ... its fourteen regular lecturers became teachers of the University ... As Mackinder's post was only part-time it was not until May 1902 that he was elected an "Appointed Teacher of the University in Economic Geography"' (Cantor 1960, p. 160).

[25] In 1903 M. lectured once a week at the Oxford School (in Hilary term on The Historical Geography of Europe). His sixty lectures at the LSE were made up of 'Thirty lectures on: i The Geographical Basis of Trade; ii The Economic Geography of Britain; iii World Routes and Trades' and 'Thirty lectures for candidates for the Intermediate Examination for the degree of B.Sc. in Economics'; these included a course of ten lectures on 'The Economic and Strategic Geography of the Great Powers during the Nineteenth Century'; he also held a seminar in geography 'throughout the year'. At Reading, besides his duties as Principal, he gave a course on 'The Geography of Europe' (*Geogrl Teacher* ii (1903), pp. 33–9).

1903 he finally gave up his Oxford Extension work and resigned his Reading post, but only to become instead Director of the London School of Economics. Yet for undergraduate audiences at Oxford he remained the star performer: 'his were the only official University lectures at Oxford which regularly concluded with applause' (Gilbert 1947, p. 95). Despite the setting-up of the new School of Geography, his impact continued to be mainly on the History school where it was by no means negligible. In 1904 he writes that his 'lectures on historical geography are regularly attended by a class of 120, the great majority being candidates for honours in modern history. To my knowledge, at least two firsts have been given mainly for excellence in geography' (*The Times* 22 Nov. 1904).

Mackinder returned from Africa not only to his various administrative and lecturing responsibilities, but also to sit down and write a geography of the British Isles, thus putting precept into practice. The result was *Britain and the British Seas*, 'one of the few classics of modern geographical literature' (Gilbert 1947) for, 'In lucidity of language which is used to clothe the thoughts of a clear and brilliant brain, it has never been surpassed' (Stamp 1947). It was reviewed in the *Manchester Guardian* (7 Feb. 1902) as 'the raising of geography from the dead'. Forty years later it was 'still the only substantial geographical work by a British writer to treat the regional geography of the country as a whole' (Baker and Gilbert 1944). And although now inevitably out of date in some respects, in others it has not been bettered; much of what he wrote intuitively has since proved to be valid. This is true both of the physical and of the human aspects. The author could boast (1927) that the famous geologist, Gregory,[26] had several times written to tell him that 'now this and now that theory of mine had been substantiated by his detailed work'. Three-quarters of a century after his book appeared, it could be said (Dickinson 1976, p. 37) that 'his concept of "Metropolitan England", as the area of the south-east that is dominated by association with London' was 'still one of the dominant realities of our day, one to which we are still seeking means of adjustment in terms of regional and

---

[26] John Walter Gregory (1864-1932). Professor of Geology at Melbourne 1900-4 and at Glasgow 1904-29; an active and intrepid traveller and explorer who died by drowning in Peru.

national planning. The thinking of Mackinder was a generation ahead of his time.'

Inevitably much of the everyday running of the Oxford School fell upon his assistant Herbertson, and in 1902 C. R. Beazley was appointed to lecture instead of the Director on the history of geography. Discontent with Mackinder's absences grew and his re-appointment after the initial period of five years (1899-1904) was said to be 'in danger'. The Readership was, however, renewed, though at a reduced stipend. Mackinder himself now realized that his position was becoming untenable: he resigned his University posts and gave up his Studentship at Christ Church as from 1 July 1905.[27]

The School of Geography, like University College, Reading, was very much Mackinder's own creation, and a monument to his efforts to raise geography to a higher status in Britain. It offered a one-year course for graduates who could thereby, if successful in the examination, add a Diploma in Geography to their qualifications. The first diploma examination was held in June 1901 when there were four successful candidates. The geography taught was practical—to ensure that students could make and interpret maps, physical—to provide the essential fundamentals, regional—to illustrate the geographical synthesis of environment and community, and historical—to bring out the significance of the geographical factor in history; to these were added the history of geography and geographical discovery.[28] Herbertson was in complete accord with this presentation of the subject, and Mackinder was doubtless quite happy to leave him in charge. From the School there went forth a generation of 'new' geographers to head departments in universities and to man teaching posts in schools, and thus the Mac-

[27] For further detail, see Scargill (1976).
[28] The programme for Hilary term 1903 was as follows:

Mr Mackinder—Historical Geography of Europe
Mr Dickson—Surveying and Mapping
           —Climatic Regions of the Globe
Mr Dickson & Mr Darbishire—Military Topography
Mr Herbertson—Regional Geography of Continental Europe
              —British Isles
              —Types of Landforms
Dr Grundy—The Historical Topography of Greece
Mr Beazley—The Period of Great Discoveries 1480-1650 (*Geogrl Teacher* ii (1903-4), p. 44).

kinder gospel was spread throughout the land. Many of his hopes of the 1880s had become realities in the 1890s, and with such achievements behind him the visionary could now walk new paths and dream other dreams.

Chapter 2

Life and Work 1900–1947
London

The first part of Mackinder's life had been filled by his love of geography, and by his determination to establish it as a respected part of the British educational system. It had culminated in a remarkable degree of academic distinction and pluralism, and in the writing of *Britain and the British Seas*. The second part of his life can be said to have been governed above all by love of his country and concern for its Empire. This was an enlightened patriotism, based on knowledge gained as a lecturer who had travelled all over the country, meeting and talking with all classes of people, and upon the work undertaken for his book; this had given him an unmatched knowledge of many vital aspects of national life. It was an anxious patriotism, because his unique understanding of Britain had made him aware of some serious shortcomings, and also because his perception of the relationship between history and geography enabled him to see why empires rose and fell. He was immediately concerned with the rise of German power, but he realized also that only a united British Empire would be able to match the inevitable transformation of America and Russia into superpowers.

Politics, geopolitics,[1] public service, and concern for the Empire now became his main interests, but he did not cease to practise geography, and to defend and support it; he also retained his special interest in education. He was probably nursing political aspirations from 1895, and one reason for his desire to have the new geographical institute established in London rather than at Oxford was probably that it would have enabled him the more easily to combine an academic with a political career. Once his association with the London School of Economics had begun, he was soon making contacts

[1] M. did not like this word, but it is now in general use for the geographical basis or aspects of foreign policy and strategical planning.

of a range and importance that could only be found in the capital.

As a young man Mackinder had worked for the Conservative candidate at Gainsborough, but he had now joined the Liberal Imperialists. The 'Limps' supported the British Empire, but held that its preservation required social reform and greater efficiency. They were led by Lord Rosebery; other prominent adherents were Haldane, Grey, and Asquith. In the late 1890s Mackinder began to provide Liberal Imperialism with an intellectual basis; he is found explaining its economic foundations to the Institute of Bankers in 1899. In 1900 he contested Warwick and Leamington as a 'Limp', his opponent being Alfred Lyttelton,[2] the sitting member, a Liberal Unionist. He was after electoral experience; he did not expect to win, and was not even too anxious to defeat Lyttelton who was absent in South Africa, and whose views did not differ so much from his own. Mackinder supported the Boer War, and his imperialism did not go down well with traditional Liberal voters. However, he was seen in the Lyttelton camp as 'a formidable candidate' (Lyttelton 1917, p. 248), and did well in the circumstances, getting 1,954 votes to Lyttelton's 2,785.

In 1901 Mackinder demonstrated his support for the Empire by joining the Victoria League, recently founded to give hospitality to visitors from the colonies, and to arouse interest in and give information about the Empire. The Princess of Wales was patroness. In 1902 he became a member of the committee and was active for some years in its educational work. Also in 1901 (*aet.* 40) he became a member of the University of London's Board of Studies for Geography. It was dominated by five geologists, four of them professors: there were three geographers (Mackinder, Chisholm, and Keltie of the RGS), and Hewins, the first Director of the LSE, an economist.[3] When geography was included as an option in the new matriculation examination in 1902, Mackinder found himself fighting to get a truly

[2] (1857–1913), lawyer, politican, and cricketer; first elected for Warwick and Leamington in 1895; Secretary of State for the Colonies 1903–5.

[3] William Albert Samuel Hewins (1865–1931). Like M. he had worked in Oxford University Extension; he organized the LSE as its first Director 1895–1903. He was Professor of Economic Science at King's College, London, 1897–1903 and Professor of Economic History at London University, 1902–3. In 1903 he resigned his academic posts to devote himself to tariff reform and the cause of Empire.

geographical rather than a geologically-slanted syllabus adopted. 'The principles at issue were important', he wrote, 'and the two conceptions very distinct.' In the end Mackinder's syllabus was adopted, one of the geologists and the economist joining the three geographers (Cantor 1960, pp. 162-3).

By 1902 Mackinder had been admitted to a group of young intellectuals, journalists, and politicians which included the Webbs, Bernard Shaw, Bertrand Russell, H. G. Wells, R. B. Haldane,[4] and Edward Grey.[5] He was a founder-member of the Coefficients, a dining club instituted by the Webbs in 1902. The twelve original members were, besides Mackinder, Amery,[6] Bellairs, Dawkins, Grey, Haldane, Hewins, Maxse,[7] Pember Reeves—who succeeded Mackinder as Director of the LSE— Bertrand Russell, Sidney Webb, and H. G. Wells.[8] Mackinder (1931a) tells how the club came to be named: 'for some weeks, while writing a book, I was lodged in a country cottage and near at hand, also rusticating, were Mr and Mrs Sidney Webb. One day, as we rode our bicycles, Mrs Webb sketched a Dining Club ... her husband, who was riding just ahead, threw over his shoulder the word "Coefficients".' He claimed that the declared purpose of the club—to study 'the aims, policy and methods of imperial efficiency at home and abroad'—was his suggestion.

The Coefficients first met on 6 November 1902. Mackinder commented: 'Wells was a trifle in the clouds, wanted subjects of discussion which were not practical and has evidently no political sense—as yet. We got on well and I think the Club is going to make friends of a useful group of men' (qu. in Cantor 1960, p. 33). Wells himself (1934, vol. ii, p. 761) said that it 'played an important part in my education', and 'included the queerest diversity of brains'. Sidney Webb's letters (Mackenzie

[4] Richard Burdon Haldane (Viscount Haldane of Cloan) (1856-1928), Secretary of State for War 1905-12, Lord Chancellor 1912-15 and 1924.

[5] Sir Edward Grey (Viscount Grey of Fallodon) (1862-1933). Foreign Secretary 1905-16.

[6] Leopold Charles Maurice Stennett Amery (1873-1955), journalist, imperialist, and Conservative politician; First Lord of the Admiralty 1922-3, Colonial Secretary 1924-9, Secretary of State for India 1940-5.

[7] Leopold James Maxse (1885-1946), journalist, imperialist, and political writer.

[8] Among those who joined later were Lord Robert Cecil, J. L. Garvin, Henry Newbolt, Lord Milner, Michael Sadler, and Josiah Wedgwood (Hewins 1929, p. 65; Wells, 1934, vol. ii, pp. 761-2).

1978) give some idea of the subjects discussed, e.g. 'Last night at the Co-efficients there were present Haldane, Mackinder, Wells, Dawkins, Hewins, Newbolt, Amery and myself. We discussed the monarchical institution—general opinion in favor of it and its development, as necessary to the Empire. Wells alone dissenting' (15 November 1904), and 'Last night I went to the Co-Efficients—9 present, including Lord Milner. I propounded the Poor Law Reform Scheme. They were all favorably impressed and made little criticism, except ... [Mackinder and Newbolt] fearing medical opposition' (18 June 1907). There was a tendency, however, to split into two groups:

Over our table at St Emin's Hotel wrangled Maxse, Bellairs, Hewins, Amery and Mackinder, all stung by the small but humiliating tale of disasters in the South African war, all sensitive to the threat of business recession and all profoundly alarmed by the naval and military aggressiveness of Germany, arguing chiefly against the liberalism of Reeves and Russell and myself, and pulling us down, whether we liked it or not, from large generalization to concrete problems. (Wells 1934, vol. ii, p. 764)

Bertrand Russell proved the least tolerant and soon left the club in some dudgeon after an argument.

Merely to list some of Mackinder's activities in 1902 (*aet.* 41) is to portray his titanic energy, yet the year was not untypical. Riding the Great Western Railway several times a week to lecture in Oxford, Reading, and London, to supervise the School of Geography, and to direct Reading College; guiding the latter's transition to a university college; completing *Britain and the British Seas* and passing the proofs; visiting Paris to meet the doyen of French geographers, Paul Vidal de la Blache; planning and running the first of a series of biennial summer schools at Oxford; attending each meeting of the Coefficients with well-thought-out views on the evening's topic; and contributing to the *Morning Post* three long articles on the necessity for extending both liberal and technical education to all classes of the community. He had supported the 1902 Education Bill as a step in the right direction, despite his party's opposition. It was in this year also that he was invited to stand for the College division of Glasgow, but he lacked the means, writing in his diary that it was ludicrous to be 'coquetting with Parliament' while in debt.

The year 1903 was decisive in Mackinder's life. His wife had left him and he felt restless and dissatisfied. He resigned his Reading post early in the year to make more time available for London and politics, and with his income thus reduced, was prepared to 'trust to his wits and face some poverty' (qu. in Blouet 1975, p. 19). Then on 15 May Chamberlain publicly abandoned free trade for imperial preference and retaliatory tariffs. The new development proved fatal to the 'Limps', who were now forced to choose between their liberalism and their imperialism: 'Chamberlain's attack on free trade ... had the effect of breaking up the politics of the centre which lay at the root of Liberal Imperialist thinking ... calm discussion of the future of imperial unity could no longer be contained within small dining clubs in which rational men could agree to differ' (Matthew 1973, pp. 100-2).

Three tariff-reforming Chamberlainite Coefficients, Hewins—Mackinder's Director at the LSE, Amery, and Maxse persuaded him to join them, and he became one of a small group of Liberals who signed a letter to *The Times* on 21 July 1903, suggesting that the time had come to jettison free trade. But most Liberals united in favour of it; Mackinder left the party, and by way of the Liberal Unionists, became a Conservative.

Tariff reform was not to prove popular electorally and the Liberals won a resounding victory in the 1906 election: the Conservatives were not to return to power until Mackinder was over 60. He had been widely regarded as a 'coming man', and Amery (1953, p. 224) thought 'he would almost certainly, if he had stayed with his party, have risen to high office in the 1906 Parliament'; he was 'a more forceful personality and a more powerful brain than either Grey or Haldane'. In 1902 Beatrice Webb had written, 'If he got his foot on the ladder he might go far towards the top' (qu. in Blouet 1975, p. 18).

The Tariff Reform League, newly formed to promote Chamberlain's policy, hoped to have Mackinder as their Secretary, knowing that he would make 'the sheer intellectual case against Free Trade ... with sufficient vigour and persistency'. They were frustrated by the interest in the League of C. A. Pearson, wealthy proprietor of the *Daily Express*:

Pearson remarked that Mackinder might be a very able man, but would obviously try to run the League, and that he, Pearson, as chairman, meant to run it himself, and preferred to have a secretary who would do as he was told. We looked at each other in some bewilderment. But nobody ventured to question his authority and Cousens was chosen. (Amery 1953, vol. i, p. 239)

Amery goes on to say 'this was a disaster, for neither Pearson nor Cousens had any real idea of the formidable task before us or of the kind of propaganda required'. They soon left the scene, but by then Mackinder had accepted the Directorship of the London School of Economics and was no longer available. However, from his base at the LSE, drawing on the knowledge and ideas developed for his lectures on commercial geography, he provided 'the theoretical foundation for tariff imperialism', as in his 'Man-Power as a Means of National and Imperial Strength' (1905) and *Money-Power and Man-Power: the underlying principles rather than the statistics of Tariff Reform* (1906). His geographical eminence was also recognized in 1903: he was awarded the Silver Medal of the Royal Scottish Geographical Society and elected an Honorary Member of the Berlin Geographical Society.

Sidney Webb's offer of the Directorship of the LSE not only gave him the challenge and the income he needed, but also took his mind off the break-up of his marriage. He gratefully acknowledged this later in a letter to Beatrice (1908):

I shall never forget what I owe to you and Mr Webb. I came to London at a venture, low in spirit after the one great blow of an otherwise happy career, and I owe it to you and Mr Webb, more than to anyone else, that I weathered the depression and started afresh. At the School you gave me the new task which I needed, and you welcomed me at your house at a time when that welcome meant more than you knew. If I now feel at home and hopeful in London, it is mainly your doing. (qu. in Cantor 1960, pp. 42–3)

Early in 1904 a dining club on similar lines to the Coefficients was formed by a group of leading tariff-reforming imperialists. Named the Compatriots, it included Amery, Hewins, Garvin,[9] Buchan,[10] and Maxse as well as Mackinder. And it was on 25

[9] James Louis Garvin (1868–1947), journalist, editor of the *Observer* 1908–42.
[10] John Buchan (1875–1940), a writer of fiction; as Baron Tweedsmuir he became Governor-General of Canada in 1930.

January that Mackinder delivered before the Royal Geographical Society a paper entitled 'The Geographical Pivot of History'—the first statement of his famous 'heartland' theory, 'a
thesis of world power analysis and prognosis which for better or
worse has become the most famous contribution of modern
geography to man's view of his political world' (Hartshorne
1954, p. 174). In the summer he conducted the second biennial
Oxford summer school in geography, noteworthy because the
leading American physical geographer, W. M. Davis, conducted instructional river trips on the Thames.

In 1905 Mackinder resigned his Oxford posts, so that his
work was now wholly centred in London. He was still Lecturer
in Economic Geography at the LSE as well as Director; but
there is a perceptible change of emphasis in his teaching, with
more stress on the application of geography to modern economic
and political questions, and less on purely historical geography.
The terms of his London appointment are sufficient to account
for this, but undoubtedly it fitted in well with his political work
and his growing preoccupation with the future of Empire. However, his famous 1904 paper shows that he did not abandon the
historical perspective in explaining the present and suggesting
the future.

Mackinder furthered the cause of Empire by serving as representative of the Victoria League on the Visual Instruction
Committee of the Colonial Office, the purpose of which was to
spread knowledge of Britain throughout the Empire, and of the
Empire in Britain.[11] Since 1903 he had been organizing the
production of lantern slides and making lecture notes to accompany them. These were published as *Seven Lectures on the United
Kingdom* (1905) and *India: eight lectures* ... (1910) by George
Philip & Son Ltd, who were also bringing out his series of
school-books written to serve the needs of the growing army of
geography teachers and their pupils. The first of these, *Our Own
Islands* (1906), sold almost half a million copies and reached a
19th edition in 1935; it was followed by *Lands beyond the Channel*
(1908). His work on these school-books, the excellence of which
is beyond question, did not prevent him from concurrently
writing an historico-geographical classic, *The Rhine, its valley and
history* (1908). Several more textbooks came from his prolific

[11] For further detail, see Blouet (1975), pp. 23-5.

pen in the pre-war years, and the royalties they earned were one
of his chief sources of income.

In 1906 Mackinder was asked by Haldane, now Secretary of
State for War, to organize at the LSE a course for senior army
officers—which came to be known as 'Haldane's Mackindergarten'; it was held annually until 1914. Mackinder himself
lectured to the officers on strategical geography. He was highly
gratified with his first class:

In my opinion, no class of students could have worked more assid-
uously or with greater enthusiasm. I say this not lightly, but after
more than 20 years' experience. It is rarely indeed that one can find
a class numbering 31, of which every single member studies seriously.
We must bear in mind, moreover, that the average age was 39 years
and 2 months, and that there were three times as many Majors as
Captains. (qu. in Cantor 1960, pp. 175–6)

The innovation upset the Commandant of the Staff College,
who saw it as a usurpation of that College's own function; he
was 'determined to fight it for all he was worth', and proposed
to attend as many of the lectures as possible 'so as to be in the
best position to fight' (Bond 1972, p. 252). His opposition was
of no avail; on the contrary, the War Office was delighted with
the success of the courses:

We should like to acknowledge the invaluable services of Mr Mackinder himself in connection with the work which has been done. His
unflagging zeal, and the energy and discretion with which he has
organized and carried out a scheme which was entirely original and
in several ways was full of difficulties, all of which have been successfully overcome, deserve the highest praise. (ibid., p. 176)

This advance on the military front was offset by a reverse on
the civil side. Another of Mackinder's old Liberal Imperialist
and Coefficient associates, Grey, now Foreign Secretary, proposed to drop geography from the Foreign Office and Diplomatic Service examinations, on the ground that those appointed
could easily pick up any essential geographical knowledge. In
a letter to *The Times* (3 Dec. 1906) Mackinder wrote:

Geography has its own mode of thought and its own points of view,
which are not to be obtained in a hurry. The handling of geographical
facts with power and ease is as much a matter of training as the

handling of historical or economic facts ... The Army requires a fairly stiff geographical test for entry to the Staff College ... Surely geography is as necessary to the diplomat as to the soldier.

And in 1907 he gave an address at the LSE on 'The advantage of adopting for civil administrators and business men certain principles of training already accepted in the British Army' (*The Times*, 18 Jan. 1907).

He was somewhat perturbed that the growing body of academic geographers was mainly concerned with advancing the subject on the university front and seeking the establishment of university chairs. He thought this premature, believing strongly that the fight should be for more geography in school-leaving, university-entrance, and civil-service examinations: 'geographical reformers should concentrate their efforts upon the door that is half open. Once geography is seriously taken up by the public schools, the Universities will experience a demand for teachers trained in the subject. They will in consequence have to strengthen their geographical departments' (*The Times*, 30 Nov. 1904). He was concerned to promote not only geography but also enlightened educational policies generally, and this was recognized by his election in 1906 as President of the Froebel Society, formed to promote the progressive ideas of Friedrich Froebel, originator of the kindergarten; in his presidential address he pointed out that increased urbanization resulted in a different outlook on life, and this required a new attitude on the part of teachers (*The Times*, 30 March 1906).

In June 1908 Mackinder (*aet.* 47) resigned as Director of the London School of Economics. He had been very active in University affairs: he was representative of the Faculty of Economics on the Senate, a member of the Senate Academic Council, and a member of eleven Senate committees. As early as 1902 he had fervently maintained that if London was to be a real university, the constituent colleges, schools, and administration should be gathered within 'a single quarter of the Metropolis', ideally near the British Museum. That London University is now largely concentrated in Bloomsbury can be attributed to Mackinder's determined opposition to a proposal in 1905 to use a site that had become available in South Kensington. All his powers of leadership, well thought-out strategy, and combative tenacity were deployed. On the occasion of the opening of the Senate House in Bloomsbury in 1933, he recalled the 1905 controversy:

A majority of the Senate were for accepting the bird in the hand, but our group was united in the view that the University must be in the centre of London, in a building erected for the purpose, which every cabman would know as the University, and that it should be near the British Museum, and within the belt of great colleges aligned from Bedford College to King's College. (*The Times*, 30 June 1933)

In the end, at a Senate meeting held on 7 March 1906, the 'idealists' as he called his own party, triumphed over the 'practical men'.

In view of his experiences in the building-up of new institutions it is not surprising that the LSE grew and prospered under his guidance, nor, from what is known of his abilities, that he ran it 'with two fingers of one hand' (Beveridge 1953, p. 168).

He quickly stamped his style on the running of the school. He introduced a printed Director's Annual Report, established advisory committees in connection with railway and insurance courses and thus brought some leading industrialists and financiers into direct contact with the institution. The Board of Governors was strengthened in a similar manner. The quality of the public lectures was upgraded and in general the whole image of the institution was strengthened by the association with able men well known in public life ... The railway and insurance industries put additional funds into the school. He gave the development of the library a high priority, pressed to establish sociology in the curriculum, and worked hard to find additional resources to buy up open sites around the school for future expansion and in order to get a main entrance 'upon the new Kingsway'. (Blouet 1975, pp. 26–7)

The Army was brought into the School's orbit with Haldane's 'Mackindergarten'. Along with this high-level activity, involving negotiations with ministers of the Crown and chairmen of companies, went a concern, already demonstrated at Reading, for the students' well-being. A refectory was added along with other amenities; the *Clare Market Review*, the student magazine, was begun in 1905; and the first of the 'students' parliaments', which were to become such a feature of the LSE, was held in 1907. Mackinder worked too 'to gain the School a sound footing within the structure of London University and in 1906 guided

it safely to a Treasury grant'.[12] The number of students more
than doubled during his Directorship.

Much of the credit for Mackinder's success must go to Sidney
Webb who, as chairman of the trustees, was remarkably clear-
sighted, co-operative, and open-minded. This is clear from his
letters, e.g.:

Mackinder wants to spend £1,500 this summer on structural altera-
tions at the School, in order to get further accommodation. I have
agreed to his bringing this forward. Our business is growing, and we
must make more room to meet the demand. (18 June 1907)

and

He and I discussed plans: and the best course seemed to be to go for
an even further enlargement by increasing Geography, if we can get
Sir George Taubman-Goldie[13] . . . to take it up and get us the money.
We may thus be able to make Geography and Ethnology together,
with the several subsidies that they bring, pay well for both, and also
our deficit. It is a hazardous game; and I am alive to the risks. (22
Feb. 1908)

It is not surprising that when, in 1910, Webb was accused of
letting his socialism affect his trusteeship of the School, Mackinder defended him robustly, asserting that 'on no occasion
did he seek to bias the teaching given':[14]

On the contrary, one of the greatest of his many great services to the
School was the consistent support which he gave me in my effort to
secure that all shades of opinion should be represented among the
students, the teachers, and the governors . . . Any influence which Mr
Webb may exercise among the students is solely due to his admitted
eminence in research.

Mrs Webb wrote in her diary:

For the last months we have known that his resignation was imminent,
he intending to devote himself to the affairs of the Empire, in preparation for Parliament and office in the next conservative ministry. He

[12] Speaking at the tenth annual dinner of the Students' Union in 1908 M. said that
the LSE was 'the only school, the only college on the list [of university institutions
sharing the Treasury grant], which was not either a University, or one of those little
Universities called University colleges' *The Times*, 2 March 1908.

[13] President of the Royal Geographical Society.

[14] *The Times*, 24 Oct. 1910. Hewins, M.'s predecessor as Director, joined in the
defence of Webb. See also Cole (1949), p. 49.

has been the best of colleagues, during these four years, and has improved the internal organization and the external position of the School. Indeed so competent a director has he been, that he has virtually run the whole business; Sidney trusting his initiative and executive capacity. We part company with the highest regard for him, and I think he for us. (qu. in Blouet 1975, p. 28)

Former students have left no doubt of their high regard. Hilda Ormsby pictured him,

as tall, erect, distinguished, he strode, always a few minutes late, up the gangway of the Great Hall packed with eager and impatient students, to the rostrum, as he paused a moment or two to take in the array of maps that hung there, and then, turning to his audience, delivered in his sonorous voice, without ever a note, a perfectly argued and presented synthesis. (*The Times*, 17 March 1947)

Sir Horace Wilson, the prominent civil servant, wrote:

I soon had reason to be glad that I had included Economic Geography in my list for I found Mackinder a masterly lecturer in that subject. I remember clearly the sweep and scope of what he said and always looked forward to the hour under him. His tall commanding figure and rich voice seemed to typify both the magnitude of his subject and the depth of his knowledge of it. I can see him now in my mind's eye explaining the economic (and the politico-economic) significance of the Urals, the Alps, or the Andes as if he were atop of one of them—or was indeed a part of them.[15] (qu. in Cantor 1960, pp. 186–7)

Although Mackinder gave up his Directorship of the LSE in 1908, he 'remained with the school as one of its most brilliant lecturers' (Hayek 1946, p. 16). He was in fact Reader in Geography until he became Professor in 1923.

Mackinder resigned his Directorship because another avenue had opened up to his ever-questing crusading spirit. A group headed by Lord Milner offered to employ him to promote the cause of Empire on terms repeated in a letter to Amery dated 22 May 1908:

[15] An American student, Martha Wilson Morse (Mrs Sydney John Morse), claimed in a letter to one of M.'s executors, dated 5 Aug. 1952, to 'have struggled for twenty-six years to forward your uncle's philosophy (he himself worked for forty without much appreciation)' and to have produced a *magnum opus* on him; publishers were 'appalled by the length'. She tells how he 'gave himself fully and freely' in her two years at the LSE and that since then she had had 'the feeling of responsibility—the hope of recording him fairly and placing him squarely in history'—Mackinder Papers, School of Geography, Oxford.

I understand that the proposal is that I am to devote myself to furthering to the best of my ability the cause of imperial unity generally, more especially in connection with the forthcoming Imperial Conference. Subject to the general approval of Lord Milner, and consultation with yourself I am to have a free hand to organize my work to this end as I may find most effective, and in particular to be free, if I consider it desirable for the purpose, to go into Parliament. To enable me to do this I gather that a sum of £850 a year for four years will be available, of which it is understood that I shall have to pay about £200 a year for working chambers and clerical assistance. It is understood that I shall retain my Readership in Geography in the University of London, and do such other Geographical work as naturally falls to the holding of that office. I am also to be free to accept any earnings, e.g. journalistic or lecture fees, which may come to me incidentally. If during the four years permanent sources of income, e.g. directorships of companies, should present themselves, I may consider myself free to accept them provided that acceptance is compatible with my work in the imperial cause. (qu. in Blouet 1975, pp. 29-30)

In pursuance of his new task Mackinder went to Canada in the summer of 1908 'as a guest of the Atlantic fleet which accompanied the Prince of Wales ... to the tercentenary of the foundation of Quebec' (Mackinder 1931a). He spent several months in the Dominion and returned with an understanding of its problems, politics, and aspirations, and these were set forth in three masterly addresses to the Compatriots' Club in November and December. He pleaded powerfully for the granting of tariff preference for Canadian wheat in order to arrest Canada's growing involvement with the American economy. 'Canada', he declared, 'was essential to the Empire. If all North America were a single Power, Britain would, indeed, be dwarfed. That great North American Power would, of necessity, take from us the command of the ocean' (*The Times*, 15 Dec. 1908).

Early in 1909 he contested a by-election at Hawick Burghs as Unionist candidate. He campaigned for tariff reform as the means to reduce unemployment and strengthen imperial bonds: 'Among the great and growing nations of the world, the only chance this country has of holding its own is to knit itself, by ties of commercial interest no less than sentiment, to the younger Britains beyond the Seas' (qu. in Cantor 1960, p. 46). But the

Liberal defeated him by 520 votes. Soon afterwards he found another constituency, the Camlachie division of Glasgow, and here, in the general election of January 1910, he was successful. At the second general election in December he retained the seat only narrowly.[16] Once elected, he wasted no time before speaking. The new Parliament opened on 15 February 1910, and on the 23rd he spoke in favour of tariffs in the debate on the Address.[17] From then on he was a frequent speaker and active Member, involved primarily with tariff reform, colonial preference, education, and of course, Scottish affairs. After 1912 he was increasingly concerned with the growing power of Germany and with naval rearmament. He did not, however, confine his attention to such topics.

On 23 April 1913 (Shakespeare's birthday) he proposed the motion that 'there should be established in London a National Theatre, to be vested in trustees and assisted by the State, for the performance of the plays of Shakespeare and other dramas of recognized merit'. Even to this subject he brought the imperial theme:

a nation is held together by the fact that you can appeal to the members of it with a common history, if you will to a common religion, and to a common literature, and for that reason, I want as an Imperialist that our British race, coming to this London, visiting it either as Rhodes scholars or as Statesmen responsible for the Dominions, that when any of them come here on a pilgrimage, it may be once or twice or thrice in their lifetime, he should have the opportunity of seeing the great national dramas presented.

[16] He increased his share of the poll, but a shift from Labour to Liberal put the seat in peril. The details of the two 1910 elections were:

	January	December
Unionist (H. J. Mackinder) .	3,227	3,479
Liberal	2,793	3,453
Labour	2,443	1,539
Woman suffragette . . .	—	35
Unionist majority . . .	434	26

The electorate totalled 9,819.

[17] Austen Chamberlain (1936, p. 204) thought the debate was 'remarkable for the ... excellence of the maiden speeches' and includes M. among those who 'made their mark'.

In the event, there were 96 votes in favour, only 32 against, yet the motion failed 'because it was not supported by the majority prescribed by Standing Order No. 27' (P.D. 1913 lii, 461-2, 495). A few days later he spoke in favour of a national theatre at the annual dinner of the Incorporated Stage Society presided over by Mme Pavlova (*The Times*, 10 May 1913).

Membership of Parliament, though not in itself a source of income, made it easier to get company directorships, and he soon appears in yet another guise as business man. British industrialists were becoming interested in tariff reform; some found themselves sharing a common platform with Mackinder, and so his business contacts increased. It is not so surprising, therefore, to find him elected President of the British Machine Tool and Engineering Association; being the man he was, it is even less surprising that he should, in that capacity, organize an engineering exhibition at Olympia in 1912 (*The Times*, 24 Oct. 1912).

All this time he remained an active member of the executive and educational committees of the Victoria League; he lectured for it, and his brain was fertile with suggestions for new ways of promoting knowledge of the Empire. He was responsible, for instance, for a system of pen-friend exchanges between British and colonial schools.[18]

He was busy too as Reader in Geography. Sometimes he had to rush from the House of Commons to the LSE, having had no time to prepare his lecture, and speak extempore from a wall map or a page of statistics. Many thought he should be appointed Professor, and in 1911 the Senate resolved that he was qualified; but as the Board of Studies for Geography made no recommendation, the matter lapsed. Either Mackinder or the Board itself may have thought that such a move would be inappropriate while he was an active MP and the busy spokesman of a Unionist Party 'ginger group'. In 1913 he became Chairman of the Geographical Association, which he had founded twenty years before, and remained in that office for over thirty years. He did occasionally get away for a brief holiday abroad, and in the summer of 1913 was in the Austrian Tyrol.

Mackinder remained an MP throughout the 1914-18 war,

---

[18] For details, see Cantor (1960), pp. 314-16.

but almost immediately he was called upon for assistance. Recruiting was going badly in Scotland, and Haldane told Kitchener to use Mackinder's oratory. Kitchener sent for him and said, 'Haldane tells me I should send you to Scotland, will you go?' He replied, 'Yes, on two conditions. That you give me a letter over your own name and that you give me the power to spend money.' 'You shall have both', was the reply. Mackinder (*aet.* 53) soon discovered that 'no oratory was wanted but organization. In three days we had organized several hundred recruiting stations all over Scotland' (Mackinder 1931a).

Mackinder was proud to have been the initiator of the National Savings Movement. He had explained his war savings plan in the House of Commons in 1915 and:

When I sat down Mr McKenna, then Chancellor of the Exchequer, beckoned me behind the Speaker's chair and told me that he would set up a Treasury Committee under the chairmanship of Mr Montagu, his Financial Secretary, and that he expected me to serve on that committee. At the second meeting of the Montagu Committee I presented a scheme for the organization of Savings Associations ... Thus the National Savings Movement was inaugurated. (ibid.)

During the war Mackinder widened his speaking brief in the House to include almost every subject that came under discussion: e.g. the availability of ploughmen, the housing of the working classes, margarine, and the price of coal. He showed an anxious concern for the economic and social conditions of Britain after the war, being one of the few who saw that even victory would leave the economy dislocated and the fabric of society damaged. On the political scene he was unhappy about coalition government which divided the House on great issues, not between party and party, but between the combined front benches, insulated from criticism and the impotent back benchers: 'I think that when the Coalition Government has been in power for a time it will grow increasingly out of touch with the nation' (P.D. 1915 lxxv, 1230).

As a Member of Parliament Mackinder had opportunities of visiting the front. He was at the western front in 1916 and the Italian front in 1917. In April of that year he visited 'the district in France which was devastated during the German retreat,' and wrote a long letter to *The Times*. Hatred of the Germans had increased to fever point during that desperate year, and the atrocities he listed must have fed that hatred. His feelings took a vindictive form when he agreed to present the Rhodes Trustees' Bill to remove their duty under Rhodes's will to provide scholarships for Germans after the war.

There was still time for geography and education, and in 1916 he served as President of the Geographical Association. No doubt he noted with interest the first honour schools of geography at Aberystwyth and Liverpool in 1917. At London he still took an active part as head of the geography department at the LSE.

His work for imperial preference went on throughout the war, and in 1917 he became Chairman of the Tariff Reform League, with Austen Chamberlain as President. His business interests also continued, and he was chairman of the Electro-Bleach and By-Products Company, a Cheshire firm, from 1914 to 1920, when it was taken over by Brunner, Mond and Co., thus finding its way into the future ICI complex (*The Times*, 22 April 1918, 24 July 1920).

Mackinder was returned by a large majority[19] at the 1918 general election. In the first post-war year, 1919, it became clear that he (*aet.* 58) was now regarded more as a trustworthy public servant than an aspiring politician. The splendid rhetoric, the commanding manner, the originality of thought, the irrefutable logic, the unquestionable knowledge, the amazing grasp of detail, all oddly combined with utopian visions, these and much more that made up the style and content of his speeches, do not seem to have gone down so well in the Commons as they did in the lecture hall. Reading the debates one gets the impression that here is a far-sighted thinker, with an extraordinary knowledge of many aspects of national and international affairs, standing up amongst men of lesser intellectual capacity, from whom it required too much mental effort to follow the arguments that were for them either incomprehen-

[19] The Camlachie result reflected the nationwide triumph of the coalition between Lloyd George Liberals and the Unionists:

Coalition Unionist (H.J.M.)	13,645
Labour	7,192
Liberal	860

sible or far-fetched. Probably too, his outstanding success with captive and passive audiences in the classroom, combined with the self-assurance that arises from mastery of one's subject, gave him an unconscious touch of arrogance which the House of Commons did not like, although generally he does not appear to have been a conceited man. But he could not resist correcting those who spoke after him and who had not understood him; he had scarcely been in the House six months before the Speaker told him 'to prefer to think his arguments distorted than to be constantly interrupting' (P.D. 1910 xix, 1477).

The sharp logic with which he cut through woolly and verbose debate may not have been liked. He ridiculed the Temperance (Scotland) Bill of 1912 which gave local option to the individual wards of Glasgow: 'You will have public houses on one side of a street and not on the other. What effect could that possibly have on a reduction of drunkenness? The effect will be not to reduce but solely to concentrate. You will have a piebald city—black and white. You aim at making the good better, but you allow the bad to become worse' (P.D. 1912 xxxvi, 897).

In the devolution debates of 1919 he maintained that a federation of the five nations (England, Scotland, Wales, Southern Ireland, and Northern Ireland) could not work because of the overwhelming importance of England. This predominance would generate extreme nationalism and anti-English sentiment. His solution, to divide England into three parts, London, agricultural England, and the industrial North, caused astonishment, and members had a field day making fun of it. The speech of Sir Ryland Atkins was representative of its reception:

I hope that Members in all parts of this House who were prepared before the Honourable Member spoke to support the Resolution will not be hindered from doing so by their enjoyment of his speech, by their delight in its rhetoric, or the way in which he managed to drown facts in most elaborate sentences of delightful fancy ... it shows how a perversion of historical perspective can give as much delight as the fairy tales of our childhood.

Atkins then spoke of the long struggle to achieve a unified England:

And now in the twentieth century there comes down the honourable and learned Gentleman, adorning his discourse with every kind of picturesque illustration, nearly all inaccurate, to find an argument, or where he cannot find it to invent it, in order that the House of Commons may be induced to adopt a form of devolution which, whatever else it does, will cut our England into three parts ... Fancy Birmingham partially digested in agricultural England! And beyond that we are to have a northern non-industrial area in which the sparse districts of sterile land which still rear sheep and grow oats are to realize their deep subordination under teeming artisans who tyrannize over them ... I hope the grave and serious question which the House ... is asked to discuss today, will, although adorned by this excursus, not be led away by it to attach importance to this fantasy of political destruction. (P.D. 1919 cxvi, 1930-2)

Leading politicians would be wary of an individualist with such far-fetched—or far-sighted—notions. But as he was highly respected as an able, honest, and courageous patriot, they were happy to use him in public service. In 1919 he was put on the Royal Commissions on Income Tax and on Awards to Inventors.

   Beatrice Webb looked upon him now more as a man being overtaken by events, than one who foresaw their course:

H. J. Mackinder lunched with us: we had not seen him since the outbreak of war. He is still a stalwart imperialist and tariff reformer—a survival of the faithful few who believe in triumphant capitalism dominating the world. He still talks in continents and waterways, in mass movements and momentums ... But he has become uncomfortably aware of another kind of mass movement, of another type of momentum—the uprising of the manual workers, within each modern state, organized as political and industrial democracies, to oust those who own the instruments of production from their property and their power ... it is an uncomfortable shadow falling across his admirable maps of the rise and fall of empires. (Webb 1952, pp. 157-8: 6 April 1918)

Mackinder was concerned with the rise and fall of empires in his *Democratic Ideals and Reality* (1919), a book intended for the Versailles peace-makers, and 'one of the most pregnant and provocative works of the first half of the century' (Dickinson 1976). Forcefully and imaginatively it developed the theme, first advanced in 1904, of the strategic and economic importance of the Russian territory as the 'heartland' of the World

Island; it forecast a struggle between Germany and Russia for the control of Eastern Europe as the gateway to this 'heartland', and prescribed preventive measures, not only for this danger but for economic and social problems also.[20] It went almost unnoticed in the Anglo-Saxon world; yet it was to prove 'perhaps the most widely—though not immediately—influential book ever written by a geographer' (Fisher 1965). As Haushofer acknowledged, German geopolitical doctrine in the Nazi years was based upon its ideas, and it has 'its repercussions in thought and strategy, directly and indirectly, on American policy in the post-war generation' (Dickinson 1976).

It was seen by some of his political associates, however. In June 1919 Lord Milner, having just read it, suggested Mackinder as British representative on the commission to delimit the Saar territory,[21] as he was a man of 'great ability, a geographer, a traveller, an excellent French scholar, and ... well at home in German' (Blouet 1975, p. 38). This suggestion was not adopted, but immediately Curzon[22] became Foreign Secretary in October 1919, he asked Mackinder to go to South Russia as British High Commissioner. A British military mission had been helping the White Russians, who had made a successful offensive; the High Commission was to help administer White-controlled territory. But Curzon's enthusiasm soon cooled as Denikin fell back and opposition to intervention mounted. He was irked by Mackinder's ambitious preparations and his delay in starting off, writing to him (20 Nov. 1919) that:

I am rather shocked at the dimensions to which your mission is expanding in respect more particularly of staff establishment ... After all Denikin at the moment is a shrinking not an advancing force, and there may be something tragic in the spectacle if you appear upon the scene with a great appanage ... As to dates I was in hopes that you would be starting in a week or ten days time. But I learn that in view of your preparations this is unlikely. (FO 1919-20, 33-5)

[20] For a brief statement of its arguments, see Gilbert and Parker (1969).

[21] The coal-rich industrialized Saar Basin Territory was detached from Germany by the peace treaty and placed under League of Nations control; France was given the exclusive right to develop the coal mines for 15 years. In 1935 the territory reverted to Germany after a plebiscite.

[22] Curzon had known M. as an undergraduate in the Oxford Union; he was a prominent member of the RGS and interested in geostrategic questions; M. had doubtless presented him with a copy of *Democratic Ideals* which gave much attention to the problem of eastern Europe. On Curzon as a geographer see Goudie (1980).

Mackinder replied:

You told me that I had to be ready to advise General Denikin on every subject except military matters ... I am sure my staff is the minimum with which I could hope to form an independent judgement ... As a fact there has been very little delay which would not have been inevitable because of one's tailor! I have only just got delivery of the warm clothing without which it would have been mad to go into a Russian winter ... I recognize it would be somewhat tragic to arrive with a strong staff just when Denikin collapsed. On the other hand to arrive inadequately equipped in a position which I could have saved appears to me to contain the elements of a worse tragedy ... The Treasury debated every appointment with me and ended by agreeing that my reasons were sound. (ibid., 29–30)

He eventually arrived in South Russia in late December, and

that grand old sailor, Admiral de Robeck,[23] lent me a battleship and told me that I might take her anywhere I would in the Black Sea ... I remember one evening addressing seven hundred bluejackets at the desire of the Captain and explaining to them why we were there [at Novorossiysk] and why they could not be allowed ashore. The whole ship was discussing high politics the next morning. (Mackinder 1931a)

But Denikin's forces, 'wracked by disease and suffering terribly from the bitter cold of the Russian winter, their discipline almost completely gone' (Ullman 1968) were in confusion and retreat. Mackinder's position was further undermined by the Government at home deciding to halt military aid. This put him in a difficult position; he attempted to bolster the morale of the White officers by promising the evacuation of their wives and children, and on 16 January 1920 he left Odessa for home.

On the way out he had stopped at Warsaw, Bucharest, and Sofia to promote co-operation between the Poles, Rumanians, Bulgarians, and White Russians. In Russia he persuaded Denikin to agree to *de facto* recognition of the independence of the border peoples. He was thus able, in his report to the Government, to put forward reasoned arguments for the organization of an anti-Bolshevik alliance between these peoples and the White Russians, and for giving financial and commercial support to this alliance. On 29 January, after Mackinder had

[23] Sir John Michael de Robeck (1862–1928), senior naval officer who held important commands during the 1914–18 war.

expatiated on his report, the Cabinet rejected his plan; not even Churchill lent him any support and Curzon was absent (Cab. 23/20 1920, p. 59). Anti-interventionist feeling was strong, and H. A. L. Fisher[24] wrote in his diary, 'Cabinet on Russia—Mackinder's absurd report.'[25] If it was any consolation, his knighthood 'for public and parliamentary services' was announced in the New Year's Honours List on 1 January 1920. Lord Hardinge[26] wrote: 'I greatly deplore the coincidence of your appointment to this post with the approach of collapse in South Russia. With more favourable opportunities I have no doubt that your mission would have achieved invaluable results; as it was, I fear the situation did not afford good scope for your abilities' (FO 1919–20, 71, 10 Feb. 1920).

Mackinder, now an authority on Eastern Europe, spoke in a debate on British policy towards Poland in May. The Poles had attacked Bolshevik Russia and Mackinder defended their action. They knew the Russians and were acting defensively:

What is it that you expect is going to happen in Russia? ... Do you expect that a democracy is going to evolve ... ? I do not think a democracy is likely to evolve ... there is a danger that you will arrive at a centralized and military power once more ... Whichever despotism you get in Russia ... they will be out to reconquer the old Russia. (P.D. 1920, cxxix, 1717–18)

Although his speech was well informed and highly relevant, it was about 'a far away country' and the Speaker was probably reflecting a weariness in the House when he interrupted Mackinder and told him to keep to the point.

After returning from Russia in 1920 Mackinder was soon again active in public service. He was chairman of the standing House of Commons committee which amalgamated the railway

[24] Herbert Albert Laurens Fisher (1865–1940), historian and Liberal politician; President of the Board of Education 1916–22.

[25] For detailed accounts of M.'s High Commissionership see Blouet (1976a) and Ullman (1968, 1972). The account in Mitchell (1919) unjustly portrays M. in a poor light. He is described as a 'reluctant missioner' who, when he arrived in Russia was 'shaken' by the situation. He is said to have composed 'a cagey but encouraging report' for the Cabinet. The author continues, 'This was just the kind of talk that the Cabinet, and especially Lloyd George ... wanted to hear. It was not long before Mackinder was knighted.' There is no basis for this interpretation of M.'s part: a pro-interventionist report was the last thing that Lloyd George wanted to hear, and M. was in fact knighted before his report was written.

[26] Permanent Under-Secretary of State for Foreign Affairs.

companies into four great systems—the LNER, LMS, GWR, and SR. He was also appointed Chairman of the Imperial Shipping Committee, where he rendered valuable service—service close to his heart because of the vital importance of sea communication to an overseas Empire; he did not overstate when he claimed that by the committee's work 'the Empire was saved some acrimonious, if not dangerous disputes' (Mackinder 1931a). In 1921 he protested strongly against abandoning the airship, because of its imperial potential: 'it would be a disaster if, even at this moment of financial strain, the chance of the immediate trial of airships on an Empire scale were sacrificed' (*The Times*, 5 July 1921). Ominously the year 1921 saw the publication of a booklet in which Haushofer, the German geopolitician, first made use of Mackinder's ideas as a basis for formulating the foreign policies to be followed by Germany and Japan (Kruszewski 1954, pp. 12-13). In that year also he was presented with the Cross of the Commander of the Crown of Rumania, presumably in recognition of his championing of East European independence. In 1922 he was elected as Honorary Member of the Hungarian Geographical Society.

In 1922 the question arose of finding money for the Russian refugees whom Mackinder had been responsible for saving from the Bolsheviks in January 1920. It was a penny-pinching time and Mackinder was blamed for this expensive obligation. He wrote to *The Times* (9 March 1922) justifying his action: rumours were running through the White Army of the imminent withdrawal of British help:

General Holman reported that many of our Military Mission were involved in isolated groups in the confusion of the retreat. Black looks had taken place of the former friendship, and at any moment a mad cry of British treachery might endanger the lives of our men. An instant decision was necessary. It seemed to me unthinkable that these poor women and children should be forsaken and left to their terrible fate by those who for a year past had encouraged and supported their husbands and fathers in a heroic if futile endeavour.[27]

In the general election of 15 November 1922 Mackinder, with 11,459 votes lost his seat at Glasgow Camlachie to the

[27] For parliamentary criticism of M.'s action, see P.D. (1922) cli, 114. According to Denikin the evacuation was part of a bargain, and promised in return for his agreeing to recognize the border states (Denikine 1930, pp. 340-1).

Labour candidate who polled over 15,000. The Liberal again came a poor third. He probably expected defeat for he was aware of the spread of Marxist ideas in Glasgow and understood the reasons, in spite of what Beatrice Webb had written. 'Marxian catchwords', he wrote, had 'taken the place of Biblical texts' on the banks of the Clyde. Social conditions were bad; such palliatives as the dole and old-age pension, and such escapist devices as the cinema and football pools were but *'panem et circenses'*. 'The revolt of some of our young people against such a state of affairs is not in itself unhealthy.'[28] Parliament could ill afford to lose his enlightened attitude, rare as it was, but a year later he told the secretary of his Unionist Association that he did not intend to stand at the next election.[29] He had been an MP for twelve years.

In April 1923 it was announced that Sir Halford was to be chairman of a committee to survey the price of building materials, a job he held for two years. In October the Imperial Economic Conference met; it praised his work as Chairman of the Shipping Committee and decided to set up an Economic Committee as well. The first Labour government was unwilling to implement this decision, but in March 1925 the new Conservative Colonial Secretary, L. S. Amery, set up the Committee with Mackinder as Chairman. In the meantime he had visited Canada (April 1924), and besides his official business as Chairman of the Imperial Shipping Committee, he gave talks on Empire questions in towns across the Dominion. He returned in time to take part in the Wembley Conference on Empire Settlement in May. In June the President of the Board of Trade announced that 'it had been decided to give a salary of £2,000 to the Chairman of the Imperial Shipping Committee, Sir Halford Mackinder, who had rendered valuable services and who had hitherto carried out the work without remuneration. The work had now become very onerous, and it was right that a salary should be paid' (*The Times*, 20 June 1924). Soon afterwards he was put on the Royal Commission on Food Prices,

---

[28] *The Times*, 23 Nov. 1922; see successive issues for correspondence criticizing M.'s letter, and his reply (4 Dec. 1922).

[29] Had Lord Curzon become Prime Minister in 1923, as was generally expected, instead of Baldwin, more use might have been made of M. who may then, perhaps, have been less ready to give up politics.

and in July 1926 (*aet.* 65) he was sworn a Privy Councillor. In 1926 also he travelled to the United States and to South Africa where he met Smuts and Herzog. In 1927 he went to Nova Scotia and Newfoundland.

His academic work as Reader in Geography at London University had continued into the post-war years, and in 1923 he accepted the personal title of Professor. In January 1925 he was at Reading for the ceremonial announcement of the grant of the royal charter by which his own creation, University College, Reading became the University of Reading. It was in these early 1920s that he was a member of the Confrères, a dining club reminiscent of the Coefficients and Compatriots of his pre-war days. Membership was drawn from those who held high office in London institutions. Sir Ernest Barker[30] wrote in 1953: 'What discussions we had nearly thirty years ago, especially when Sir Robert Donald, a very great journalist, and Sir Halford Mackinder—a past master of versatility, skilled in geography and affairs—were present to take a hand.' However, in 1925 Mackinder, after only two years as Professor, had to retire from his London University post because of the age limit then in force.

His retirement by no means ended his geographical work. In 1928 he read a paper on 'The Content of Philosophical Geography' at Cambridge; in 1931 (*aet.* 70) he delivered a brilliant address to the British Association for the Advancement of Science entitled 'The Human Habitat';[31] in 1935 he spoke to the Royal Geographical Society on 'The Progress of Geography during the Reign of George V'; in October 1937 he travelled up to Scotland to address the Royal Philosophical Society of Glasgow; and in 1942 (*aet.* 81), in the middle of the war, he was down at Exeter talking on 'Geography as an Art and a Philosophy'. These papers are neither regurgitations of past work nor senile effusions. Each is a freshly-conceived contribution to geographical thought, characterized by originality of concept and individuality of style, and testifying not only to a long and rich experience, but also to a breadth of knowledge and depth of understanding which none of his younger contemporaries in the

[30] (1874–1960); he was Principal of King's College, London, 1920–8.
[31] Described by Weigert *et al.* (1957, p. 256) as a 'memorable lecture' and 'a classical piece of geographical definition'.

field could match and few of them approach. He also held office in geographical societies: in 1928, for instance, he was President of Section D of the International Geographical Congress, and in 1931 President of Section E of the British Association for the Advancement of Science; from 1928 to 1936 he served on the Council of the RGS and he was Vice-President from 1932 to 1936; in 1932 he succeeded Sir Patrick Geddes as President of the Le Play Society.

He was still a business man, and in 1933 he is found chairing the twelfth annual meeting of Sheffield Steel Products, which had, however, been badly hit by the depression. In 1936 *The Times* has a photograph of him as the company's chairman (15 Oct.). In February 1937 he was the speaker at 'the first of a series of luncheons ... to bring together people in the London area who are anxious to advance the work of the Council for the Preservation of Rural England'. He made two observations which, though commonplace now, were far-sighted in 1937: 'the danger is that those who go out to enjoy that beauty will themselves destroy the thing they are enjoying', and 'we can do as much damage by unskilful and unsympathetic planning as the speculators themselves' (*The Times*, 12 Nov. 1937). He travelled from time to time, and in 1939 was in Portugal. His London clubs were the Athenaeum and the Alpine.

In 1939[32] (*aet.* 78) Mackinder resigned the Chairmanship of the Imperial Shipping Committee, probably because of increasing deafness. It had been exacting work, for it meant reconciling the interests, often divergent, of the UK and the seven self-governing dominions, with those, also sometimes apparently mutually irreconcilable, of the shipbuilders, shipowners, merchants, and manufacturers. Yet every one of the Committee's thirty-eight reports was unanimous, an extraordinary fact that speaks for itself (Imperial Shipping Committee 1939, p. 6). His health in old age seems to have been good, although he had an operation in a London nursing home in May 1937. This had 'prevented him from obeying Their Majesties' Command to be present at the Coronation' (*The Times*, 26 May 1937).

Then came the war of 1939–45, and in 1941 the German offensive against Russia, the Japanese attack on Pearl Harbor,

---

[32] Not 1945 as in Stamp (1947, p. 530) and Gilbert (1961, p. 16). He had resigned the Chairmanship of the Imperial Economic Committee in 1931.

and the entry of the United States into the conflict. Americans became suddenly aware of geopolitics, and the news that an English writer, back in 1919, if not as long ago as 1904, had forecast what would happen and explained why, made Mackinder, and his German disciple Haushofer, household names. Magazines and newspapers carried maps and diagrams to illustrate Mackinder's 'World Island' and his 'Heartland'. Scholars realized at last that he had 'arrived at a profounder understanding of modern strategy than any of the leading military experts of his times', and that his conclusions as to the 1939–45 war had been shown to be 'the most accurate political and military prophecy' (Strausz-Hupé 1942, pp. 143, 145). The American Geographical Society hastened to award him the Charles P. Daly Medal. It was presented at a ceremony in the American Embassy on 31 March 1944. The Ambassador, Mr John G. Winant, told the recipient that his name was 'world famous to-day as the first who fully enlisted geography as an aid to statecraft and strategy' and went on:

You previsioned the true basis of what to-day has won fashion as geopolitics. Unlike less worthy successors you have always been mindful of the responsibilities owed by science to democracy and you have furthered democracy's cause in your writings and in service to your country. You were the first to provide us with a global concept of the world and its affairs and we hope it will be given us to establish the global peace for which your tireless mind has only recently set forth the pattern and inspiration. I am proud to place in your hands this medal in recognition of the reverence in which your name and services are held both in your country and in mine. (*Geogrl J.* ciii, p. 131)

The Ambassador's eulogy, though an accurate appraisal of Mackinder's achievement, erred in its final sentence. He was indeed appreciated in America, but it cannot be said that he was accorded the same recognition in his own country. The British political and academic establishments and the communications media, possibly because of the low status of geography in education, but mainly because of an island history insulated from the realities of conflict, proved incapable of giving serious consideration to geostrategic and geopolitical ideas. The Royal Geographical Society did not honour him until, stung perhaps into action by what its American counterpart had done, it awarded him the Patron's Medal in 1945 (*aet.* 84).[33] On this occasion the RGS President said of Sir Halford:

By his first ascent and survey of Mt Kenya in 1899, his name is established in the history of African exploration. At Oxford and later in the University of London, he has inspired and guided successive generations. But to him geography has been not merely the concern of the schools: he has striven to secure the recognition of its fundamental role in national life, and its value as a bridge between science and philosophy. To many his 'Britain and the British Seas' has revealed for the first time the fascinating interplay of environment and human society. As a political geographer his reputation is indeed world wide. (*Geogrl J.* cv, p. 230)

His last years were spent at his brother Lionel's home in a suburb of Bournemouth.[34] Here he was cared for by his sister-in-law until his death on 6 March 1947 at the age of 86. He was cremated—he had spoken in favour of cremation at his first Oxford Union debate in 1880. He was survived by Lady Mackinder with whom he had been reconciled. She had lived in Italy on Capri but now resided in Switzerland where he had recently visited her. The only child of the marriage had died in infancy and before it could be baptized, a tragic event that may have contributed to their parting.

A memorial service was held at Reading on 17 March 1947. He left only two or three thousand pounds, bequeathing legacies of £100 each to his wife and other relatives. Of his wife he said, 'I do not leave more to her because she has her own villa in Capri and the income from Canada which I provided for her in my life time.'[35] He left the balance to his sister-in-law. Lady Mackinder wrote to her: 'I am more than glad he made this return for all you have done for him, though I am sure it does not cover the financial losses involved by your loans. And you have done so much else for him in ways for which no return can be made, in giving him your care and affection and in bringing peace and happiness into his life.'[36] That Mackinder had to borrow from relations is indicative of the penury he had often experienced while serving the state honestly, unselfishly, and

[33] And then he could not receive it because of wartime restrictions on the use of gold.
[34] At Elville, Kimberley Road, Parkstone, Dorset.
[35] Mackinder Papers, School of Geography, Oxford.
[36] Ibid.

often without monetary reward. He had been one of those who, in Pope's words, 'dare to love their country, and be poor!'[37]

In 1961 a plaque was unveiled in his memory at Queen Elizabeth Grammar School, Gainsborough, by the Lincoln branch of the Geographical Association. In 1966 another plaque was placed on Elswitha Hall, his birthplace. It reads:

Sir Halford John Mackinder, P.C. Geographer, Administrator, Author, Explorer, Politician, Public Servant. Born in this House 15th February, 1861.

In 1971 the University of Oxford established a Halford Mackinder Professorship of Geography.[38]

[37] 'On his grotto at Twickenham'.
[38] First held (from 1974) by J. W. House, himself a graduate of the Oxford School of Geography.

Chapter 3

Patriot and Imperialist

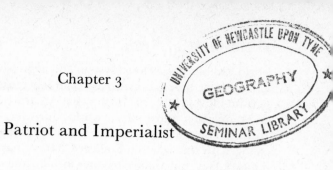

During his long life Mackinder expressed views on a wide variety of subjects, and almost always he was moved to speak out of concern for his nation—the English, his country—the United Kingdom, and the Empire over which his sovereign ruled. Like Heylyn (1657) he could say, 'as I have taken on myself the parts of an Historian and Geographer, so have I not forgot that I am an Englishman'. He was a discriminating patriot who passionately desired that England should remain powerful and secure, democratic and free. His love of country did not blind him, however, to social and economic deficiencies which offended his sense of justice and his respect for his fellow men. Unlike most politicians he took the long view, and so well was he intellectually fitted to do this, that many of his dicta, regarded as far-fetched, if not fantastic, when they were uttered, were to make good sense later. Had his advice and warnings been acted on, the rapid deterioration of Britain's position might well have been averted.

A first-class brain and the power to visualize the unfolding of historical processes within their geographical constraints enabled him to harness his scientific, economic, and political knowledge to the chariot of his disciplined imagination. For in such matters, as he himself remarked (1909a), 'Foresight of a generation's length is not excessive where the vital questions of territorial productivity, national man-power, strategical position, and imperial organization are under consideration.' His biological and historical training had developed a consciousness that the world was a dynamic place where states expanded and contracted, and where nations flourished and decayed; but momentum from the past disguised change and so gave the British people a false sense of the permanence of their power and prosperity.

There were two factors which made change more likely and both could operate to Britain's disadvantage. One was that the world had become a closed system and aggressive energies could no longer be diverted overseas: 'The repercussion of every important blow in any part is felt in every part. In the future every great question must be a world question ...' (Mackinder 1916a). The other was impending revolutionary technological change: 'In this war the English Channel has still existed as a military fact, but we are passing into an age of which wireless telegraphy, aeroplanes, zeppelins and submarines are but the first indications' (ibid.).

He was wary, however, of concentrating on technology to the neglect of social factors. Certainly, 'the advance of scientific knowledge and invention' had placed great power in the hands of mankind, but this power was conditional upon 'social organization' which was a complex mechanism, the maintenance of which could not be taken for granted. From this it followed that, 'The assumption of some scientific enthusiasts that the study of the humane arts had ceased to be important will not bear examination; the management of men, high and low, is more difficult and more important under conditions of modern reality than it ever was' (Mackinder 1919, pp. 16–17). Where power was resource-based, the exhaustion of vital fuels and raw materials could also lead to change: 'the command that the West has exercised over the vacant seas and almost vacant lands of the outer world' had been 'intensified by a temporary cause; Western men have led the way in the exploitation of the coal, oil and iron ore', but the effects of their eventual depletion could be delayed and masked by momentum and inertia (Mackinder 1931, p. 12).

This awareness of change enabled him to see that, despite the apparent unassailability of its power, Britain could fall into rapid decline within a relatively short period:

Foreign markets may be lost, and employment for British workmen reduced: capital may be repaid by debtor countries, and the annual interest may cease to be received: the carrying trade may dwindle, and shipping be transferred to other flags: the preference of later generations of colonists may grow weaker, and they may buy more impartially from the competitors of the mother country: finally the coalfields at home may be exhausted, and no fresh supply of energy be available. Grown poorer, Britain may no longer have the means of building and maintaining an adequate fleet, and may lose command of the sea. Other empires have had their day, and so may that of Britain. (Mackinder 1902, p. 350)

Yet he realised that a Britain whose power had decayed would still have a vital part to play in Western strategy, for although 'in this little island we have not productivity sufficient to base an empire which shall hold its own with the great continental empires that are developing', the Dominions and the United States would find an offshore island base essential in warding off any threat from the continent (Mackinder 1909a, p. 474).[1]

Mackinder's biological training, and the theories of evolution and natural selection may have affected his thinking. Like Ratzel[2] he sometimes saw a political structure as an organism and applied this term to the British Empire, 'which has to hold its place according to the universal law of survival through efficiency and effort' (Mackinder 1911, p. 83; also 1905, p. 140). But also like Ratzel, he distinguished between biological and political organisms, the latter being susceptible to moral and spiritual motivation: 'Last century, under the spell of the Darwinian theory, men came to think that those forms of organization should survive which adapted themselves best to their natural environment. To-day we realize ... that human victory consists in our rising superior to such mere fatalism' (Mackinder 1919, p. 3). Even more dangerous, however, than denying the human will a place in shaping a nation's destiny was an unthinking belief in the permanence of the political *status quo*. At the end of the 1914-18 war he wrote:

The temptation of the moment is to believe that unceasing peace will ensue merely because tired men are determined that there shall be no more war. But international tension will accumulate again, though slowly at first; there was a generation of peace after Waterloo. Who among the diplomats round the Congress table at Vienna in 1814

[1] For M. and Britain's place in the world see also C. A. Fisher (1963), p. 125. In this illuminating paper he points out that even in the post-war decade, Britain 'had tried to continue playing a great-power role, which we are no longer capable of substaining.'

[2] Friedrich Ratzel (1844-1914); German geographer whose *Politische Geographie* (1897) provided the foundation for political thought in Germany, and had much influence abroad. Although he stated that the State was a political organism, he was careful to make clear that it was not comparable to an animal organism, and that the more developed it became the more imperfect as an organism it was; 'the spiritual and moral powers that influence it increase this imperfection'. Therefore 'the comparison of the State with the highly developed organism is unprofitable' (pp. 12-13).

foresaw that Prussia would become a menace to the world? (ibid., pp. 1–2)

Powerful forces, both physical and human, were at work, making for change:

> The great wars of history ... are the outcome, direct or indirect, of the unequal growth of nations, and that unequal growth is not wholly due to the greater genius and energy of some nations as compared with others; in large measure it is the result of the uneven distribution of fertility and strategical opportunity upon the face of our Globe. In other words, there is in nature no such things as equality of opportunity for the nations. (ibid., p. 2)

At first sight the many topics on which Mackinder expressed views may seem unconnected. Yet most of his multifarious statements find a place in a unifying imperial philosophy. This was expressed in a logical theorem intended to prove that Britain's only salvation as a great power lay in consolidating round the mother country a united Empire. Britain's power and prosperity rested upon her human resource, her industrial base, her commerce, and her Navy, which guarded the trade routes. All these foundations needed strengthening if the edifice they bore was to stand: the human resource required social reform and better education; the industrial base needed tariff protection; the commerce required greater security of resource and market; and the Navy had to have more men, more ships, and more money to maintain its supremacy in a world where rivals were building great fleets. Except for the improvement of the human resource, which was a domestic matter, all these requirements could be met, and often only met, from a unified Empire—unified politically through some kind of federation, economically by a system of imperial preference, and socially by common regard, mutual understanding, and genuine equality of status. For this to happen, the British must become a well-educated and efficient people, since, having become a democracy, the whole nation would need rare qualities of judgement, foresight, and forbearance if it were to fulfil the imperial role essential to its survival. So one came back to the human resource—the British people.

Each stage of the argument was developed in books, articles, or speeches. First there was the need to demonstrate the reality of the external threats to British supremacy. Concluding his classic description of the British Isles, he wrote:

In the presence of vast Powers, broad based on the resources of half continents, Britain could not again become mistress of the seas. Much depends on the maintenance of a lead won under earlier conditions. Should the sources of wealth and vigour upon which the navy is founded run dry, the imperial security of Britain will be lost (1902, p. 358)

Three years later he warned that 'all the great Powers are building fleets and half a continent may ultimately outbuild and outman our island' (1905, p. 139). In 1906 he again pressed home the unpalatable message:

The foreign world ... is watching the rise of the tide around us, and forecasting the decay of our Empire. Ten years ago an eminent German writer, Fuchs, predicted the rise of a statesman who would try to save England as a great Power by reversing her economic policy. In the last edition, recently published, of his 'English Trade Policy', he asked whether that statesman has not come too late.[3] (1906, p. 12)

After 1909 it was not so necessary to give these warnings; the menace from Germany was becoming apparent to all. His worries about the growing strength of America and the potential Russian threat, had to give way to the common preoccupation with the more immediate danger. But whereas the German threat was seen by most in mainly military terms, Mackinder viewed it in the wider context of the differing economic and social outlook of the two nations. And as the problem itself was not wholly military, nor was the long-term solution, which needed radical changes in commercial and social policy at home. His position has been well summarized (Semmell 1958):

Mackinder had become convinced that the world of the twentieth century was not to be the peaceful world of the nineteenth. The Germans meant to do more than deprive England of industrial hegemony. What good would British capital be against German armed might? Could a nation living on foreign investments and brokers' fees, deprived of the capacity to manufacture weapons,[4] successfully defend herself against a well-trained, well-equipped nation of half again as

---

[3] A reference presumably to Joseph Chamberlain.
[4] i.e. through the destruction of its unprotected engineering industries by German competition.

many people? ... The moral was plain. In order to defend herself against Germany, Great Britain had to be transformed. (p. 559)

To combat the danger the first essential was radically to improve the human resource, which Mackinder called man-power, a term he introduced into the language.[5] He did not mean by it merely a 'body count' but 'the product of the number and the present quality' of a people. A small but talented and trained nation could vie successfully with a larger but less endowed population: 'it is probable, for instance, that the teeming millions of China do not, for lack of effective education, man for man, at present count in the balance of power against the men and women of western Europe' (1909, p. 462). He criticized the statistical evaluation of the country's prosperity, to the neglect of the qualitative assessment of man-power. In his maiden speech he told the Commons that he wanted 'to deal with this matter not from the point of view of pounds, shillings and pence ... but from the point of view of human beings who constitute the real nation' (P.D. 1910, xiv, 317).

The social conditions and mental training of the British people must be reformed. The neglect of the education, health, and welfare of the masses had resulted in an inefficient use of man-power; the upper classes too had become unfitted to meet the challenge from outside. As H. G. Wells (1934, vol. ii, pp. 763-4) put it, 'our ruling class, protected in its advantages by a universal snobbery, was broad-minded, easy-going and profoundly lazy. The Edwardian monarch, Court and society were amiable and slack. "Efficiency"—the word of Earl Rosebery and the Webbs was felt to be rather priggish and vulgar.' A very different attitude was needed if Britain was to confront her rivals successfully. Mackinder shared this view. Upper and middle class education was well suited for turning out an imperial ruling class:

The private preparatory schools, the great public schools, and the colleges of Oxford and Cambridge, receive their boys from nursery to manhood, and shape them according to class and athletic ideals. The English gentleman is the result. He has the defects of his great qualities, and we may perhaps trace them to the system under which he was formed. Neither conspicuous originality nor professional thoroughness

---

[5] 'May we, for shortness, refer to the labouring and fighting power of this country as its Man-power?' (1906, p. 21).

are engendered either by the traditions of his caste or the atmosphere of his school. But for the purpose of maintaining the honesty, the energy, the discipline and the honorary fellowship of a great ruling class it would be difficult to imagine any machinery more delicately adjusted to its purpose under the conditions which have prevailed during the last few generations. (1903, pp. 250–1)

But conditions and needs were changing. It was now time to treat 'the education of the whole nation as a single problem', i.e. we should be more concerned with 'the betterment of the race and the greater efficiency of the State', than with the welfare of 'particular social classes'.

Mackinder condemned the social condition of the working class as 'our present *regime* of weekly wages, unemployment doles, old age pensions, football betting, and cinemas'; these furnished 'a low-level security against absolute want' and 'anodyne pastimes', revolt against them was not in itself unhealthy' (*The Times*, 23 Nov. 1922). The cause of the trouble he ascribed to *laissez-faire* economics, investment abroad, changing technology, foreign tariffs, and the free entry of foreign goods. The export of capital in the form of machinery had promoted foreign competition: 'by it you have made foreign countries your rivals ... If a machine tool is manufactured here does it not matter to the worker whether it is kept in this country or whether it is sent abroad? Is there not a bench for a workman here in the one case; is there not a bench for the foreign workman in the other?' (P.D. 1910, xiv, 317). 'Let me', says Mackinder (1906, p. 22) 'make the idea clearer by a concrete instance. As the result of foreign dumping here, and of difficulty of access to foreign markets, an English manufacturer decides to establish a new factory within a foreign country. His men will supply recruits to a foreign army, and his factory will be taxed to support that army.' His profits will show up to the advantage of our balance of payments.

But what in this instance do the statistics tell us of our loss of Man-power? True, that the factory owner residing here, having studied his private interest, is probably making a greater profit than if he had established a factory in this country ... but from the point of view of our national Man-power, the loss of the wages of his operatives must far more than counterbalance any such gain. (ibid.)

Unemployment was particularly damaging to man-power:

Every great irregularity of employment, whether due to foreign competition, trade disputes, shortage of raw materials, or failure of employees, involves terrible wreckage of the capital fixed in humanity
... Our extreme division of labour renders men helpless in the presence
of changes which would formerly have meant little to them. Are not
our slums to a very great extent the scrap-heaps of abandoned and
disused portions of our national man-power? Who can say how many
men and women have sunk to a lower grade when their skill became
obsolete, and with what loss of hope and morals? No doubt a reasonable amount of competition stimulates. Some loss is also inevitable in
all progress. But we should be careful to set against our gains this loss
of humanity ... (1905, p. 142)

One-sided development was the bane of the free-trade policy 'If
the world's efficiency can only be maintained by competition,
it is well that it should be competition in which the whole
energies of the people are tested. Excessive militarism defeats
itself, no doubt, but so also does excessive commercialism, or
excessive development in any direction.' And so, 'The right
policy has for its conscious object to attain the greatest sum of
man-power in all its complexity—physical, intellectual, and
moral.' It would necessitate 'legislation for temperance, education, and better housing'. In fact, 'the real strength of a nation
lies in its workers, its thinkers, its fighters and its mothers'
(ibid.).

The remedy was not only to protect our industries with a
tariff but also to give workers 'a stake in their country beyond
a weekly budget and a State pension against contingencies'. He
saw the National Savings Movement, which he had been instrumental in introducing during the 1914-18 war,[6] as one way of
doing this. However, for good or ill the country was now,
through extension of the franchise, a democracy, and the
people's fate was in their own hands. But a poorly educated
people was unfit for democracy. Education for citizenship—i.e.
for making sound and realistic judgements, was therefore in the
forefront of the reforms he advocated.

If Britain fails in the contests of the half-visible future, it will not be
because the best products of her best education are inferior to those of
Germany or America—for they are certainly not—but because the
great majority of her soldiers, civil servants, clerks, and artisans,

[6] See above, p. 43.

whatever their advantages of character, are less professionally expert and less generally informed than are the ordinary people of other countries. (Mackinder 1903, p. 248)

He quotes the famous chemist, Dewar,[7] in support of his belief that Germans are not more intelligent than Englishmen, and that technical training would not in itself be a sufficient remedy:

'It is in the abundance of men of ordinary plodding ability, thoroughly trained and methodically directed, that Germany has at present so commanding an advantage. It is in the failure of our schools to turn out, and of our manufacturers to demand, men of this kind, which explains our loss of some valuable industries, and our precarious hold on others. Let no one imagine for a moment that these deficiencies can be remedied by any amount of that technical training which is now the fashionable nostrum.' (ibid.)

Mackinder then returns to his main point: 'Britain, with a relatively small population, but great geographical and historical advantages, may long preserve a lead in the world, but it can only be on one condition. Her people, man for man, and woman for woman, whether leaders or rank and file, must be more than the equal of like numbers in other lands' (ibid., pp. 249-50).

He deplored the loss of man-power through emigration— 'surely 150,000 of educated, adolescent human beings are an export of the finest and most cherished capital of this country' (P.D. 1910, xiv, 316). It was argued that we needed emigration because we had a surplus population, and that there was emigration from Germany as well. But Germany's booming tariff-protected industries were now employing her surplus population at home, and Britain should do the same. In any case, more man-power would be needed for defence: 'A purely oceanic policy is possible even for an insular Power only under temporary conditions which are passing away ... a world Power simply cannot limit its liabilities to the ocean, and must not therefore depend on expending men with the singular economy of sea-power' (Mackinder 1905, p. 139). It would be 'highly improbable' that we could

---

[7] Sir James Dewar (1842-1923), Professor of Experimental Natural Philosophy at Cambridge 1875, Professor of Chemistry at the Royal Institution 1877. Inventor of cordite, the thermos flask, etc.

long maintain the position of an insular Power with fleet-defended commercial dependencies. You cannot permanently insure your world position and wealth on any principle of limited liability. While there is time, perhaps a whole generation, you must so increase your white man-power ... that your friendship may be worthy of allies and that foes may shrink from your strength. (ibid., p. 141)

There was the possibility of sharing the burden with America:

A great naval Power is rapidly rising beyond the Western ocean. A league with this Power on terms of equal alliance is an attractive ideal, but the condition is strength on our side no less than the other ... Nor must we forget that we have won the Americans by supporting the Monroe doctrine; in other words, by helping to shut Europe out of South America. We have, therefore, helped to shut Germany into Europe. In supporting Japan, we are helping to shut Russia into Asia and Europe. (ibid., pp. 139-40)

The best solution was to build up British man-power in the colonies; this would enable them to help us as they had done in South Africa.

One final reason for taking care of man-power was that, if the worst came to the worst, and the Empire was lost, Britain could still find wealth in her human resources, and be 'actually, although not relatively, richer than to-day' (Mackinder 1902, pp. 351-2).

If the man-power base needed improvement by social reform and educational enlightenment, the industrial and commercial bases required protection from foreign competition. Mackinder had begun active political life as the theoretician of free-trade imperialism, describing 'with unusual insight the imperialism of capital export, anticipating at some points the later analysis of Hobson and the neo-Marxists, Hilferding and Luxemburg' (Semmell 1958, p. 554). He came soon, however, to realize that the growing wealth of London merchants and bankers, and of *rentiers* who invested abroad, was balanced by unemployment and poverty, caused by foreign competition, in the industrial areas. Germany and America had developed strong industries under the protection of tariff walls; their secure home markets subsidized the cheap export of their surpluses, driving Britain out of her markets, even within her own Empire, and actually invading the home market.

Before his conversion, Mackinder (1900b) had regarded this situation with equanimity: 'the financial importance of the City of London may continue to increase while the industry ... of Britain becomes *relatively* less'. But once he had become theoretician and propagandist for the tariff reformers, he urged the inadequacy of the mere 'accumulation of wealth' when it was achieved at the expense of 'productive powers'. Tariffs had not only given the nascent industries of foreign countries shelter under which to develop. They had enabled them to grow into formidable rivals, undermining the vital foundations of British power:

... in the case of Germany and the United States, the home market, greater than the British home market, has sufficed for the development of industries large enough to produce cheaply, and now in excess of home requirements. Hence the rise of an export trade of manufactured articles, a demand for foreign markets, and the need for a strong fleet to give support in world diplomacy. That fleet could not have been paid for except out of the proceeds of the new industries. Thus power and labour alternatively support one another. (Mackinder 1906, p. 20)

Britain also needed tariffs, not only to protect her domestic industries, but also her foreign commerce, for, 'some of the "protected countries" have grown so fast both in man-power and wealth, that it has become a question whether Britain can much longer defend her trade by keeping the "open door" to her own and neutral markets' (Mackinder 1907, p. 343). 'It is useless', he argued (1906),

to urge in reply that the totals of our trade are at present growing ... Of what good ... would it be when we come to take stock some ten or twenty years hence, not of our wealth as such, but of the basis of our power, to find that while we had a double trade and a double fleet, our principal rivals had each a triple trade and a triple fleet? (p. 13)

At present, Britain was 'losing the race' (ibid.).

Fiscal reform alone would not suffice to keep Britain strong, wealthy, and free, nor enable her to resist the challenge of her rivals. She must consolidate her Empire around her if she were to match their potential strength, and this would not be easy in the face of the powerful centrifugal forces operating in a far-flung and scattered overseas Empire. But it must be done, for the Empire was essential to Britain. 'Of what consolation', he asked (1905), 'is it to be told that we are holding our own ... as well as can be expected of a small country? Nature is ruthless, and we must build a Power able to contend on equal terms with other Powers, or step into the rank of the States which exist on sufferance' (p. 143). British power needed to be broader based, i.e. more evenly developed throughout the Empire. He even contemplated Canada developing as 'the economic centre of the British Empire' (1909, p. 474), and he hoped it would do so. In *The Times* of 19 October 1910 he wrote that, 'only by gathering together the several nations of the Empire can we cope in the international balance of power with the newly-organized continental states'.

The Empire, properly constituted as an organic whole, would supply British deficiencies. Was not New Zealand 'to all intents and purposes, a fragment of the old country lying moored in the antipodean ocean, a portion of that agricultural land which we shall need to add to this country if, with the present scale of our industries, we were to be a balanced and self-contained community?' (Mackinder 1930, p. 255). The Empire was also necessary to Britain because it could widen our reserves of man-power. Emigration could be turned to advantage if it were kept within the Empire; one of his little school-books (1906a) concluded with the paragraph:

Those who can to-day find work in Britain should stay here among their friends, but those who have no work should cross the ocean and make new homes for themselves in Canada, or Australia, or New Zealand, or South Africa. In all these lands they will remain the subjects of our King, Edward VII; the same flag will be theirs and they will not be among foreigners.[8]

Mackinder saw salvation for Britain in the Empire, but not through exploitation of that Empire. It should be a free partnership of democracies united by a common interest—the necessity to belong to a political organization large and strong

[8] At a meeting of the Coefficients on 15 May 1905 M. opened the discussion on 'How far is it practicable and desirable to guide British emigration to British colonies rather than to foreign countries?' According to the minutes 'the position of the opener met with general acquiescence, although some doubt was expressed as to whether any action could be taken which would counteract the economic attractiveness of the United States' (Mackinder Papers, School of Geography, Oxford).

enough to compete with great continental realms; but many changes and reforms were needed—constitutional, economic, and social, before this combination of inter-dependent states could operate efficiently.

Constitutionally, Mackinder hoped for closer union, possibly some kind of federation. But the strength of 'Little Englander' feeling and free-trade radicalism, along with colonial suspicions, militated against moves towards unity. The Imperial Federation League had been dissolved in 1893 and Chamberlain's proposal for an Imperial Council had been rejected by the 1902 Colonial Conference. The efforts of the Pollock Committee, 1903, first to revive the idea of an Imperial Council, and then to establish some kind of permanent colonial conference, were successfully frustrated by the Colonial Office, jealous of the creation of a rival body (Kendle 1967, pp. 57–107).[9] Mackinder was inevitably drawn into association with those who believed passionately in imperial unity and were prepared to fight on despite such setbacks. In 1908, led by Lord Milner and organized by Amery, they succeeded in raising enough money to enable Mackinder to go into politics so that he could advance their cause more effectively. He was to resign the Directorship of the London School of Economics and devote himself to promoting imperial union. In return he was to be paid £850 a year for four years (ibid., p. 127).

Mackinder had held the view that imperial union was a necessity when he was Liberal candidate at Warwick in 1900: 'No other course is open to us than to bind Britain and her Colonies into a league of democracies, defended by a united Navy and an efficient Army' (his election address, qu. in *The Times*, 22 Oct. 1903). As soon as he was in Parliament he urged a permanent imperial secretariat so as to give continuity to the discussions which the self-governing Dominions held at the imperial conferences (P.D. 1910, xviii, 981): 'A truly Imperial Government' he insisted (1911a, p. 316) 'in some way representative of all the Britains, must sooner or later come into existence.' During the war he thought that, in the period of political

[9] The Imperial Federation League, founded in 1884, included Bryce, W. E. Forster, Froude, Lord Rosebery, J. R. Seeley, and several colonial politicians among its members and supporters. The Pollock Committee was chaired by the great legal historian and jurist, Sir Frederick Pollock (1845–1937).

readjustment that would inevitably follow, 'side by side with the reorganization of Europe, you might achieve the reorganization of the Empire'. What was wanted was 'something more organic' (P.D. 1915, lxxiii, 1526). His suggestions did not bear fruit, and after the war he regretted (1925) the strong disruptive forces bearing upon the Empire:

Now, what is clear is that foreign opinion will press more and more strongly on the several parts of the Empire, tending to pull them apart owing to the immediate urgency of their local dangers and duties. Even in this island, with all our developed strength, though we resisted the Geneva Protocol, we have found it necessary to make the Treaty of Locarno,[10] and thereby to put the unity of the Empire to the test. (p. 3)

Yet he had not given up hope entirely. He was Chairman of the Imperial Shipping and Economic Committees, and these were extraordinarily successful in uniting the disparate interests of their members, and had a fine record of unanimity; he called them (1925, p. 6) 'certain experiments which I sometimes dream may prove to be the seed of great things in the British Empire'.

The economic reinforcement of the Empire would have to come from Imperial Preference or Empire Free Trade within a tariff. But although powerful vested interests urged protection of the home market, just as even more powerful interests supported free trade, there was no such force backing imperial preference; its advocates, such as Amery, Hewins, and Mackinder, had to rely upon the soundness of their arguments and on imperial sentiment. The Compatriots' Club was founded by Amery in 1904 'to act as an organizing and propagandist body'.[11]

As Mackinder saw it, imperial preference was necessary to ensure that the colonists benefited from membership of the Empire; they would then be the more willing to support its unity and participate in its defence:

[10] At Locarno (1925) Britain guaranteed the Franco-German frontier against aggression from either side; the Dominions were hostile to this involvement.

[11] 'The one anxiety felt by most of Chamberlain's younger supporters ... was that the Empire side of it should be overborne, or even side-tracked, by the growing tide of the demand for industrial protection with its more immediate appeal both to industrialists and to working men. A dozen of us met for dinner in my rooms in the Temple ...' (Amery 1953, vol. i, pp. 264-5).

Under present conditions ... what is there to induce our colonies to take a real share in maintaining the power of the Empire? ... we derive wheat and wool from Argentina, a foreign country. We derive wheat also from our colony Canada, and wheat and wool from our colony Australia. We receive the commodities on precisely the same terms from all three sources ... Yet the Canadians and Australians, and not the Argentines, helped us to fight in South Africa—helped us in other words to keep the great alternative route to India, which is the most valuable market for the manufactures of Lancashire. Therefore the Colonials assisted in securing the wages of our cotton operatives. Is it very surprising that they should ask that a part of these wages be spent buying Canadian and Australian, in preference to Argentine, wheat? If they were so spent, more wages would be paid for wheat-growing in Canada, and the Canadian population and wealth would be increased accordingly. The result would be to give the Canadian a greater interest in the maintenance of a British fleet ... we should soon arrive at a time when political federation would be called for to deal with our large common interests. (Mackinder 1906, pp. 15-16)

In the Commons he made the same point in his maiden speech, and often returned to it. In public lectures also he hammered home his case, giving the example of Canada, a country he came to know well:

There was a strong feeling against annexation by the United States, there was also a constant economic temptation to give to the United States terms which must end in political union. The independent existence of Canada would be secured ... only by an amalgamation of Canadian and British interests ... By tariff reform, by a preference on wheat now, as soon as we could do it, we should play a stroke which would not only make for the Empire, but make powerfully for the Canadian nation. (*The Times*, 15 Dec. 1908)

Mackinder was writing in the context of a Canadian offer of closer co-operation in return for preference. It was galling for him to see such opportunities lost.

Imperial preference was necessary if the Empire was to absorb more British immigration: 'What a splendid output of English-born Man-power might have been diverted from the building of the United States to that of Canada had we adopted Imperial Preference a generation ago' (Mackinder 1906, p. 22). Imperial Preference was also an essential prerequisite for a more united or federated Empire; without it, closer union 'could only make more evident the separation of our interests' (ibid., p. 16).

A great obstacle to unity was the colonists' fear of a revival of British mercantilism, but this was not what Mackinder had in mind. In fact, because he deeply appreciated the problems of Empire, and sympathized with the aspirations of the colonies, he was one of the few British statesmen who could have made a success of Empire. In 1907 (1907a, p. 34) he said:

> When the Colonial premiers arrive here in May they will, I fear, often be shocked ... by the assumption, at the back of most of our minds, that the permanent function of the Mother Country is to manufacture, and of the Dominions overseas to grow food and raw materials for the Mother Country.

There was, in fact,

> much to be said for a reasonable tariff control area even as between parts of the Empire ... complete Free Trade within the Empire might tend to that unhealthy segregation of industrials on the one hand and rustics on the other, which has been rejected by other nations. As Imperialists we should be ready to welcome the first British battleship built in Nova Scotia or New Zealand. (Mackinder 1905, p. 143)

Even when the Conservatives were in power in the 1920s, they failed to effect Empire Free Trade and Imperial Preference. Imperial tariff reformers had to be content with an improved organization of marketing Empire produce—for which Mackinder's Imperial Economic Committee was set up in 1925 and Amery's Empire Marketing Board in 1928, and with the limited agreements reached at the 1932 Ottawa Conference.[12] By 1930 (*aet.* 69) Mackinder himself had come to accept that the unification of the Empire could only be achieved, if at all, by a piecemeal or gradual approach: 'the British Empire is a great business partnership—fortunately a family partnership—and just as, in an ordinary business concern, you build each day on what was accomplished yesterday, so must it be in regard to the Empire' (Mackinder 1930). He would have liked to see industry rationalized throughout the Empire, in order to achieve the economies of scale and optimum size possible in continental empires like the United States. It would then be

[12] For a critique of Empire Free Trade and Imperial Preference, see Fisher (1963), pp. 124–5.

possible to compare such an Empire 'with a potential United States of Europe and with the actual United States, and with other great agglomerations which are not, perhaps, immediately upon us, but are yet looming on the horizon' (ibid.). What chance was there of the Empire acting as one great unit? 'It would be a sensible thing to do, but difficult under the circumstances of democracy' (ibid.).

If the survival of the Empire was dependent upon mutually beneficial economic arrangements, agreement to these arrangements could only be obtained if the social relationships were satisfactory. This meant a degree of mutual sympathy, respect, and understanding which was not yet present. It therefore behoved idealist imperialists such as himself to remedy matters through education and propaganda.

There were two meanings of Empire: 'the federation, loose or close, of several British commonwealths, and the maintenance of British rule among alien races' (Mackinder 1902, p. 346). Each had its own special relationships with Britain. For the first group, 'the several British commonwealths', she was the mother country or the 'old country', with which most of their inhabitants had 'kith and kin' ties. For the second, or 'ruled' Empire, the link with Britain lay in the 'more than ten thousand of officers, civil and military, drawn largely from the middle classes' who administered it.

The requirements of the first Empire differed from those of the second. The self-governing part consisted of democracies whose leaders and peoples had to be convinced of the need for and benefits of closer co-operation. The administered part required justice and respect for its traditional cultures. The discrete nature of Britain's Empire complicated the problem:

In most empires the ruling people has spread from its original home over contiguous regions.[13] In the process the conquerors have often lost their liberties, while the conquered have often been assimilated more or less to their masters. But Imperial Britain is unique, because wide seas roll between the islands and the outlands. This is a source both of weakness and of strength. On the one hand it renders the growth of sympathy difficult. On the other hand it preserves undiluted the chief reservoir of the Imperial man-power. To some extent, there-

[13] Mackinder could have given America, Canada, Russia, and China as examples of continental empires formed in this way. See Parker (1972), pp. 23-9.

fore, it tends to perpetuate the wide contrast of conqueror and conquered ... (Mackinder 1905, p. 137)

Mackinder illustrated the need for tact and understanding, if the goodwill of the self-governing dominions was to be retained, in a letter to *The Times* (8 Sept. 1908), which also throws light on his attitude to racial problems:

A paragraph has recently appeared in many Canadian newspapers in which sentences are quoted from certain English journals ... From the *Statist* are taken the following words:

'Canada, with a population about the size of London, occupying or pretending to occupy a territory nearly as big as Europe, takes upon itself to exclude Indian fellow-subjects, equal in number to the whole population of Europe. The Canadian people have no right to take up this attitude except the right of mere brute force.'

Sentiments such as those which I have quoted strike the average Canadian as both ignorant and unsympathetic. In an academic sense they may no doubt present an aspect of the truth, but ninety-nine out of a hundred Canadians are in no mood for mere dialectic ... Such a nation, when told in the same breath that it has no moral right to prevent itself from being overwhelmed by an inexhaustible stock of alien race and civilization, must not be blamed if it conclude that there is a wide angle between the points of view of the Mother Country and the Dominion.

If there is one object of policy on which thinking Canadians are firmly united it is that of a white Canada. Mixture of races must result either in intermarriage with physical and moral consequences which, to say the least, are deeply uncertain, or in a caste system fatal to democratic ideals ... if force be ever justifiable it must surely be for the preservation of the very texture of social order, painfully woven during long history. British statesmen will have to reckon with this fact if the Empire is to be held together. Nor need they thereby be involved in insoluble difficulties with our Indian fellow-subjects.

No one seeks to exclude the 'intellectuals' of any race or religion. For them let us have the most Imperial scope and hospitality, more sincere and better organized than they are to-day ... The vast majority, on the other hand, of every race, the normal workers, are not so conditioned. Narrow resources and dense population place them—and their wives and children—very much at the mercy of the average society around. Neither Japanese, nor Chinese, nor Indians would welcome into their venerable and civilized societies an inroad in mass of white workers, with habits and ideals good in themselves, but destructive of the very bases of Japanese, Chinese, and Indian moralities.

As for the 'ruled' part of the Empire, there must be a 'freedom from contempt for other races ... the essentially provincial contempt of other races is a vice to be fought in the education of an imperial race' (Mackinder 1907a, pp. 36–7). Although he conceded the right of Australia and Canada to remain 'white', there must none the less be equality of status

if we are to uphold the British Empire it must be by maintaining our provincial nationalities, and at the same time cultivating the idea of equality as between these nationalities. The races of India will not become English in their prejudices and their ideals, yet in the long run they will have to be treated as equals if we are to have their willing strength ... the Imperial race must be educated beforehand to tolerate the gradual rise of Indian ideals. Without this toleration equality of the component nations can never be realized except at the cost of the disruption of the Empire. (ibid., p. 40)

The idea of responsible trusteeship should replace the glory of possession: 'I am always sorry when I see Imperialism taught in our schools by means of the kind of map which is just now frequent—I mean the map on which the Dominions of the Empire, and the Protectorates, and even the ocean, are coloured over with a brilliant red to signify possession.' Instead he wanted to 'put the idea of Trusteeship into the minds of our people, and with it the idea that we have to improve ourselves because we are the trustees, and must be worthy to rule' (ibid., p. 41). It followed that an enlightened imperial education in all parts of the Empire was vital. That is why he devoted so much of his time to the Victoria League and to the Visual Instruction Committee of the Colonial Office—both aimed to spread knowledge of the Empire. He warned (1911), however, against taking too narrow a view:

'Little they know of England who only England know.' Still more truly may it be said, little they know of the British Empire who only the Empire know ... the British Empire is, as it were, threaded through the other powers as the weft through the woof of a cloth ... The significance of such a station as Hong Kong lies wholly in its relation to neighbouring China and to the eastern seaways.

Knowledge of a world-wide Empire involved knowledge of the whole world.

In the late 1890s Mackinder had thought out an ideology of imperialism tailored to the Liberal Imperialist group of which he was a member; this he expounded in four lectures late in 1899 (1900b). Although consonant with the free-trade *laissez-faire* philosophy of the 'Limps', it was an early prototype of the centre-periphery model later used by Marxist economists. It begins by postulating organizing centres amongst which there is a chief or world centre—a corollary of the 'oneness of the ocean'. The late nineteenth century had seen the 'process of suddenly occupying virgin territories, drawing their new re-sources from them; and fitting them with capital appliances', and this constituted 'for the organizing centres of the old world, a great, though necessarily passing work'. Possession of capital was the great single determinant of economic power:

those who have capital always share the proceeds of the activities of brains and muscles of other countries. It is certainly true 'that to him that hath shall be given.' The possessors take from all the world a toll on the world's traffic; and as a consequence, have ever more and more capital, and are ever increasingly monopolists. (1900b, p. 155)

Once you owned capital in various parts of the world, you had 'the biggest stakes in securing good government for the most various countries. It is for the maintenance of our position in the world, because we are the great lenders, that we have been driven to increase our Empire.' The tendency, however, would be 'towards the dispersion and equalization of industrial and commercial activity throughout the world'. But even when 'factories and warehouses are equally distributed over the world, a great organizing centre will be even more needful than at the present time . . .' (ibid., p. 271).

He justified his conversion to protection (tariff reform) on ethical as well as economic grounds. This was ironic because it was the free-traders who were generally regarded as having morality on their side. At meetings of the Coefficients[14] H. G. Wells (1934, vol. ii, p. 762) 'was still clinging to the dear belief that the English-speaking community might play the part of leader and mediator towards a world commonweal. It was to be a free-trading, free-speaking, liberating flux for mankind.' But Mackinder (1906) reminded his readers 'that Bismarck

[14] See above, pp. 30-1.

described Free Trade as the policy of the strong', and pointed out that it was accompanied by and depended upon the exercise of power: 'nothing stands out more clearly from the facts of recent history than that our power has in almost every instance been exerted in connection with some substantial market of our commerce'. With the free-trade policy one had to resort to war to protect one's interests; the retaliatory tariff was a more flexible weapon and infinitely less dangerous:

We were being forced steadily into a defensive position ... even in the United Kingdom we are experiencing dumping ... We must recover the habit of making bargains. At present our only serious weapon is power, the threat of war, and this is far too ponderous ... Yet we have the technically stronger position, if we would only use it with courage, in the power of denying access to our market here, which, to the foreign exporter, is at present the most valuable in the world. Retaliation is an ugly phrase, but no more is involved than International *business*. (Mackinder 1906, pp. 20–1)

Mackinder later (1919) expanded his argument that lack of the tariff weapon led to the costly and provocative use of military might:

Britain had no tariff available as a basis for bargaining; in that respect she stood naked before the world. Therefore, when threatened in some vital market, she could but return threats of sea-power ... Britain was *fighting* for her South American markets when her fleet maintained the Monroe doctrine against Germany in the Manila incident,[15] and for her Indian market when her fleet kept Germany at bay during the South African War, and for the open door to her China market when her fleet supported Japan in the Russian War. Did Lancashire realise that it was by force that the free import of cottons was imposed on India? ... repeatedly, both within and without the Empire, free-trading, peace-loving Lancashire has been supported by the *force* of the Empire. (p. 188)

Mackinder contested the 'idealism' of free-traders on another ground—that the regional and national economic specialization which *laissez-faire* produced was not really in the best interests of mankind. Seen from abroad, 'the generous ideals of our great Free Traders were simply a bid for universal empire ...'.

[15] At Manila Bay in the Philippines in 1898, the Americans attacked and destroyed the Spanish fleet and took the city of Manila.

In a world of general Free Trade our great industrial lead in 1846 would have made us the universal manufacturers and capitalists, and other races would have ploughed for us. With eyes open they have preferred, in the words of Adam Smith, defence to opulence. And after all, who shall say that the ideal of a balanced independent people, containing a due proportion of industrials as well as rustics, is lower than subjection to a British world metropolis of capital and industry? (Mackinder 1905, p. 141)

After the 1914–18 war Mackinder had to face a reaction against imperialism as a cause of war. He maintained that the British Empire and the League of Nations were not incompatible, and tried to answer a frequently-asked question: 'will not propaganda for the preferential buying of Empire produce generate a temper at variance with the broad humanitarian ideal wherewith we are endeavouring to kill the spirit of the Great War?' He argued (1925) further that Empire was the best means of diffusing the English tradition which had much to offer world civilization:

... there is something English which is slowly transferable, and that is the English tradition as embodied in our Common Law, our Party system, our methods of business ... In my belief this English tradition is vital to civilization as it has now developed. The race will long be needed as its standard-bearer because it can be transferred only gradually. The Empire is valuable to the world because it encloses certain areas within which the transfer has already been effected in greater degree than elsewhere.

The end of Mackinder's imperial dream came when the independence of the Dominions was recognized at the 1926 Imperial Conference, and enshrined in the Statute of Westminster (1931), without any accompanying move towards constitutional unity or co-ordinated policy.

Two parts of the Empire in which Mackinder took a special interest were the self-governing Dominion of Canada, which he visited several times and whose problems and policies he knew and understood, and India, on which he wrote a little book of illustrated lectures (1910).[16] He was proud of Britain's role in India:

---

[16] He also contributed the introductory chapter to *The Cambridge History of India* (1922).

The Indian Empire is one of the most wonderful achievements in the history of mankind. When the Great War broke out Germany looked confidently for an Indian revolution. Instead of revolution there was a very remarkable display of loyalty to the Empire ... the British work in India has been one of leadership and organization among a number of rival races and religions. (Mackinder 1924, p. 266)

The responsibility was great:

We could not withdraw now without throwing India into disorder, and causing untold suffering among three hundred million of our fellow human beings. Yet the administration of such an Empire calls for virtues in our race certainly not less than those needed for our own self-government. Above all, we require knowledge of India, and sympathy with the points of view begotten of oriental history.

Could British rule be maintained? 'Our power ultimately rests on our command of the seas and on the justice of our administration. When either of these fail, the British position in India will crumble' (Mackinder 1910, p. 133)).

Preoccupied with the Empire, Mackinder had little time for Britain's relationship with Europe and America. However, in *Britain and the British Seas* he discusses Britain's geographical position with regard to Europe. He notes how the coasts of south-eastern England 'had an almost unique character, facilitating to a remarkable degree intercourse between the continent and the island'. He goes on:

For many centuries the English were a race of shepherds rather than mariners, and the most significant feature of British geography was not the limitless ocean, but the approach of the south-eastern corner of the islands to within sight of the continent. Kent was the window by which England looked into the great world, and the foreground of that world, visible from Dover Castle, had no ordinary character. Immediately to the east of Calais is the end of the linguistic frontier which, crossing Europe from south to north, divides the two great races, Romance and Teutonic, whose interaction has made European history. From Calais eastward, in succession, were nations of Germanic seamen—Flemings, Hollanders, Frieslanders, Hansards, and Vikings. Westward was the Frenchman, and behind him the Spaniard and the Italian. To the Teutons—'Easterlings' and 'Norsemen'—England owes her civil institutions and her language; to the peoples of the west and south, her Christianity and her scholarship. Two distinct

streams of ethical and artistic influence converged upon the island
from the Rhine delta and from the estuary of the Seine; and the
balanced English character has therefore a physical counterpart in
the symmetry of the eastern and southern shores pivoted on the
Kentish forelands. (pp. 10–11)

He sums up with the epigram, 'Britain—of Europe, yet not *in*
Europe'. His thoughts would have been pertinent to the debate
on British membership of the EEC. In 1923 he wrote:

At present the little countries of Europe still stand in the foreground
of our imaginations, with conventional boundaries giving colour to
the map. But we Europeans will have to learn to see ourselves massed
into a single crowd, as already the Americans, the South Africans, and
the Australians see us. (p. 285)

In 1930 he spoke of 'a potential United States of Europe'.

As to the United States of America, he was concerned with
its growing naval and industrial strength, and with its attraction
to British emigrants who might otherwise have gone to British
colonies. But he also—at first reluctantly and then with more
interest—envisaged an Atlantic alliance (e.g. 1905, pp. 139–
140). The necessity to call for American help in 1917 forced him
to consider the idea more seriously, and in 1924 he suggested
that 'Western Europe and North America now constitute for
many purposes a single community of nations'. The 1939–45
war strengthened this view, and he reasserted it in 'The Round
World and the Winning of the Peace' (1943). Here he sees
Britain becoming 'the moated forward stronghold—a Malta on
a grander scale'. And that is what, in the postwar world, it was
fated to become.

According to Goudie (1980) Curzon 'was perhaps the only
British geographer to be a man of significance in the history of
the Empire'. The foregoing pages suggest that Mackinder also
had significance, and he has been called 'almost the scientific
counterpart of Kipling' (Gottmann 1952, p. 43). 'For many
years', as Amery (1953, vol. i, p. 228) reminds us, 'he played a
valuable, if inconspicuous part, in Empire affairs as chairman
of the Imperial Economic Committee and of the Imperial
Shipping Committee.' The remarkable record of unanimity

achieved by these committees was a practical illustration of the harmony that could have been achieved in Empire co-operation at other levels and in other fields if Mackinder's precepts and example had been followed.

Chapter 4

Democrat and Teacher

Mackinder understood by democracy much more than just the electoral practice of 'one man one vote'. The economic independence and spiritual well-being that followed from 'seeing life whole' in a 'balanced' nation or province, the freedom from the incubus of an overweening metropolis or from the centripetal pull of an advantaged and dominant neighbour, the possession of an educated and enlightened citizenry; these were more important than mere constitutional form.

Just as his imperial ideal was a federation of closely-knit cooperating nations united by a common allegiance, so his global ambition was for a world of 'balanced' autonomous communities. In this he was a generation before his time; it was not until after the 1939–45 war that a similar concept became popular under the guise of 'developed' and 'developing' nations, with the former helping the latter. It was in 1919 that he wrote:

Civilization, no doubt, consists in the exchange of services, but it should be an equal exchange. Our economics of money have assessed as equal, services of very unequal value from the point of view of the quality of the industrial employment which they give. For the contentment of nations we must contrive to secure some equality of opportunity for national development. (p. 235)

Fryer (1973) asks, 'Has anyone in the United Nations or World Bank ever said it better?'

The enemies, as Mackinder saw it, of that 'balance' which is essential to the freedom of nations, were organization, centralization, specialization, and large political and economic units. In 1921 he spoke of the dangers of the 'cult of personality' made possible by improvements in communications:

We had not only spanned the oceans and the continents, reduced the time of communication, but we had also increased in the most wonderful way the power of retailing personality, whether through the newspaper or by the film, with the result that a man at the other side of the world might speak or make grimaces to a million on this side.

The power of the organizers had increased, so that it was the prime danger to humanity. We had the military organizer, the financial organizer, the administrative organizer, and the journalistic organizer. Of course, they might have a Napoleon who combined them all. (*The Times*, 11 July 1921)

How much more convincing this would have seemed to his audience if they had known how close was the age of Hitler and Stalin!

He styled politico-economic organizations of State power 'going concerns'; if they fell into the hands of 'single-minded' or 'ruthless' organizers, freedom, whether of individuals or of nations, was lost (1919). Two years later he voiced his anxiety about the emergence of large monolithic empires:

There were people who condemned the Treaty of Versailles, and complained that Europe had been covered with frontiers ... If we got rid of frontiers, and had a horizontal class of society, it would mean the rule of one class, and ultimately of one organizer or group of organizers. If humanity was to retain freedom it could only be by insisting on provincialism. (*The Times*, 7 Oct. 1921)

Organization and centralization led to the growth of great power centres where the fate of the many was decided by the few, and which acted as 'brain drains'. The consequences for outlying provinces were dire. He found the 'horizontal' organization of the world by classes, with conflict between socialist and capitalist, particularly alarming, and advocated instead a 'vertical' arrangement of human activities by autonomous regions and unique localities, each with a full and balanced economic and social life:

As long as you allow a great metropolis to drain most of the best young brains from the local communities, to cite only one aspect of what goes on, so long must organization centre unduly in the metropolis and become inevitably an organization of nation-wide classes and interests ... the one thing essential is to displace class organisation, with its battle-cries and merely palliative remedies, by substituting an organic ideal, that of the balanced life of provinces, and under the provinces of the lesser communities. (1919, pp. 241-2)

His description of the consequences of 'horizontal' organization by classes has a familiar ring:

What is the bane of our modern industrial life? Surely monotony ...
Most of the responsible decisions are reserved for a few, and those few
are not even seen at their work, for they are away at the big centres.
What is it that in the last two or three generations has given such
strength to the Nationality movement ... It has arisen as the modern
States have not only increased in size, but have also grasped wider
functions within the Community. Nationalist movements are based
on the restlessness of intelligent young men who wish for scope to live
the life of ideas and to be among those who 'can' because they are
allowed to do.[1]
Are you quite sure that the gist of the demand for Home Rule in
Ireland, and in a less degree in Scotland, does not come mainly from
young men who are agitating, though they do not fully realise it, for
equality of opportunity rather than against the assumed wickedness
of England? ... Is there not something of the same human truth in the
refractoriness of the shop stewards in our factories against the Union
Executives away in London offices? (ibid., pp. 244–7)

In one of his most perceptive passages, he continues:

These ideas apply not only to industry but also to our educational
institutions and the learned professions. Our English system is to
buy—we must use plain words, for the element of competition among
the colleges exists—the best young brains by means of scholarships
open to national competition ... So you recruit your public schools
and your Oxford and Cambridge; from the beginning you lift your
lads out of their local environment. From the Universities many of
them pass into a centralised Civil Service, a centralised legal profession, and even a centralised medical profession ... (ibid., pp. 250–1)

Mackinder had abandoned free trade and *laissez-faire* because
they led to the specialization of each locality only upon those
economic activities that could survive in a competitive world, a
one-sided development which was inimical to freedom and happiness; for social monotony followed economic specialization.
Nations will 'be the poorer in the long run for the excessive
localization of the different industries. It takes all sorts to make
an inventive nation, where men increase ideas by the friction of
minds trained to many callings. Such a nation must soon forge
ahead of one which is socially monotonous' (Mackinder 1906,

[1] The reference is to Shaw's epigram which he has just quoted: 'Mr Bernard Shaw
says that "He who can, does; he who cannot, teaches." If you interpret the words "can"
and "cannot" as implying opportunity and lack of opportunity, then this rather cynical
epigram conveys a vital truth' (1919, p. 244).

p. 23). Commercial penetration by a foreign power was also inimical to the balanced nation, 'for the object of that penetration is to deprive other nations of their fair share of the more skilled forms of employment'. Indeed, 'whenever an industry is so developed in one country that it can be content with no less than a world market for its particular products, the economic balance of other countries tends to be upset' (Mackinder 1919, p. 229).

Another difficulty confronting the ideal of balanced nations was that of unequal endowment by nature. In fact, if history were left to run the course indicated by geography 'the grouping of lands and seas, and of fertility and natural pathways' was 'such as to lend itself to the growth of empires, and in the end of a single World Empire' (ibid., p. 2). But although everything seemed to be against the ideal of the balanced nation, it would be mere fatalism to accept as inevitable the drift towards mutually hostile super-states, bureaucratically run by organizers, and running blindly on collision courses with each other. The ideal was feasible, worth-while, and attainable, if there was a will to work towards it: 'For a hundred years we have bowed down before the Going Concern as though it were an irresistible God. Undoubtedly it is a Reality, but it can be bent to your service if you have a policy inspired by an ideal. *Laissez-faire* is no such policy; it was mere surrender to fate' (ibid., p. 247). It destroyed the independence of provincial life. Improved roads and railways concentrating on the capital 'brought the life of the country up to London, sapping it for the growth of London'. Market towns had, as a result, 'been degraded in respect of the variety of their life'. Nor did

the Londoner profit in any true sense from the change. He lives in a suburb; he is shot through a tube to an office-room in the City, and then shot back to his bedroom in the suburb; only on Saturdays and Sundays has he time for communal life, and then he amuses himself with neighbours who are tied to him by nothing essential. (ibid., pp. 248-9)

All nations should have balanced economies, with a due share of what he calls the 'higher', that is the more technologically advanced industries. This would be possible if the better-endowed countries and the more gifted peoples were to help the less well off in a spirit of neighbourliness. Where larger associations were desirable they should be federations of the free rather than exploited empires, and for this planning was necessary:

Unless I mistake, it is the message of geography that international co-operation in any future that we need consider must be based on the federal idea. If our civilization is not to go down in blind internecine conflict, there must be a development of world planning out of regional planning, just as regional planning has come out of town planning. (Mackinder 1931, p. 13)

Within the federated states, as many functions and callings as possible should be given to local provinces, regions, and communities, enabling local talent to stay at home, making for the good of the people and the happiness of individuals. The ability to 'see life whole' meant much more to well-being than the improvement of material services.

Mackinder advocated the application of the 'balanced nation' principle to two specific problems, one external and one domestic. In *Democratic Ideals and Reality* (1919) and in his secret report to the Cabinet in 1920, he suggested that the group of peoples situated between Germany proper and Russia proper should have independent statehood, with military and economic assistance from the West.[2] And in his 1919 book he argued for a measure of devolution within the British Isles. He had declared himself against Irish home rule in the debate in Parliament on 2 May 1912. His argument was one often heard in the devolution discussions of 1978–9—that it was a case of all or nothing. There were 'only two courses open to you in regard to Ireland'. One was to 'maintain the Union', the other 'to hand Ireland over to the Irish', for 'it passes the ingenuity of man to devise any system which will enable you successfully to carry out your policy of granting a certain amount of freedom, but not complete freedom' (P.D. 1912, xxxvii, 2131). However, on 3 June 1919 he voted for a motion to set up 'a Parliamentary body to consider the creation of subordinate Legislatures within the United Kingdom', and it was then that he argued that devolution would not work satisfactorily unless the predominance of England were countered. This predominance made the other nations of the British Isles nationalistic and perverse.

---

[2] The border states question is discussed below, see pp. 167–70.

It made Scotland 'assert her nationality by trying to be different in all things'. In a federal United Kingdom, 'the nationality, the separateness of action of Scotland and of the two parts of Ireland ... and of Wales, will be emphasized ten times over' (P.D. 1919, cxvi, 1922).

Mackinder suggested therefore the division of England into three, each part having devolved legislative powers. London was not only the imperial capital but a world commercial and financial centre with interests of its own; it threatened to overwhelm the whole country with its metropolitan influence; it would be detached from the rest of the country, which was to be divided between an agricultural south and east, and an industrial north and west: 'You would get real power in the hands of agriculturalists to realize the needs of modern agriculture; and you would get real power in the hands of modern industry, without interference from London to realize the material needs of the industrial community' (P.D. 1919, cxvi, 1918). At this point a Member interrupted with, 'Would my hon. Friend not go a little further and re-establish the Kingdom of Kent?' and the proposals were greeted with amusement or scorn.[3] Yet almost fifty years later, in 1968, the Liberals advocated the division of England into twelve provinces to rank with Scotland, Wales, and Northern Ireland 'to counteract the over centralization of government' (*The Times*, 19 April 1968). The establishment of English regions with devolved powers comparable to those proposed for Scotland or Wales was again seriously mooted in the devolution discussions of 1978–9.

He maintained (1902) that the idiosyncrasies of provincialism begat initiative:

The British peoples owe much to the narrow seas which have divided them from the continent; it is, however, not infrequently suggested that they have lost by the seas which have held them apart from one another and impeded fusion. But as liberty is the natural privilege of an island people, so wealth of initiative is characteristic of a divided people. Provinces which are insular or peninsular breed an obstinate provincialism unknown in the merely historical or administrative divisions of a great plain; and this rooted provincialism, rather than finished cosmopolitanism, is a source of the varied initiative without which liberty would lose half its significance. (p. 15)

[3] See also above, pp. 45–6.

As an illustration of the damaging effect of a preponderant state upon a weaker neighbour, he instances Scotland, where

the people of the highest tier of society send their sons for the most part to the English Public Schools and the English Universities, whereas the ministers of the Scottish Churches, the advocates in the Scottish Law Courts, and the doctors and schoolmasters are trained in the main in the local Universities, which are frequented by the sons of the shopkeepers and artisans to a greater extent than in England. The result, as I believe, is that the Scottish aristocracy has been, to a greater degree than in England, detached from the people ...
It is said that a certain Scottish Baronet who had eight beautiful daughters approaching, some of them, to the age of marriage, put them all on a coach and drove them away from Edinburgh to London, because all the young Scotsmen of his acquaintance who had money, or the wits to make money, had already gone thither! In the end of the eighteenth century, and the beginning of the nineteenth, Edinburgh was one of the lamps of Europe, with its own particular tinge of flame. To-day it is one more instance of the futility of trying to separate the economic from the other aspects of the life either of a nation or a province. (Mackinder 1919, pp. 252-3)

Perhaps the greatest danger to democracy in Mackinder's view, was the over-zealous reformer—the unrealistic, and therefore destructive, idealist. For society and the productive economy were complex and interlocking mechanisms which, if put out of joint, could collapse into confusion: 'A great and advanced society has, in consequence, a powerful momentum; without destroying the society itself you cannot suddenly check or divert its course' (ibid., p. 3). In such circumstances people abandoned democracy and called for the organizer:

The Nemesis of democratic idealism, if it break from the bonds of reality, is the supreme rule of the organiser and of blind efficiency. The organiser begins innocently enough; his executive mind revolts from the disorder, and above all from the indiscipline around him. Soldierly efficiency undoubtedly saved Revolutionary France. But such is the impetus of the going concern, that it sweeps forward even its own creator. (ibid., p. 21)

Napoleon was so swept forward, and finally 'impelled to his Moscow'. He might also have cited the essentially similar example of Cromwell. He did, however, prophesy that single-minded organizers would arise from the chaos in which war and revolution had left Germany and Russia: 'Even with the revolution in Germany let us not be too sure in regard to its ultimate effect ... The end of the present disorder may only be a new ruthless organization, and ruthless organizers do not stop when they have attained the objects which they at first set before them' (ibid., p. 201). As for Russia, 'autocratic rule of some sort is almost inevitable ...'.

Idealists, he says, 'are the salt of the earth'; he is on their side because they counter 'blind materialism'. But there are historically, he points out, two very different phases of idealism. There is the older religious one, 'based on self-denial' and the newer, 'based on self-realization'. They correspond

with two developments of reality. In older times the power of nature over man was still great. Hard reality put limits to his ambitions. In other words the world as a whole was poor, and resignation was the only general road to happiness. The few could, no doubt, obtain some scope in life, but only at the cost of the serfdom of the many ... But the modern world is rich. In no small measure man now controls the forces of nature, and whole classes have become imbued with the idea that, with a fairer division of wealth, there should be a nearer approach to equality of opportunity. (ibid., pp. 9-10)

Mackinder is sympathetic to this latter ideal, but not with its pursuit by methods revolutionary enough to imperil society. Trying violently to get one's hands on the means of production defeated its object. For, 'Human riches and comparative security are based to-day on the division and co-ordination of labour, and on the constant repair of complicated plant which has replaced the simple tools of primitive society. In other words, the output of modern wealth is conditional on the maintenance of our social organization and capital' (ibid., p. 10). For this maintenance of capital he regarded capitalism as essential. It must not, however, be the *laissez-faire* capitalism of the free-traders, but an enlightened, socially-conscious capitalism. This was not only consistent with democracy but necessary to it. For initiative and incentive, freedom and enterprise, which only capitalism could promote, were as essential to liberty as they were to productivity. Employers and employed were all part of the same mechanism, to which they could cause irreparable harm by their strife. He told the citizens of Glasgow (1921a) that they were in truth all capitalists. They depend for very existence on a running organization and world-wide goodwill which have come down to them from their predecessors. That is not to say that they should totally abstain from healthy contention among themselves, for the going concern must be improved as it runs if it is not to be left behind by upstart competitors. But it does signify that their economic strife should always be tempered by the consciousness that they are guardians of a society for their children which they can destroy but never create.

Mackinder (1906) insisted that it was productivity rather than wealth that mattered in the modern age; productivity depended not on the mere possession of capital, but upon the way it was exploited by manpower, the quality of which was therefore of supreme importance. This was 'a revolutionary idea' (Malin 1944, p. 67) and was the key to his enlightened capitalism: 'the idea of Man-power gives the economic basis for a wise philanthropy' (Mackinder 1906, p. 23). *Laissez-faire* and free-trade policies were wrong because they sacrificed manpower to the accumulation of capital and to a narrow view of efficiency:

If you pursue relentlessly the ideals of efficiency and cheapness, you will give us a world in which the young will never see life but only an aspect of life; national and international organisers will alone hold the keys admitting to the Observatory of the complete view. Is it in that way that you will get a continuous supply of fruitful brains, and happy, because intellectually active workers? (Mackinder 1919, pp. 258–9)

Laissez-faire economics looked with indifference on the destruction of an industry by foreign competition—it could and probably would be replaced by another industry.

But the labourer's skill cannot so easily be transferred to a new trade. No small number of the unemployed are men for whose skills there is no longer an accessible market ... their good habits are broken ... they become unemployable, and a burden to the community. The nation, if not the employer, should set down the loss of Man-power in its balance sheet. (Mackinder 1906, p. 23)

During his term as a Member of Parliament Mackinder showed more interest in the mechanics of democracy. In 1911 he spoke in favour of a referendum to decide the great Lords-versus-Commons constitutional issue:

I do not believe if the Referendum were established it would often be taken ... I believe the very existence of the Referendum would tell deeply in a favourable sense upon the conduct of affairs in this country. Neither the Government nor the Opposition would challenge a Referendum lightly ... the result would be that we should have, very generally at any rate, a sweeter reasonableness in the matter of legislation than we have at the present time. (P.D. 1911, xxiv, 1846)

In 1917 he put down an amendment for the reform of the House of Lords, arguing that a 'sufficiently strong Second Chamber, well founded on a sufficiently democratic basis, is surely part of the equipment of any enduring freedom' (*The Times*, 22 May 1917). But he remained opposed to women's suffrage, and urged a referendum to see whether it was really wanted:

My chief reason for opposing women's suffrage is that I believe a fair body of women ... do not wish to have the vote ... if a majority of women do not wish for a vote, you are doing violation to the best views of the sex by forcing the vote upon them because the minority want it. Convince me that the majority of women want the vote [by taking a referendum] ... Why do you shrink from it? The machinery is easy. (P. D. 1917, xciv, 1701)

Later he supported an amendment to the Representation of the People Bill for the introduction of proportional representation (*The Times*, 23 Nov. 1917).

Mackinder regarded a well-educated citizenry as essential if democracy was not to be exploited by demagogues or to adopt specious policies. 'Half-educated people' were 'in a very susceptible condition'. They were capable 'of seizing ideas', but they had 'not attained to the habit of testing them and of suspense of mind in the meantime' (Mackinder 1919, p. 243). He set forth the aim thus:

I have no illusions as to what is possible in a democracy, but still I believe that the people must and can be sufficiently trained to distinguish clap-trap from reality, so that they may be able to compel their leaders, whether they be newspaper editors or party politicians, to place at any rate rational stuff before them. (Mackinder 1913, p. 8)

When he was forty he wrote of devoting the rest of his working life 'to the modernizing of our English education' (Blouet 1975, p. 16), for he saw serious limitations in the system. It was limited as to class—only the upper classes received a good education. This was tolerable when they alone provided the ruling establishment, but now the franchise had been extended the populace were the masters. 'The system of our public schools is a wasteful one', he wrote in 1903, and 'the classes whose homes are simple, who cannot afford £200 a year or more for each son, must in day schools of the first rank—of which a few already exist—obtain for a quarter·of the boarding school payments an education that shall prepare them for the highest university or technical training'. He supported the 1902 Education Bill,[4] even though his then party vehemently opposed it. He likewise backed the 1918 bill which gave all children full-time education to the age of 14. He supported these measures because they were steps forward, not because they were adequate.

The curriculum was too limited, too academic, too specialized, and too categorized; and he 'deplored that tendency in the recent development of education to multiply subjects unduly. There was too little of the philosophical aggregation of subjects; in other words too little of the real world, which, of course, was not partitioned into subjects at all' (Cantor 1960, pp. 200-1).

A cardinal drawback, as he saw it, was the division into arts and sciences, which produced the two cultures, the chasm between which he had spoken of in 1887,[5] seventy-two years before C. P. Snow popularized this theme in his Rede lecture. It was particularly deplorable that higher education was wholly divided into Arts and Science, for men and women who 'saw the world whole' were needed in government, civil service, and elsewhere:

a rift divides the organization of our higher education so deeeply that almost every teacher and almost every student must definitely take his stand on one side or the other ... the effect of it has been to press most educated people, including the teachers in our public and secondary

---

[4] The 1902 Act has been described as 'among the two or three greatest constructive measures of the twentieth century' (Ensor 1936, p. 355). But M. had doubts about putting secondary education on the rates—'after all', it was a 'national rather than local' matter (1903, p. 260).

[5] 'One of the greatest gaps lies between the natural sciences and the study of humanity', and this was 'upsetting the equilibrium of our culture' (M. 1887, p. 145).

schools, into one or other of two moulds ... (*Times Educational Supplement*, 7 Sept. 1916)

As a result, 'a large number of our scientific men really cannot express themselves in good English and a considerable number of our literary men are not ashamed to be absolutely ignorant, let us say, of the first elements of electricity, or of the transmutation of various forms of energy' (Mackinder 1917a, p. 51). The division was aggravated by class distinction and was reinforced by the gulf between the older academic institutions and the newer technical ones: 'the influence of the linguistic arts has permeated from the top downward, while that of the physical sciences has penetrated slowly upward. Not a little of the asperity of the conflict has been due to the social distinctions thus connotated by the rival educations' (Mackinder 1903, p. 237). He suggested a way of bridging the rift which was to be widely adopted later:

Might we not do something in the way of brigading subjects in a university under, say, a score of leading professors instead of in two faculties? There could then be many permutations of curriculum, each internally consistent with some leading idea, but each complete in that it aimed at imparting definite knowledge, inquisitive outlook, and the trained power of welding ideas in languages. (*Times Educational Supplement*, 7 Sept. 1916)

Geography was the key subject to bridge the gap between arts and sciences. It drew from the latter just that information and those explanations which the educated and influential person needed to know, and it added to the former the essential environmental factor which specialists in the humanities sometimes neglected. Geography would do for modern education what the classics had done before science loomed so large in life—impart a catholic sense of values.

Education designed for those going on to do research should not be the standard for everybody:

research compels specialization, and specialization as a consequence pervades the teaching of science. This is inevitable where the training of researchers and of the technicians who apply the results of research is in question. But what of the training of that great majority who will not be engaged in research but must give themselves just to living? In these days they too must know something of science, but as part of their equipment for the business of life in the big world, not in the laboratory. (Mackinder 1935, p. 7)

A great danger to democracy and to civilization was the abuse of scientific knowledge, and this was facilitated by ignorance of science among the public at large. Scientists produced by the present system, although 'wonderful in research and in industrial technique', were ill-fitted to diffuse the essentials of their knowledge throughout the community. They lacked 'outlook' (Mackinder 1937, pp. 180–1).

In one of his last addresses Mackinder (1942) maintained that we could not 'any more afford ten years of concentration on two dead languages for many of those fitted by intellect and character to be leaders in our national life'. What statesmen required was the foresight and judgement that came of 'accurate imagination' or vision based on reality, and 'we train imagination in the great outlook subjects—history, which implies outlook in time, geography, which implies the outlook into space' (Mackinder 1904a, p. 191). With history, geography provided 'a mental foundation for judgement in action':

The problem is to arrive at an organically coherent discipline for the upbringing of the cultivated and efficient men and women who in various capacities must run our democracy in the next couple of generations. They must have a global outlook … they must also have a trained power of judging values and be capable of long views in framing policies for the future; and they will, of course, still need an understanding of the momentum with which both Man and his environment come up to the present from the past … (Mackinder 1942, pp. 129–30)

It was becoming essential for a ruling class to have some understanding of science, and geography gave this in a natural way, because it offered scientific explanations at just those points where science impinged upon real life (Mackinder 1937, pp. 180–1).

Geography was a unified and integrated discipline in which causal relationships between man and his environment were studied within areas, with a view to looking at such relationships ultimately on a global scale. The widespread treatment of the subject in two separate parts, physical and human, he regarded as destructive of its unifying and therefore of its real educational role. A unified geography would have two immense practical advantages: as an aid to statecraft and as an education for citizens. Both for the 'top people' who ran things, and for the masses upon whom democracy was imposing awesome responsibilities, it offered the philosophical abstraction from the arts and sciences of all that was essential for the understanding of the fundamentals of modern existence; and this essential knowledge could be assimilated because it was integrated in real places—actual localities that could be lived in or visited, seen and understood. As he once said (1932, p. 191), 'it takes a trained grasp of brain to seize and hold, in order and not chaos, the data of our modern existence on this Earth.' Geography gave that training.[6]

In 1887 Mackinder claimed that the geography he had described would satisfy the 'practical requirements of the statesman'; in 1895, he maintained that 'as a merchant, soldier, or politician', the geographer 'would exhibit trained grasp and initiative when dealing with practical space problems on the earth's surface'; many Englishmen had a natural bent that way, 'but England would be richer if more of such men, and others besides, had a geographical training'; in 1911, that geography 'went far to make the statesman, whether in politics, or strategy, or commerce', and 'the man who has once acquired the habit of geographical thinking approaches every problem of great affairs with more surety and resourcefulness'. In 1890 (*aet.* 28) he gave a brilliant example:

Suppose that I am told that a certain sample of wheat comes from Lahore, and that I do not know where Lahore is. I look it out in the gazetteer and ascertain that it is the capital of the Punjab ...If I know nothing of geography, I shall get up with the idea that Lahore is in India, and that will be about all. If I have been properly trained in geography, the word Punjab will ... probably connote to me many things. I shall see Lahore in the northern angle of India. I shall picture it in a great plain, at the foot of a snowy range, in the midst of the rivers of the Indus system. I shall think of the monsoons and the desert, of the water brought from the mountains by the irrigation canals. I shall know the climate, the seed time, and the harvest. Kurrachee and

[6] M. would have seen it as tragic that his geographical synthesis had not been able to hold arts and sciences together, but that instead, the great divide had pulled geography itself apart into two distinct subjects, a physical geography aiming to be a physical science, and a human geography calling itself a social science.

the Suez Canal will shine out from my mental map. I shall be able to calculate at what time of the year the cargoes will be delivered in England. Moreover, the Punjab will be to me the equal in size and population of a great European country, a Spain or an Italy, and I shall appreciate the market it offers for English exports. (1890a, pp. 3-4)

Forty years later, having lived through one great war and foreseen another, he warned that 'geography must underlie the strategy of peace if you would not have it subserve the strategy of war' (1931, p. 15).

In stressing the need for a geographical training for the ruling class, Mackinder was indirectly pleading for a better place for geography in the universities and public schools. In advocating it as the core of education for citizenship in a democracy, he was working for more and better teaching of geography in the maintained schools. The capacity for 'outlook' was needed by all, and not just by the classes who benefited from secondary and university education:

For every man or woman who goes to a secondary school there are, unfortunately, fifty whose schooling must end when they go to work at fourteen. Yet these fifty are pilgrims in a scientific world and citizens in a democratic state. It may not be theirs to lead, but they have to judge and to accept or refuse the lead which is offered to them by others ... (Mackinder 1914, pp. 46-7)

For the elementary education of the masses in a democracy the 'three Rs' were not enough: 'A man may read and write, and sum quickly and accurately, and yet be at the mercy of every plausible statement which finds its way into print. He may be so confused by the multiplicity of impressions he receives that he has less judgement than many an illiterate ...' (ibid., p. 14). Two years later he returned to this theme:

When we teach languages and mathematics and science we are teaching very valuable things, we are training powers of expression and we are teaching definite facts, but we have only done two out of the three vital things of education. The third must be achieved by ... that training of the mind which shall enable you to keep your poise in the midst of all the vast sea of half-known facts in which you have to live your life. (Mackinder 1916, p. 275)

For this third and most important part of education the 'out-look' subjects, geography and history, could be taught together at the lower levels of education:

So shall we impart the historical sense in regard to the affairs of to-day, rather than a merely romantic interest in the past. Moreover there is a practical reason in favour of this course. In these days, when international affairs have become world wide, it is necessary that the great human contrasts which are the outcome of universal history should be generally known, and that—to take only a single category, by way of illustration—the distinction of Christian, Mohammedan, Hindu and Buddhist should be generally realized in some degree of historical perspective. (Mackinder 1911, p. 82)

He would have agreed with Heylyn (1657, p. 19) that, without geography, 'the study of History is neither so pleasant or so profitable, as a judicious Reader will desire to have it', but that 'if joined together' they 'crown our reading with delight and profit'. Mackinder likened the two subjects to 'the two blades of a pair of scissors', which although they 'may be separately made ... do their work only when screwed together'; in another analogy, to teach them separately was 'as though we sought to train one of our eyes at a time, forgetful of the fact that we have two eyes for stereoscopic vision'.[7] He suggested that the 'outlook' subjects could form the focus for general political, constitutional, economic, and social material, and that together they might form a course in civics.[8]

Mackinder's was an essentially liberal and humane education, centred upon and radiating out from the 'outlook' subjects, linked with the sciences through geography and with the humanities through history. But during and after the 1914–18 war a more wholly practical and technical education was widely

[7] Although he advocated teaching history and geography together to the young, M. insisted that they must be regarded as distinct disciplines in higher education. He had made this position clear in his very first paper (1887): 'In their elementary stages they must obviously go hand in hand. In their higher stages they diverge' (p. 154). In a letter to *The Times* (9 Feb. 1905) he was very severe with Major-Gen. Warrand who had urged that history and geography should be taught together for Army entrance, and had repeated Heylyn's (1657) view that they were 'like two sisters'. M. rejoined that 'it does not follow that they are Siamese twins'; and to distance geography from history as far as possible, he defined it as 'a branch of physics'.

[8] M. wrote a book on Civics (1914a). The chapter heads give an idea of his method: e.g. 1, An agricultural village—production; 3, A market town—bankers and lawyers; 4, A county town—administration; 8, The textile industries—the collective bargain of labour; 10, A great port—foreign commerce; 16, The army—international relations.

advocated. To meet this threat, in 1917, he ranged the Geographical Association alongside the Classical, English, Historical, and Modern Language Associations in the 'Five Associations' defence of humanistic studies. He was not against the strengthening of the technical side, provided the liberal element was safeguarded. He had long before (1890a) called for a dual-purpose education:

What do we expect to find in an educated man? Do we not expect to find him possessed of a double nature—an expert, i.e. a specialist in his money-earning capacity, but the very antithesis of a specialist as a citizen, a parent, as a member of 'general society'? ... Intermediate and higher education should be both liberal and technical.

However, in the 1920s he himself was advocating more scientific and technical education because technological progress would give rise to new industries which would require more advanced skills (*The Times*, 16 May 1924).

It follows from the priority which Mackinder attributed to education in a democracy that he regarded the teacher's function as crucial. He himself was a professional teacher for the forty years that separated his taking up University Extension in 1885 and his laying down the professorship at London in 1925. Although a university teacher himself, he regarded teaching as a single profession, equally important at all levels. He was also a teacher of teachers, looking upon this function as essential to the furtherance of his subject. For almost sixty years, from his first extension lecture to his last words to the Geographical Association in 1943, he was addressing teachers of geography at all levels on aims and methods, going about the work with his usual missionary zeal and grasp of detail.

He thought teaching was too closely linked with research. Research bred specialists, but a knowledge of the world at large was more important to the teacher, who above all should be possessed of 'outlook'. Scientists at schools and universities 'knew how to train ... recruits for their own specializations' but these were but 'a small minority of their pupils'. Teaching postulated 'a living philosophy, ever assessing, co-ordinating, and presenting with balance and accuracy a wide range of the results of research and practical experience' (Mackinder 1937, p. 181).

He was therefore against specialized teacher training, believing it essential that teachers should have some experience of the economic and social problems of their communities. There was, indeed, 'no more dismal or narrowing system than that of the residential training colleges' (Mackinder 1903, pp. 254-5). Although his reformed education centred on geography, he was aware (1917a, p. 50) of the practical difficulty of finding teachers who had 'an adequate literary and historical training on the one hand, and yet a sound grounding in the natural sciences on the other'; but, 'until you have them you cannot have a really sound teaching of geography'.

He was sceptical about costly teaching apparatus, believing that there was no substitute for the enlightened and stimulating teacher in direct personal touch with his pupils. Because a teacher's main function was to train the imagination in 'accurate visualization', he was against the use of the cinematograph. It would make for lazy minds, doing for the pupils the 'visualizing' they should do for themselves:

The young child loves the battered doll, which amply serves to focus the imagination. Similarly, I believe that the good teacher can make the blackboard and the lantern slide speak to better educative purpose than he could the cinematograph. The picture palaces of the present moment debauch the imagination by relieving the spectator of all effort. The picture painted by the artist is more stimulating than the photograph for the very reason it suggests rather than reproduces.[9] (Mackinder 1911, p. 86)

Obviously he would have held a similar view of the indiscriminate use of television. He would not have notes and exercises in his textbooks because 'so far as I can remember my boyhood' they 'made school-books repellent', and he believed 'that commentary and question can only come with vivid interest from the living teacher' (Mackinder 1910a, vi).[10]

Mackinder was a strong believer in adult education in which he had much experience.[11] He valued University Extension

---

[9] This view was elaborated in a letter to *The Times*, 28 Feb. 1913.

[10] But this did not stop his publisher from commissioning someone else to make them and from issuing them as companions to his books (Taylor 1915).

[11] 'The years between 1886 and 1892 marked the period of his greatest endeavours, and during them he gave almost five hundred lectures in over fifty centres, ranging from Manchester to the Isle of Wight and from Canterbury to Plymouth' (Cantor 1961, p. 26).

because it was the only means by which the humanities were brought to the mass of working people. But he would have preferred a thematic series of related courses connected with 'the political and economic working of the nation', and running over a period of two or three years, to the piecemeal offering of unrelated topics (Cantor 1960, p. 203). His experience with the 'Mackindergarten'[12] had convinced him that a return to education in later life was of immense value and should be more widely applied. Civil servants and business men could with advantage to the nation return to a period of full-time study; it would be more effective than increasing the school-leaving age; supplementary evening classes were no substitute because they were given to tired men (*The Times*, 18 Jan. 1907). He also favoured the employment of graduates in industry, and welcomed (1930, p. 265) the growth of the practice between the wars.

Most of Mackinder's work for teachers of geography and history was concerned with the early years, the years for which he wrote his series of school-books. In these he mingled geography and history together, scorning the idea of learning by separate subjects. The object was to satisfy the child's curiosity in a constructive and realistic way:

the vast majority will increase their knowledge ... by reading this or that cheap book, by reading the newspapers, by talking with friends, and by seeing what they can when travelling. Therefore what is important is not to send them out with the rudiments of History as such and the rudiments of Geography as such in their minds, but to send them out with some sort of orderly conception of the world around them. (Mackinder 1913, p. 6)

He envisaged the combined subject being taught 'to the end of the fourteenth or fifteenth year', and his popular series of school-books was designed for such a course. As infants, the children would model, draw, and study the cycle of life and the circulation of water in their home area. They would be told of wonderful things that had happened 'once upon a time' and 'in a distant land'. They would meet the 'moving globe'. Then, at the age of nine, they would be ready 'to enter Bookland' and browse for themselves. Mackinder says that he has written his

[12] See above, p. 35.

little books 'in the attempt to realize my ideal of what a child's book on geography and history should be ... My high ambition ... has been to supply for the masses of our children that kind of writing which in another sphere is known by the name of humane letters.' The first book, *Our Own Islands* (1906a), was mainly geographical; but there is history in it too: he explains, for instance, how the Church came to build churches and the barons to build castles:

Now I have no doubt you are asking, 'What has all this to do with geography and the map of England?' It has a great deal to do with it, because wherever a bishop built a cathedral, or an abbot an abbey, or a baron or the king built a castle, there, for the sake of security, a large number of people gathered, and set up their wooden houses round the stone walls of the great church or castle. In this way many of the towns of England were founded. (p. 272)

The next book, for the ten/eleven-year-old, was *Our Island History*, traced upon the stage described in the first: 'the map of Britain is already familiar. We are going to enrich it with historical associations' (1914, p. 87). *Lands beyond the Channel* (geography and history intermingled), *Distant Lands* (predominantly geographical), and *The Nations of the Modern World* (largely historical and political) followed to fill the remainder of the primary school course.

Both the idea of teaching geography and history together and the concentric method[13] of teaching the former have been criticized. The latter, because it is usually thought that the geography of Britain is more difficult than that of, say, Australia. But Mackinder (1903a) thought, perhaps rightly, that the increased difficulty should come in method rather than in subject matter: 'Now if geography is to be generally accepted as a valued discipline ... it must be characterized by a similar progression of method ... in each successive year you must employ more effective, or rather, more nearly mature methods, and not learn of successive regions by precisely the same methods at all stages of mental development' (p. 96). He was ambitious for young children studying the home area:

---

[13] i.e. doing the home region first, then the home country, the home continent, and finally the most distant lands.

I mean by the home area that every child in London should study, say, the Thames Basin and the Weald, and every child in the North some area as large as, say, Lancashire and Yorkshire. My reason is this: if you consider the Thames Basin and the Weald, you have in the chalk strata a great yet simple basis of physical structure. The hills and valleys all comment on that structure. (ibid., p. 99)

By this method people would learn to understand landscapes, thereby greatly increasing their interest in travel: 'it is not possible to travel intelligently if you do not think of the land-scape intelligently' (ibid.).

It says much for his courage and tenacity that, despite the many calls on his time and his activities as politician, public servant, and business man, he repeatedly chose to come forward to champion a cause which, if not quite lost, was regarded by many as futile or unworthy. Few inside or outside the academic world were prepared to recognize his arguments, so strong was the English belief that Geography was a matter of practical common sense at best, of memory at worst, and not seriously to be considered along with the established academic disciplines. Those who knew and admired him thought that the geograph-ical virtues he sang were personal to him and not really capable of wide inculcation.

Fifty years after he had gone to Oxford as Reader in Geog-raphy, he recalled (1937, p. 176) that then 'there was more than neglect, there was prejudice', and 'it was objected to me, quite seriously and repeatedly, that the study of maps by the young promoted strategical, that is to say militarist and imperialist, ways of thinking ... Men were accustomed to think in verbal formulae; patterns and plans were suspect; geometry was taught through the verbal logic of Euclid.' He doubted 'whether even to-day Geography is much better than tolerated in the elder ranks of the educational world'; two years earlier he had said (1935, p. 10): 'Let us recognize that academic opinion ... still undervalues the potentialities of geography', and he mentioned 'the still prevalent scientific suspicion and depreciation of geog-raphy'. One reason for his passionate advocacy of the necessity for a unified geography, with its own distinctive philosophy and methodology, was his belief that in this way only would its status come to be fully recognized.

Chapter 5

Geographer

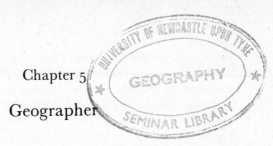

Mackinder had many occupations throughout his long life, but from his schooldays he thought of himself foremost as a geographer. He found geography of inestimable value in illuminating the various questions with which he, as a public man, was concerned, and he passionately believed that if all statesmen and others of influence were trained in geography as he conceived it, the world would be a better governed, better ordered, and more peaceful place. Although he was a busy man, throwing himself whole-heartedly into the various academic and public duties which came his way, he never ceased to think, talk, and write about geography. His published work on the subject, from the first in 1887 to the last in 1943, forms an unparalleled corpus of geographical thought in English.

Much of his work went unheeded and for the most part unread by English-speaking geographers, including those few who concerned themselves with the philosophy of the subject. Although Hartshorne used over four hundred and fifty works for his *The Nature of Geography* (1939), he refers to only one by Mackinder. He later ascribed this neglect to his inability to find any reference to Mackinder's views 'in the methodological literature'. It has been said (Crone 1951) that Mackinder 'had made his main contribution to geography' by 1905, although most of his published work on the philosophy of the subject comes after the date. Freeman (1980) does not discuss Mackinder's geographical contribution after 1902 except to say that it has been 'overpraised', and Stoddart (1980) concludes that 'his career lay not in the intellectual development of the subject ... but in political life.' Yet scarcely a year went by without some contribution from him to the nature, methodology, and philosophy of the subject.[1] When one remembers his intellectual

---

[1] See the Bibliography. Besides his articles and adresses, M. throughout his political career and after, regularly attended the meetings of the RGS and the GA, often taking part in the discussions; he was also a frequent correspondent to *The Times* in defence of geography as a discipline.

stature, his broad academic base in science, history, and economics, the extraordinary breadth of his knowledge, the depth
of his understanding, and the fact that he was so highly regarded
for his brains by many of the leading thinkers of his time, and
when one considers that he practised geography as a public
servant, exposing his ideas not only to academic criticism but
also to the examination of practical men of affairs, who yet held
him in the highest respect, is it not astounding that what he had
to say about geography was largely ignored by his contemporaries and those who followed him? When his geographical work
has been mentioned, it has, as often as not, been denigrated or
misrepresented. It has even been suggested that 'his writing
hurt geography' (Sylvester 1968, p. 56). Although his geography revolved about man, he has been described (Gregory 1978,
p. 16) as the most typical exponent[2] of the Victorian natural
science tradition whose 'early practitioners eschewed any close
involvement with man himself'.

Tributes by British geographers to Mackinder's geographical
work have been few. Although there are flattering references to
his 1887 paper, little has been said about his life's work in geography as a whole. However, in 1935, his contemporary, H. R.
Mill, spoke of his 'remarkable genius in grasping the "scheme
of things entire" and showing the wide aspects of geography as
it permeates all human thought, raising geography from a
science to a branch of philosophy and carrying it forward to
enlighten the practical affairs of daily life' (*Geogrl J.* lxxxvi, p.
13). E. W. Gilbert (1951) paid elegant tribute to Mackinder as
a geographer, and hoped that his teachings would 'continue to
illuminate the path of geographical learning'.[3] In 1970 R. P.
Moss wrote that 'he was a giant who towered above his contemporaries' and that 'he originated certain ideas which ... are
particularly apposite today'. J. W. House (1976) remarks that
he was 'the founding father of an applied geography, in the
service of the state and the community, seeking to solve the
problems and to meet the needs of the times'.

[2] The actual words are 'the party line was captured most precisely by Sir Halford
Mackinder'.

[3] Freeman writes, 'Later publications by Gilbert on Mackinder seemed to some to
exaggerate his academic strength' and that, 'To some geographers it seemed ... that his
[Gilbert's] work ... was marked by excessive hero-worship' (in Freeman and Pinchemel
1979).

In order to understand the significance of the 'new geography' that Mackinder popularized, some idea of the subject's position in the educational system of mid-Victorian Britain is needed. In the primary schools it appears to have been satisfactorily 'taught according to a generally precribed method which, if carried out everywhere with intelligence and enthusiasm, would be nearly all that could be desired' (Keltie 1886, p. 13).[4] This could hardly be said of secondary education, which had not yet been taken under the wing of the State. Mackinder (1937) remembered that the 'great public schools for boys' had 'replied haughtily to a questionnaire from the Royal Geographical Society that they did not teach the subject'; it was found more often in girls' schools, and Thackeray had 'gibed at Miss Pinkerton's Academy for young ladies because it advertised geography and the use of the globes as a principle subject of education'. Where it was taught in boys' schools, it was usually by unqualified and uninterested teachers and to the duller sort of pupils. If they were lucky the geography taught was physical, using Huxley's *Physiography* (1877) or Geikie's *Physical Geography* (1873), for here some principles were illuminated. If it was general or 'political' geography, then 'no drearier task' could 'be set for the worst of criminals' than that of studying the textbooks then in use (Green 1880, p. vi). Hughes (1863) wrote: 'The geography still taught in too many of our schools is miserably defective—hardly, indeed, worthy of the name. It consists, too often, in little more than a dry or dull routine of names, appealing to the memory alone.' Educated people, looking back to their schooldays, could 'recollect little but a confused list of proper names and statistics, learnt by rote' (Warren 1887, p. 262).

Geography was not a recognized subject at any university, although at Oxford some knowledge was required for Ancient and Modern History.[5] There was a professor of geography at

[4] But it was reported in 1897 that, 'Geography unfortunately is now an optional subject in the elementary schools of Great Britain . . . Geography is taught in two-thirds of the schools in England and Wales, and about 95 per cent of those in Scotland' (BAAS 1897, p. 371).

[5] Candidates for the degree of Literae Humaniores were required to have such a knowledge of classical geography 'as shall be necessary for the profitable study of the authors and periods which they offer'; Modern History required 'such a knowledge of geography, Political and Descriptive, as is necessary to the understanding of the Political History of England' (Firth 1918, p. 5).

King's College, London, after 1863, and some geography was also taught at Victoria College, Manchester. It was the absence of geography as a subject in its own right at Oxford and Cambridge which made it not worth while for the public schools to take it seriously, and which resulted in the lack of qualified teachers.

Geography was split into two quite unconnected parts. Physical geography or physiography[6] was the science of the features of the earth's surface, which it described, classified, and explained; it was regarded as a branch of geology, and was in the hands of geologists. General geography detailed factual information about the earth's features, produce, and divisions; it listed mountains by height, rivers by length, lakes by area, and capes and bays in the order in which they succeeded each other round the coast; or it could be 'political', with tables of countries or counties, their areas, their chief products, their capital cities, etc. In schools these lists were learned by heart in the same way as the multiplication tables or Latin declensions.

The only organization with any concern for the position was the Royal Geographical Society, founded in 1830 as a travellers' club. Its main interest was in travel and exploration, and its membership was made up largely of people who liked to come and hear a tale of adventure from some intrepid globetrotter. Fortunately there were also those who thought the Society should have some care for the status and well-being of geography as an academic discipline; their anxieties were increased by a remarkable exodus of the many geologists and scientists who had once been fellows of the Society (Stoddart 1980), for they took physical geography with them, leaving the Society with the lifeless general geography. The first need therefore was for a conception of the subject that would, at one and the same time, reclaim physical geography from the geologists, breathe life into general geography, and unite the two into a single discipline. The next task would then be, armed with this new conception, to persuade the universities to adopt it, so that the schools would feel it worth their while to teach it. Such a geography had developed in Germany, where it was a well-established

[6] The word was first used in this sense by Huxley in his lectures at the London Institution in 1869; previously it had been a mineralogical term (Huxley 1877, p. vi).

academic discipline concerned basically with the interaction of man and nature within regions.

Such an idea of geography had emerged in mid-nineteenth-century England. Hughes[7] had written (1847, p. 15), 'There is no mental pursuit which makes so clearly evident as an extensive knowledge of Geography the harmonious arrangement which subsists between all departments of the Kingdom of nature, or which enables the mind to trace so completely the connection of one of these with the other, and of the whole with the condition of mankind ...' Mary Somerville had expressed a similar view in her *Physical Geography* (1848). Hughes (1870) anticipated Mackinder in suggesting that, 'All geography has physical geography ... as its basis ... political geography cannot be studied or taught without constant regard to the physical aspects of nature ... Geography ... is one subject ...'[8] Many others, including Oxford historians like Bryce, were familiar with this theme, as were leading members of the Council of the RGS. In 1871 and 1874 they approached Oxford and Cambridge on behalf of this new geography, but in vain. In the 1880s a fresh campaign was mounted with Freshfield[9] and Markham[10] as the prime movers. They were anxious to strengthen their case with proof that such a geography flourished elsewhere, and by producing a man who could formulate, practise, and defend it in the academic world. Keltie[11] was appointed (1884) to report on the state of geography in Britain relative to other countries; Mackinder was to be the standard-bearer and, at the Society's invitation, read his paper, 'The Scope and Methods of Geography', a full exposition of the new geography, in January 1887. The paper argued that physical geography was not a matter for the geologist, but belonged to, indeed was essential to, 'political' (human) geography' and that distributions of phenomena on

[7] William Hughes was Professor of Geography in the College of Civil Engineers in the 1850s, and from 1863 to 1876 at King's College, London. Despite the laudable principles he expressed, Hughes's books were factual in the extreme, with little if any explanatory or cause-and-effect argument, but with numerous tables and lists.

[8] Hughes also objected to the inappropriate use of the term 'political' geography—'It might with quite as much (perhaps more) propriety be entitled "social"' (1870, p. 3).

[9] Douglas William Freshfield (1845–1934), mountaineer; the chief driving force behind the efforts of the RGS on behalf of academic geography.

[10] Sir Clements Robert Markham (1830–1916), traveller and writer; Hon. Sec. of the RGS, 1863–88, and later President.

[11] See cap. 1, fn 10, p. 7.

the earth's surface, both physical and human, were geographical only in so far as they explained—or were explained by— each other; the physical distributions formed natural regions and the human distributions formed communities; the interaction between them was the stuff of geography.

Mackinder had already set forth these principles in his 1886 Extension lectures. His enunciation of them in 1887 has been generally regarded as heralding the renascence of British geography: 'he startled the Royal Geographical Society with his famous revolutionary paper on the content and teaching of the subject' (Ormsby 1947). Baker (1963, p. 120) wrote that Mackinder 'preached what he, wrongly, believed to be a new geography'; but in fact he had said, 'I do not pretend that these suggestions are new' (*Proc. RGS* ix (1887), p. 160). His 1886 Extension lectures were justifiably entitled 'The New Geography' because they marked a revolution in the way the subject was taught; for he put into perfect practice the estimable precepts which had, to some degree, been preached by others besides himself.

Mackinder was perhaps influenced by Keltie, who, having returned from his investigations on the continent, set forth his ideas of what geography should be, both in a lecture in December 1885 and in his superb report (1886). As Mackinder probably heard the lecture and would certainly have read the report, and as he claimed that his meeting Keltie in December 1885 changed the course of his life, it is not unlikely that he found inspiration here. He did not begin to lecture on the New Geography until 1886, his lectures in 1885 having been on physiography. Keltie's report foreshadows Mackinder's paper:

[In geography] various sciences are co-ordinated in such a way as to present a vivid picture of the different regions of the world, and a clear statement of the causes that determine the resemblances and contrasts of those regions. The forms of the land and their origin, the climates of the globe, the distribution of plants and animals, and the causes that have regulated it, the influence of the variations of climate, soil, and topography upon the history of man, the reaction of man upon nature—these, and a thousand other connected problems, form the subject of the highest kind of geography. (p. 32)

Mackinder took a theme familiar to many who had thought about the subject and developed it into a comprehensive and well-reasoned analysis, such as had not existed in English before. James Bryce, the distinguished historian, having listened to his 1887 paper, commended its 'singular clearness, logical cogency, and width of philosophical view' (*Proc. RGS* ix (1887), p. 170). Although many of its ideas were not original, there is still justification for calling it 'the founding document of modern British geography' (Wooldridge and Linton 1955, p. 152). He was to speak again and again on the nature of geography over the next fifty-six years, expatiating on this or that aspect, but many have been content to read no farther than his 1887 discourse, regarding it as in itself a sufficient statement of the 'new geography'. Its success meant that the RGS was now able to go to the University of Oxford, not only with a strong case for a geographical appointment, but also with the ideal man to fill it. Mackinder was made Reader in Geography, and as he said, 'a platform had been given to a geographer'; he was to make brilliant use of that platform.[12]

As a man of powerful brain, intellectual self-assurance, and an unusual breadth of learning and variety of training, it is unlikely that Mackinder was greatly dependent for his geographical thought upon external influences. His mind had been absorbing countless impressions from a myriad sources since childhood, and from them he created his own distinctive ideas. It is quite possible, however, that, listening to Keltie he found the key to geography as a unified discipline that he was searching for. Troll (1952) suggests the influence of the German masters, and Freeman (1975) asserts that he 'looked to them for inspiration'. In his 1887 paper there is only a single reference to Germans and that a critical one: 'It is a mistake, especially of the Germans, that they include too much in geography.'[13] It is unlikely that even a Mackinder could have accomplished the formidable task of reading the German 'literature' by 1887; in the three years since graduation he had read a second honour school, won a university prize in yet another subject, completed a legal education, been called to the bar, and travelled all over England giving Extension lectures, 'getting up' for these such

[12] A lecturer was also appointed at Cambridge in 1887 (see Stoddart 1975). For more detail on the RGS negotiations with Oxford see Unstead (1949) and Scargill (1976).

[13] This is remarkably like Keltie's phrase of the previous year: 'some German geographers seem to claim too much for their subject' (1886, p. 33).

topics as the economics of wealth. By 1895, however, he was
able to give a detailed address on German geography; yet this
is by no means deferential—he arbitrates the debate between
Ritter and Peschel with masterly detachment.

Darwinian influence has also been suggested (e.g. Troll 1952,
Freeman 1975, Stoddart 1976, Gregory 1978), and Mackinder
himself acknowledged Moseley's influence at Oxford.[14] It is
difficult, however, to detect much 'biologism' even in Mackinder's early geographical writing, with its concern for man in
society, although his geopolitical thought may reveal traces of
it. Fleure (1953) may be right in claiming that 'he seems to have
felt but little the influence of Darwin'. Dickinson (1976) prefers
to see Mackinder's thought as independent of both German and
Darwinian traits, though open to the ideas of his colleagues and
contemporaries:

He established a distinctive brand of British geography ... He was
closer to the thinking of Patrick Geddes[15] than to that of foreign
scholars, and his view of geography was far more balanced and mature
than Davis's 'influences of physical geography on human activities' or
Mill's 'mobile distributions', both men being essentially natural scientists who viewed man on earth as dependent upon his physical environment. From the maturity of his views one suspects that he was influenced by his close association with distinguished contemporaries in
other fields ... (p. 37)

Mackinder popularized the 'new geography' in Britain. He
equipped it with a robust methodological constitution and with
sufficient intellectual *savoir-faire* to take care of itself as an un-
wanted intruder into the academic family. Yet it did not survive
as he had conceived it—much of what his successors practised
he would not have recognized as geography. Why did he fail?

There are many reasons. One was that his geography required a rare combination of skills: some training and ability as
a scientist, humanist, and philosopher; a love of maps; the power

[14] Henry Nottidge Moseley (1844–91). Naturalist on the *Challenger* expedition (1872–
6), FRS 1879, Linacre Professor of Human and Comparative Anatomy at Oxford,
1881.

[15] Sir Patrick Geddes (1854–1932), trained as a biologist but became better known as
a sociologist and town planner; he anticipated and may have inspired some of M.'s
ideas—cf. his remark, 'Our greatest need to-day is to see life as a whole, to see its many
sides in their proper relations'; in 1892 he set up a sociological laboratory in Outlook
Tower, Edinburgh, which became 'a museum of civic geography with a world outlook'
(Joerg 1922).

to visualize accurately; and the facility to write in lucid colourful language. In fact Mackinder's geography was so ambitious that only a Mackinder could practise it. H. G. Wells (1903) wrote that 'one of the things that the educational reformer must guard against' was 'the persuasion that what an exceptional man can do' could be done by everyone else: 'Mr Mackinder teaches geography—inimitably—just to show how to do it', but 'this sort of teaching is not within the capacity of such teachers as we have, or are likely to have' (p. 183). His successors could not sustain it: 'he was followed by lesser men', all of whom 'to some extent ossify the vitality of the ideas of the patriarch' (Moss 1970, p. 35).[16]

He had himself (1921) warned that 'Geography is inherently not an elementary but an advanced subject' because 'no one can appreciate geographical correlations without some mathematical, some physical, some economic, and some historical knowledge' (1921). Later (1935) he acknowledged the criticism that his ideas were 'a counsel of perfection' and that 'their application would postulate a supply of sound philosophers which, at any rate in geography, is not available'. Today there is growing recognition that geography is 'a much more difficult enterprise than many of us have been prepared to admit' and that 'it may even be one of the most difficult of all' (Gregory 1978, p. 170). Perhaps the verdict on Mackinder's geography should be that pronounced on Christianity: 'not "tried and found wanting" but "found difficult and not tried" '.

Hostility to the subject in the Board of Education was fatal. Its 1917 regulations on Advanced Courses, which were to determine the pattern of secondary school education through the inter-war period, 'proved disastrous to geography', for it was 'the one and only main subject of a liberal school education, which it is impossible to take as a main subject in any of the Board's advanced courses' (Mackinder 1921). As a result only the dullest pupils took geography in the upper forms and the subject remained basically a test of the ability to assimilate factual knowledge. Those who distinguished themselves were the patient plodders with good memories, the very opposites of

[16] See also Gyorgy (1944, p. 281) 'Ever since Mackinder "dropped the torch", British political geographers seem to have lost their awareness of fundamental political forces ...'.

the versatile, intuitive, perceptive, and imaginative scholars envisaged by Mackinder. There were exceptions—often those who had come from other subjects where their intellectual worth had already been tried and who had come to geography, not because their industry and memory had made them appear good at it, but because they were attracted by its theme.

Mackinder was the intellectual equal of his academic colleagues and did not lack self-assurance in expounding or defending his subject. But he admitted (1935) that, 'The Professor of Geography is at times conscious that beneath the friendly comradeship of the Common Room there is a covert denial of his real equality of status.' C. G. S. Crawford (1955) the archaeologist, found that 'going from Greats to Geography was like leaving the parlour for the basement; one lost caste ...'.[17]

The reaction of the undistinguished English-speaking geographical establishment to the hostile and contemptuous attitude confronting it, was to play for safety and avoid giving offence by retreating to impregnable citadels of accumulated facts or unimpugnable techniques. Their early attempts to operate Mackinder's cause-and-effect argument, perpetrated without his grasp of historical perspective and without his perception of the varied forces and realities involved, brought on their heads a charge of 'crude determinism', whereupon they drew in their horns, avoided causality like the plague, and stamped out environmentalism wherever they found it. Far from standing out for a unified geography, they hastened, according to their inclinations or qualifications, for shelter to the umbrellas of wholly arts or wholly scientific organizations. Mackinder had said (1935) of the low opinion of geography widely held in universities that it would not matter but for its effect on the geographers themselves. Too often they tried 'to appease the critic by differentiating between physical and human geography', so sacrificing unity to specialization.

It seemed like a new dawn for English-speaking geographers when, in the 1960s, in place of the difficult and seemingly

[17] p. 44. However, he 'immediately felt at home in the new environment of maps and things of this world, so refreshingly different from the musty speculations about unreal problems that had hitherto been my fare'. But this was Oxford, where Herbertson, who understood and shared M.'s views, was a worthy successor. Unfortunately Herbertson died in 1915 aged only 49. The injury done to British geography generally and to Oxford geography in particular was incalculable.

unattainable discipline sketched out by Mackinder, it was boldly asserted that by abandoning the aim of unity in the regional synthesis, and by applying to the spatial aspects of the various contributory sciences the methodology of those sciences, geography could hold its head up as a real science in one or other of two loosely-associated groups—the earth sciences or the social sciences. Furthermore, their intellectual deficiency could now be hidden in jargon borrowed from those sciences and elaborated into a system of closed communication between those who wrote for each other rather than for the world at large.

Another reason for Mackinder's failure lies in the nature of geography itself. The geographer inevitably comes into contact with other subjects of study: for many it is simpler and more satisfying to work with the geographical aspects of one of these subjects on the circumference, than to face the baffling task of co-ordinating in the centre. Furthermore, the abler may even attain to a certain proficiency in the contributory subject and perhaps, by a useful contribution earn recognition—even membership of the Royal Society or the British Academy. And if they wish to fund their research, they must declare themselves to be either natural or social scientists. The real geographer is, from the administrative point of view, neither fish nor fowl, and from the academic standpoint, not even good red herring. Mackinder (1935) has some appropriate words:

Since success in research is to-day the chief criterion of academic distinction, and since purely geographical research is not ... of a kind that, however excellent, normally wins entry to the Royal Society, there is the standing temptation for the Professor of Geography to pursue his investigations in some borderland ... The Fellowship of that Society is the noble compensation of those who submit for a great end to the self-denials of specialism. But geography must have leaders of a different kind of ambition if it is to carry science as a vital strand into the new humanism demanded by the conditions of our time. (p. 11)

Many who found their way into academic life as geographers discovered, after tasting the contributory subjects, that they were really geologists or historians or economists *manqués*. Perhaps at school they had not qualified for the classes which studied the essential preliminaries for higher work in these subjects. But in some branch of systematic geography they found the opportunity to bypass the eliminating competition they would otherwise have met.[18] Or they may have been abler men who developed an interest in these subjects later in life, having been brought into touch with them by geography. Inevitably they will resent the suggestion that they are not really geographers and that they constitute a threat to the unity of the subject. However disparate their fields of interest they will combine to reject the idea of a single coherent discipline. And so, 'British geography became dominated by the notable achievements of individual geographers in certain systematic disciplines, and, as their work became more scientifically and academically respectable, so their links with the 'New Geography' of Mackinder became more tenuous' (Moss 1970, p. 32).

There are signs of a reaction. Because of improved status in the schools and more awards at the universities, a new generation of talented geographers has arrived; many of these are not content with a geography that lacks unity, ignores values, and disregards the interaction of places and people. Perhaps, when the centenary of 'The Scope and Methods of Geography' falls in 1987, its message will be more in tune with the age than at any time before.[19]

MACKINDER'S GEOGRAPHY

The statement that follows summarizes Mackinder's view of geography as he elaborated it over a period of almost sixty years. In the subsequent pages each assertion in this statement is substantiated from his work and considered in the light of the subject's later development.

Geography analyses the distributions of phenomena on the earth's surface, in order to explain them and to establish the relationships between them. Physical geography analyses the natural environment, with a view to understanding the relationships between its constituent parts and between it and

---

[18] There are also those 'who started as geologists, but who failed to secure geological appointments and who ultimately became lecturers in geography *faute de mieux*' (Stoddart 1980, p. 198).

[19] And in America too: 'The last quarter-century of this Association's first hundred years could well see the end of this dichotomy (i.e. physical v. human)'—Presidential address to the Association of American Geographers, 1979 (Marcus 1979, p. 532).

man in society. Human geography traces the interaction of man in society and so much of his environment as varies locally. Physical geography and human geography are complementary, inseparable, and essential parts of one subject. Man in society forms local communities and the natural environment may be marked off into natural regions: natural regions influence the development of the communities inhabiting them; communities modify the regions they inhabit; the regions, so modified, influence the communities differently than before; and so the interaction continues.

Regional geography synthesizes the interacting distributions within a region, arranging them in a logical sequence linked by cause and effect. This synthesis requires the accurate mapping of related data, and the ability to visualize and describe such mapped distributions associated together in actual landscapes. Although practicality requires a regional treatment, there is no complete region less than the whole world.

The distributions of geographical data form global shapes which, combined, form the map of the world. They constitute six spheres: lithosphere, hydrosphere, atmosphere, photosphere, biosphere, and psychosphere; these in combination form a complete conspectus of geography. Physical geographers have been obsessed with the lithosphere; but the atmosphere and the hydrosphere are more important geographically because their global circulations shape the lithosphere and are vital to the biosphere; the hydrosphere sets the limits of geography and gives it unity.

Man is part of the biosphere, in which his mobility gives rise to circulations comparable to those which agitate the atmosphere and hydrosphere. But ideas constitute an independent force which grows in strength with improved technical knowledge and social organization, and may be termed the psychosphere. Now that all parts of the world have been discovered and explored, the interplay of the forces of the psychosphere has become a closed system; their action in any part of the world is felt throughout the whole.

Geography draws upon both sciences and humanities for its data, seeing knowledge whole within areas. In its analysis of the distribution of phenomena and in their representation on the map, it is a science—the science of distribution; but it is not a science in the sense that physics and chemistry are, as the patterns formed by its distributions are unique. Because the test of relevance of its data is from a human standpoint, and because it applies human values, it cannot be wholly objective. In its explanatory descriptions of landscapes it is an art. It is both science and art, and this enables it to build a bridge between the sciences and the humanities.

Geography has its own philosophy; this justifies its claim to be an independent discipline. For it asks the question 'Where?' with the object of posing the further question, 'Why there?'. This question may be asked in a genetic or in a dynamic sense: it may mean 'how does it come to be there?', an historical question, or 'why is it there and not somewhere else?'—a geographical question inquiring into present phenomena and their interactions. Although the genetic approach has its place in geography, particularly in geomorphology, the dynamic is more geographical. Geography must, however, take account of momentum from the past.

Stoddart (1976) writes: 'it is clear, viewing his work as a whole, that only by rigorous selection can one recognise the "clear and unified view" of the "content and functions" of geography that Unstead (1949) ascribed to Mackinder.' Admittedly there is change of emphasis and occasionally some shifting of ground during the half-century and more covered by his geographical writing, but the selection problem in the following pages has been to choose from a mass of supporting testimony rather than to search for it. Perhaps they will go some way to provide the 'close analysis of Mackinder's substantive papers' and 'of their contribution to contemporary debate', the absence of which Stoddart (ibid.) rightly deplores.

Geography analyses the distributions of phenomena on the earth's surface in order to establish their causes and the relationships between them.

This is the gist of 'The Scope and Methods of Geography' (1887):

it is necessary that we should . . . consider what relations hold between the distributions of various sets of features on the earth's surface and what are the causes of those distributions. (p. 160)

At Manchester later in the same year he expanded this:

The basis, a descriptive analysis of the earth's surface, including in that term the atmosphere, the hydrosphere, the form of the lithosphere, and the material of its surface. From this we shall reason backwards to causes, and forwards to effects. The causes largely geological, the effects mainly on man. (1887b, p. 699)

He never wavered in this conception of the subject, repeating it fifty years later in almost the same words (1937, pp. 178–9).

Physical geography analyses the natural environment, with a view to understanding the relationships between its constituent parts and between it and man in society.

In his 1887 lecture Mackinder stated that 'the mind which has vividly grasped in their true relations the factors of the environment is likely to be fertile in the suggestion of new relations between the environment and man' (1887, p. 144). In his early work he was at pains to stress the primacy of the physical basis, giving the impression of a deterministic approach; but such emphasis must be seen in the context of a time when human (then called 'political') geography was divorced from the natural environment. Like Wooldridge (1949) he wanted the 'ge' put back into geography, and this meant stressing the physical side:

Geography is double sided. It has a physical and human aspect. Physical geography is the more important, and a thorough grounding in this is essential to *all* sound geographical knowledge. (1888b)

I regard physical geography as the foundation of the whole subject. (1888d)

Later he became concerned that the growing interest in geomorphology, which he had at first welcomed, was turning physical geography from its main purpose and destroying the newfound unity of the subject:

... treat the physical geography as the data for your human geography; do not treat physical geography as an end in itself. In so far as you treat physical geography as an end in itself you are merely pursuing so many different chapters of other sciences. (1916, p. 277)

Geomorphology, as it has now developed, has internal coherence and a consistent philosophy, and in their hunger for these joys many of our geographers, it seems to me, have blinded themselves to the fact that as geomorphologists they are not in the centre but on the margin of geography. (1931, p. 4)

When Mackinder began his fight for a new unified geography, he had found physical geography in the hands of the geologists and taught as physiography, a systematic study of the physical features of the earth's surface. His first Extension lectures had been on physiography and dealt with 'Winds', 'Mountains', 'Currents', 'Rivers', 'Climates', and 'Geographical

Changes' (1885). But by 1887 he was at pains to differentiate physical geography from physical geology:

The true distinction between geology and geography seems to me to lie in this: the geologist looks at the present that he may interpret the past, the geographer looks at the past that he may interpret the present. (1887, p. 146)

... physical geography ... has been abandoned to the geologists, and has in consequence a geological bias. Phenomena such as volcanoes, hot springs, and glaciers have been grouped into chapters, irrespective of the regions in which they occur. (1887, pp. 147)

Although physical geography was the foundation for the whole geographical structure, it legitimately included the inter-relationships between different kinds of physical distributions, such as between landforms and climate, climate and soils, etc. This is clear from Mackinder's own work:

Every hill has its influence upon the rains which are degrading its substance; every headland bends the currents which are reducing its salience. The solid features and the fluid circulations are, therefore, delicately adjusted to one another: a correlation which gives intricate unity to the varied theme of geography. Climate has closely co-operated with rock structure in determining the features of Britain, and these features are in turn among the chief causes producing variety of climate ... (1902, p. 148)

Physical geography was also of value in satisfying a natural curiosity about the landscape (1887, p. 148).

Mackinder's pleading notwithstanding, a narrow and morpho-genetic geomorphology, oblivious of climatic vagaries, careless of the vegetational cover, and ignorant of man, tightened its grip on physical geography, consummating the divorce from human geography and leaving climatology and biogeography as detached orphans. More recently, however, there has been a partial return to Mackinder's holistic view, for both theoretical and practical reasons. The rejection of the seductive Davisian cycle and the development of applied physical geography, serving man as Mackinder would have wished, have been steps in this direction:

As long as physical geography is taught as theoretical geomorphology or as an extension of historical geology it provides a most unsuitable base on which to build the geographical synthesis. The study, in isolation, of planation surfaces and denudation chronology, or the relative movements of land and sea in the Pleistocene, offers little if anything of value to the human or regional geographer. (Walton 1968, p. 5)

... many physical geographers ... have recognized a potentially profitable convergence of their interests with public environmental concern, so that, for example, the traditional geographical stronghold of man-environment relationships has attracted an increasing number of physical geographers. (Cooke and Robson 1976, p. 85)

There has been something close to a publication explosion of work stemming from the application of physical geography to engineering, planning, land and resource management problems. (Doornkamp and Warren 1980, pp. 102–3)

... physical geography is a correlative natural science, the geography of the physical world. As such, its future growth and that of geography generally are best served by integrating geomorphology and climatology, physical geography and biogeography, and environmental geography as a whole with human geography. (Orme 1980, p. 146)[20]

Human geography traces the interaction of man in society and so much of his environment as varies locally.

... the function of political[21] geography is to detect and demonstrate the relations subsisting between man in society and so much of his environment as varies locally. (1887, p. 144)

The human aspects of geography—for which 'political geography' is an insufficient term—should aim at exhibiting human movements and settlements as depending on physical features, or overcoming them. (1888b, p. 2)

Geographers were to prove unable to cope with one side of the man–land relationship—the influence[22] of the environment

[20] Professor Orme, who believes 'in the fundamental unity of geography', refers to M. (p. 143).

[21] Although M. at first uses the current term 'political geography', he was soon to substitute 'human geography', after toying with 'anthropogeography'.

[22] Kristof's footnote (1960, p. 16) on the use of the word 'influence' is relevant: 'The notion of "influence" is unacceptable to many American geographers ... The British and French are somewhat less adamant on the subject ..., and the Russians are wholly unperturbed and speak of "influences (vliiania) of the geographic environment". The Americans argue that nature does not initiate, at least not consciously and purposefully; hence it is a passive factor and cannot be said to *influence* anybody. Omitting certain philosophical questions, it remains whether such a position is correct from the semantic point of view. Does the common and professional ... use of the English language justify such an interpretation and limitation of the meaning of the word "influence"?'

upon man. It came to be regarded as too dangerous to touch, for fear of accusations of determinism, and after much debate about 'probabilism' and 'possibilism', English-speaking geographers came generally to the conclusion that any form of environmentalism was best eschewed.[23] One of the most valuable contributions which the geographer could make thus disappeared, and the West rode unwarned by geographers into the environmental crises of the late twentieth century. There was less inhibition in asserting man's power over nature.

Had Mackinder's successors read his work, they would have found a safe-conduct through territory they were too timorous to cross. This was his formula that the interaction of the environment and man was governed by his civilization or culture, the main elements of which were technology (know-how and tools) and society (the economic, political, and social organization). Generally, as civilization advanced, the power of nature over man lessened while his power over nature increased; but as man was himself part of nature and depended on it for all his material resources, any control he exercised was conditional. He carried this idea further by pointing out that man's culture affected his perception of the environment, a fact the significance of which was not fully recognized for half a century or more: 'in considering the influence of the geographical environment on human history, it is essential . . . that we should bear in mind not merely the facts as we know them, but also man's former beliefs concerning them' (RGS 1893). Later he wrote (1919):

The influence of geographical conditions upon human activities has depended . . . not merely on the realities as we now know them to be and to have been, but in even greater degree on what men imagined in regard to them . . . our view of the geographical realities is coloured for practical purposes by our preconceptions from the past . . . human society is still related to the facts of geography not as they are, but in no small measure as they have been approached in the course of history.[24] (pp. 38–41)

[23] Thus Freeman (1980, p. 115) regards 'geographical control' as an 'emotive' term. Spate (1952, p. 421) believed that, although 'To speak of "controls" is doubtless nearly always illegitimate', it is not always so, and that the 'fear of controls seems to lead to a horror of admitting quite reasonable influences'.

[24] Spate (1952, p. 419) criticizes this, saying that 'the facts of geography are the facts as they are approached; there is no other geographical way of looking at them.' This is to say there is no difference between reality and illusion. A river is a geographical fact, but the culture of the people approaching it will determine whether it is to be a barrier

His writings yield examples of determinism—when he has reason to believe that environmental control has been direct or compelling, but there are many others illustrating exercise of choice.[25] Although the facts of geography represent reality, they can be challenged or surmounted by peoples who are inspired by ideals, and the human spirit is often victorious, at least in the short run. On his return from Canada in 1908 he spoke of

an unparalleled struggle between the physical environment of a nation and a designed policy based on a national ideal, to control by means of modern material resources and the political policies which could be based on them, the destinies of a race, rather than to allow that race to be controlled by the blind forces which in the past had so very materially managed men and mice. Again and again one had heard the same expression, 'Ours is a geographical problem', meaning 'Ours is a problem of conquering geography'. (*The Times*, 1 Dec. 1908)

The theme that geographical reality can be challenged by human determination is also the theme of his *Democratic Ideals and Reality*. In the long run, however, those who are working in harmony with environmental influences will triumph over those who strive against them. Notable successes can and will be achieved by the latter, but their permanence would need an unlikely succession of talented leaders and self-denying peoples. Sooner or later the line of least resistance will be followed. These extracts illustrate his practice:

... comparatively undisturbed strata usually underlie wide plains and wide plains seem specially favourable to the development of homogeneous races, like the Russians and the Chinese. (1887, p. 157)

The relative importance of physical features varies from age to age according to the state of knowledge and of material civilization. The improvement of artificial lighting has rendered possible the existence of a great community at St Petersburg ... The invention of the steam engine and the electric telegraph have rendered possible the great size of modern states. (ibid.)

---

or a means of communication, a water supply or a source of power: one geographical fact, several human approaches. Much confusion has been caused by the selection of rivers as boundaries because such rivers were approached in ignorance of their true nature.

[25] Fleure 'stoutly' maintained to Cantor (1960, p. 235) that M. was 'essentially a possibilist'.

... the resistance offered by a given feature to man's movement, or the facilities of a given area for his settlement, are for ever varying with the state of his civilization ... a daring leader, a mechanical discovery, a great engineering monument, may revolutionize man's relations to geography in the third of a generation. (1890, p. 79)

Sometimes human genius seems to set geographical limitations at defiance, and to introduce an incalculable element into every problem of anthropogeography. Yet, as we extend our survey over wider periods, the significance even of the most vigorous initiative is seen to diminish. Temporary effects contrary to Nature may be within human possibilities, but in the long run Nature reasserts her supremacy. (1895, p. 8)

... do not attempt to ... explain everything human in terms of geography. You cannot and it is well you should not. The initiative is in the soul of man: the only control under which he works is the environment around him. (1916, p. 277)

In this age of flying and wireless telegraphy it may be true that man is no longer cabined and cribbed by geographical obstacles, but it is still true that he conquers nature like an artist by understanding the properties of the material in which he works. (1928, p. 8)

... the facts of physical geography have determined that there should always be a predominant English people in the south of the island, whether as foe or partner of the Scottish and Welsh peoples. (1919, p. 70)

Mackinder looked at man–land relations as he found them. He was not inhibited by a preconceived attitude embodied in some '-ism', and made no attempt to apply a universal law. His successors' attitude that it was unscientific and unsafe to suggest anything that was incapable of proof, brought to an end fruitful hypotheses about the land–man relationship. 'Who', asked Roxby (1914) in a review of one of Mackinder's books, 'shall attempt to estimate the relative importance of natural forces and of human personality on the course of history?' If early geographers overvalued these natural forces, the tendency of many historians was to overestimate the significance of 'the human personality', and as Mackinder suggests, however dramatic the achievements of peoples and their leaders, natural forces, acting through human cultures, tend in the long run to prevail. Peter the Great made Petersburg the capital of Russia in the teeth of a hostile geography and cultural factors made its continuance technically possible; in the short run the Tsar appeared to have triumphed, and for two centuries the great Russian Empire was ruled from this magnificent 'folly'. But in the end it was the centripetal pull of Moscow that won the day. It is doubtful whether the exercise of the human will could have more than delayed or hastened the rise of the Superpowers, the decline of Europe, or the fall of the British Empire. Because historians have been more numerous, more highly regarded, and much more influential than geographers in the formation of British attitudes, the power of human volition has been exaggerated, and geographers after Mackinder lacked the confidence and conviction to protest. Ironically, it has been left to a few historians to insist upon geography as a history-shaping factor.

Deprived of its links with its physical counterpart, human geography became a social science, analysing human distributions, studying their spatial relations, and mapping behaviour patterns, without reference to the physical environment: it became 'spatial' history, 'spatial' economics, 'spatial' sociology, 'spatial' politics.[26] There are now 'geographies' of all kinds of economic, social, and political phenomena—e.g. a geography of crime (Harries 1974) and a geography of prostitution (Symanski 1974).[27]

Mackinder's human geography was intended to help 'man in society' by illuminating his relationship with his varying environment, an environment where places differed because in them individual kinds of community inhabited distinctive localities. He believed that the true freedom of man lay in the preservation of the independence and individuality of regions or provinces from centralized control by distant metropolises. Modern human geography, with its concept of space to be ordered from above rather than of place belonging to people, has developed in the service of this very control. Its function has been 'to provide "objective" and by implication, *unobjectionable* solutions, legitimized by the compelling force of science

[26] For a comprehensive survey of modern human geography, see Johnston (1979).

[27] 'The light-hearted prophecy I made in 1959 that we might soon expect to see the full 57 varieties of geography has since been almost literally fulfilled' (Fisher 1970, p. 373).

rather than the free consent of society' (Gregory 1978, pp. 71–2).[28]

Physical geography and human geography are complementary, inseparable, and essential parts of a unified subject.

In 1928 Mackinder spoke of the failure to maintain this unity. Despite the favourable reception of his 1887 statement with its emphasis on unity, there was soon

a fresh tendency to break the subject up again, and to attach the chapters of geography to the several sciences to which they are cognate ... The Universities established more schools of geography, but at the same time published curricula containing often very little real geography. The critic was once more emboldened to deny that geography could exist as a reputable study. (1928, p. 4)

When he went to Exeter in 1942 the 81-year-old patriarch heard the Principal of the University College of the South West welcome the Geographical Association thus:

I have sought to discover from likely persons what Geography ... is and what it aims at. These persons became instantly embarrassed. I was told of Human Geography, and Physical Geography, and Historical Geography, and rather more vaguely of Economic Geography, and still more vaguely of Social Geography, and I was told that Geography was Regional Psychology. Many geographies, but no Geography! (Murray 1942, p. 117)

Mackinder was not optimistic about the future for it was an age of growing specialization, and the demand for 'scientific' method made the intelligent speculation and the large generalization suspect. Yet the trained ability to speculate and generalize was essential to statesman and citizen alike, and this training was the greatest benefit a unified geography could confer:

Its inherent breadth and many-sidedness should be claimed as its chief merit. At the same time we have to recognize these are the very qualities which will render it 'suspect' to an age of specialization. (1887, p. 159)

The Principal, a classicist, took up this point at Exeter:

... this is a gathering of orphans. Whether it is the desire for reunion with the Mother that has brought them to Exeter, I do not know. The

[28] See also Relph (1976) and Buttimer (1974).

desire may have cooled away. They may even think that orphanhood sits well on them. Perhaps the Mother might be neither comfortable nor welcome among her offspring. She might disturb specialist self-sufficiency by importing a measure of discipline, or shall I say of unity ... The canon of humane value has been pushed away out of sight behind the imposing facade of scientific method, and the meticulous procedures and the esoteric diction of the specialists. (Murray 1942, p. 117)

Worse was to come: the 'scientific' approach and the quantitative techniques of the 1960s favoured the multiplication of geographies of separate kinds of phenomena or behaviour. More recently, however, there has been renewed recognition of the necessity to take the natural environment into account in the economic, social, and political fields, and thus to admit the value of a unified geography:

the opportunities for co-operative man–land focussed geography have never been greater, and to ignore them is to abrogate a major tradition and raison d'etre of geography ... the blinders[29] that steer many of us along narrow, sub-specialized paths should be removed. Specialties are essential, but need not cause loss of geographic perspective ... geography must seek new concepts, approaches, and models which explain and/or help interpret the man–land relationship. (Marcus 1979, pp. 523, 530)

Which is a return to Mackinder.

Man in society forms communities and the natural environment may be marked off into natural regions; natural regions influence the development of the communities inhabiting them; the communities modify the regions they inhabit; the regions, so modified, influence the communities differently than before, and so the interaction continues.

Although Mackinder's suggestion that geography should study the earth–man relationship had been made earlier, his 1887 statement that this relationship was between social communities on the one hand and natural regions on the other was a significant advance. It highlighted the importance of social groupings and structure on the one side,[30] and of the variability

[29] US for 'blinkers'.
[30] Gregory (1978, p. 16) argues that M. gave little weight to 'man in society', relegating its mention in 1887 to a footnote. This is not so. Earlier in that paper he had written that the function of human geography was to 'demonstrate the relationship

of the earth's surface on the other. The interaction at once became more complex and more realistic, for it was between variable patterns of human societies and variable patterns of the natural environment.[31] Mackinder had used the concept of the natural region in the 1886 Extension lectures. The South-West Peninsula and East Anglia were among the regions he treated; he also lectured on 'the natural regions of the world'. There follow some of his dicta on regions and their relationships with the communities inhabiting them:

'An environment' is a natural region. The smaller the area included the greater tends to be the number of conditions uniform or nearly uniform throughout the area ... So with communities. 'A community' is a group of men having certain characteristics in common. The smaller the community, the greater tends to be the number of common characteristics. Communities are of different orders—races, nations, provinces, towns ... (1887, pp. 156-7)

Man alters his environment, and the action of that environment on his posterity is changed in consequence. (ibid., p. 157)

We are all familiar with the saying that it required the Greeks in Greece to develop the Athenian civilization, and that neither the Greeks elsewhere, nor any other race in Greece, would have been equal to the achievement. It would be easy for a Peschel to demonstrate the falsity of the assertion that the Greeks owed all to Greece, but on the other hand, the Ritters and Buckles were in error in attempting so simple an explanation. What seems to have been constantly omitted from these speculations is the fact that communities can move from one environment to another; that even a given environment alters from generation to generation; and that an existing community is often the product of two or more communities in past generations, each of them subject to a different environment. (1895, pp. 6-7)

---

between man in society and so much of his environment as varies locally' and his footnote is but a subsequent reminder. His best-known work, *Democratic Ideals and Reality* (1919), although usually thought of in connection with the Heartland theory, is in fact largely devoted to society and its organization. Gregory gives more attention to the ideas of M.'s French contemporary Vidal de la Blache, and following Buttimer, says that the *tradition vidalienne* 'stood out from other European schools of thought by virtue of its "vision of collective man" '. This vision is implicit in M.'s use of the terms 'man in society' and 'communities' in his 1887 paper.

[31] The principle of communities of living things in occupation of regions is found in modern biogeography—see Morgan and Moss (1965, p. 339).

... but for their different relations to the metropolis, the south and south-east of England would form a single natural region, symmetrical in structure, in system of drainage, and in conditions of settlement. (1902, p. 247)

In a manner all south-eastern England is a single urban community; for steam and electricity are changing our geographical conceptions. (ibid., p. 258)

The natural region is no mere convenient generalization; both by origin and effect it is a fundamental fact. (1931, p. 7)

Consideration of separate communities and regions inevitably raises the question of the boundaries between them; some regional geographers became obsessed with demarcation lines, but Mackinder looked at boundaries individually, giving them importance according to their nature, location, function, and effects:

I sometimes think that this strange straight line which forms the boundary between Canada and the United States is the most remarkable feature on the map of the world ... [it] may very well last for a long time owing to what I have called geographical momentum. You have two societies, organized on each side of the frontier. In each of these societies you have an organization of men such that they look towards widely separated centres ... Thus what was at first merely an imaginary line becomes in fact a frontier of the most marked character. It is as important as any natural feature. (1911b, p. 377)

... I have no respect for the definitions that you find in your text-books as to what Europe is and what it is not. The text-books set children to learn precisely where is the boundary which separates Europe from Asia. But though I have spent a great many years thinking about things geographical, I say frankly I do not know where this boundary is. (1917, p. 5)

[Regions] cannot be accurately delimited, for their boundaries are inevitably zones of compromise as between limits based on different criteria. (1943a, p. 69)

Regional geography synthesizes the interacting distributions within a region by arranging them in a logical sequence linked by cause and effect.

Mackinder introduced regional geography, already well established in Germany, into Britain: 'I believe I was the first habitually to use the expression "regional" in this connection' (Mackinder 1921, p. 379). When the School of Geography was established at Oxford in 1899 he gave his chief lieutenant, Herbertson, the title of Lecturer in Regional Geography. He then planned a series of books, 'The Regions of the World', of which his own *Britain and the British Seas* (1902) was the first to appear.

It was within the region, large or small, natural or political, continent, country, or province, that the unity of geography would find expression in a synthesis of contributing factors. These would be arranged in a logical sequence, starting with position, continuing through lithology, structure, relief, climate, natural vegetation and wild life, to the economic activities of man; and concluding with the distribution of population, human settlements, and other anthropological features. Each factor was to be dealt with not in isolation, but so as to bring out its relationships with those that had gone before.

It was in regional geography that British and American geographers attempted to follow Mackinder most closely, keeping to his form even when unable to infuse it with his spirit. But the various chapters were often undigested and unrelated borrowings from the contributory subjects with little attempt at synthesis; the most fundamental factor—position—was often omitted altogether. His own *Britain and the British Seas* (1902) is permeated by the significance of the geographical location of the British Isles. The book may fall short of his ideals,[32] but it was an experimental prototype: he was trying out ideas and following intuitions with nothing of the kind extant to guide him, and no body of accumulated research to draw upon.[33] He

---

[32] But Dickinson (1976) says of it: 'This work stands as a classic in modern British literature, and shows a more mature and sounder approach to a regional interpretation than Vidal de la Blache's *Tableau* or Ratzel's *Deutschland*. It is a remarkable essay in regional synthesis.' Freeman (1980) writes, however, 'As a regional geographer he was completely outclassed by many people working at his time, particularly by Vidal de la Blache.'

[33] This is the answer to Freeman (1980) who writes that the book is 'inadequately provided with bibliographical references'. M. (1908b) thought that, 'No really adequate geographical account of the British Isles will be possible until we have a much richer local literature from which an author may mine.' He had supported Mill's abortive scheme for a series of local geographies based on the OS one-inch maps (1896), and himself set in motion a similar project at the LSE in 1910, repeating that 'until this spade-work has been accomplished, no exhaustive book on British geography will be possible'. For details see Cantor (1960, p. 183).

had more excuse for any shortcomings than his successors, few of whose regional geographies even approached the quality of his work. Had they done so, regional geography might not have collapsed so readily before the onslaught of the spatial scientists. Some of his statements about the regional synthesis follow:

[The geographer's] first business is to define the form, or relief, of the surface of the *solid* sphere, and the *movements*, or circulation, within the two *fluid* spheres. The land-relief conditions the circulation, and this in turn gradually changes the land-relief. The circulation differentiates climates, and these, together with the relief, constitute the environment of plants, animals, and men. Shorn of complexities, this is the main line of the geographical argument. In the language of Richthofen, the earth's surface and man are the terminal links. (1895, p. 2)

Humboldt's *Essai politique sur la Nouvelle-Espagne*, published in 1809, must take high rank among the efforts of the new geography[34] ... Here, for the first time, we have an exhaustive attempt to relate causally relief, climate, vegetation, fauna, and the various human activities. (1895, p. 4)

The facts of geography are obviously capable of two kinds of treatment ... In the former case, our book should *as a whole* observe the order of what has been called the geographical argument; in the latter case each chapter ... should exhibit that order complete ... By whatever name we call it, however, it is clear that the treatment by regions is a more thorough test of the logic of the geographical argument than is the treatment by types of phenomena. (1895, p. 4)

... geography reaches its highest development in the regional synthesis. (1903, p. 100)

There is the bass of geology; there is the tenor of meteorology; there is the alto of agricultural, botanical and zoological studies; and there is the treble of social, economic and strategical[35] studies. Now geography is a harmony of all four. (1927, p. 214)

Most British and American geographers became fearful of developing his cause-and-effect argument within regions. Gregory (1978, p. 30) notes that even Hartshorne 'avoids mention

[34] These words imply that by 'the new geography' M. had meant, not something that he himself had invented, but the geography developed by the Germans earlier in the century.

[35] M. uses this word in the wider sense of 'planning', rather than as a purely military term.

of causal mechanisms', for 'causality was still uncomfortably close to the discredited thesis of environmental determinism'. Regional geography thus becomes ' "mere description" and classification of facts by area ... constituting as Mackinder observed, "a mere body of information" ' (Moss 1970, p. 32). But the regional idea still lives on: 'Ever since regional geography was declared to be dead ... geographers, to their credit, have kept trying to revivify it in one form or another' (Gregory 1978, p. 171).

This synthesis requires the accurate mapping of related data, and the ability to visualize and describe such mapped distributions associated together in actual landscapes.

Here are brought together the three essential requisites for the successful practice of Mackinder's geography: the map, showing phenomena in spatial association and fertile in suggestions of interaction; trained imagination—the power to visualize landscapes; and the ability to write prose equal to the task of depicting such landscapes. The ideal geographer

is a man of trained imagination, more especially with the power of visualizing forms and movements in space of three dimensions—a power difficult of attainment ... He has an artistic appreciation of landforms obtained, most probably, by pencil study in the field; he is able to depict such forms on the map, and to read them when depicted by others. In this cartographic art he possesses an instrument of thought of no mean power ... maps can save the mind an infinitude of words. A map may convey at one glance a whole series of generalizations ... (1895, p. 9)

By geography ... I refer rather to a special mode and habit of thought, to a special form of visualization which I cannot otherwise describe than as 'thinking geographically'. The mind has an eye as well as an ear, and it is possible to train this eye. (1911, p. 80)

I would have the young geographer practised in the use of an almost Ruskinian, purely descriptive language, with terms drawn from the quarryman, the stone mason, the farmer, the alpine climber, and the water engineer. (1931, p. 14)

The historian *qua* historian writes his narrative in words, and the geographer *qua* geographer draws his map; it is the essential limitation of literature that it must make its statements in sequence to the mind's ear, whereas geography presents its map to the mind's eye and states many facts simultaneously. (1942, p. 142)

He was against the use of jargon and foreign words in geographical writing because he wanted it to be read by as wide a public as possible:

It is no doubt easy when you are talking to experts, to describe with precision by the use of a technical jargon. It is a very hard thing to write a good plain English sentence. But if we adopt the easier method, and shirk the harder, then geographers are throwing away a great opportunity which lies before them ... You can move by your subject ... the whole Anglo-Saxon race in a rational direction. For this reason I care far more that our terms should be harmonious to the ear and powerful, than I do as to whether they are genetic or analytic. There are words like 'peneplain', which are not beautiful. There are others, often taken from English dialect, such as 'scree' and 'crag', which will be adopted readily by the literary writer. (1909, p. 321)[36]

These principles he put into practice. *Britain and the British Seas* and *The Rhine* abound in graphic descriptions enlivened by the use of strong adjectives, picturesque phrases, and striking analogies. In his introductory chapter to the *Cambridge History of India* (1922) even the simplest geographical facts are made arresting or interesting by the skilful use of comparison, contrast, and epigram. There has been such writing by the French masters, but as Gilbert (1951) said, 'little contemporary writing in the English language has approached the level set by the great master of the subject'.

Although practicality requires a regional treatment, there is no complete region less than the whole world.

As he grew older Mackinder came to see limitations in a regional treatment; it was not so much a change of mind as a realization that the world was changing. Improvements in communications were increasing the volume, vigour, and extent of the inter-regional or horizontal movement of men, materials,

[36] M. was, perhaps surprisingly, taken with the Davisian terminology, and he resisted criticism of it by H. R. Mill: 'Dr Davis has done a very valuable thing indeed in giving us terms which, with all due deference to Dr Mill, I cannot regard by any means as so uncouth as those with which most sciences are equipped' (1896, p. 625). He used them in *Britain and the British Seas* (1902) and was duly criticized by Mill (*Geogrl J.* xix (1902), p. 493). In 1921 he referred to them as 'often laughed at but none the less provocative of fruitful and systematic study'.

and ideas across the face of the earth; these horizontal links were being forged at the expense of the intra-regional, vertical links between communities and the land on which they lived. He saw these horizontal human circulations as somewhat comparable to the world-wide movements which agitated the atmosphere and the hydrosphere,[37] and as reinforcing the need to set regions in a global context. He was thus the first to grasp a fact that was used to effect in the post-war attack on regional geography. But he did not draw the drastic conclusion that regional geography was obsolete; he was content to warn that, while the geographical synthesis must still take place within regions, they should be regarded as within and subordinate to global patterns. They were still 'fundamental facts'. In 1943 (*aet.* 82), however, he seemed prepared to base his teaching—at least for children— on a global systematic geography rather than upon natural regions. Regions were not excluded, but they were based on 'focal points' (which might to-day be styled 'cores'), and they had indeterminate boundaries.[38]

Just as his dicta emphasizing the primacy of the region come from his earlier work, so those which stress the world view are from his later years:

... we seek to attain the practicable by the study of special regions. But we must ever hark back to the whole world conception ... every regional study is in the nature of a first approximation ... (1928, p. 7)

We had hardly settled down to this distributional or regional conception of geography, when we were compelled by the rapid march of events in the world of action to adapt our minds to a further conception. *There is no complete geographical region either less than or greater than the whole of the earth's surface* (1937, p. 179)

To-day, for the first time, the habitat of each separate human being is this global Earth. The tempo of affairs has quickened, and the fields of action have widened in a single generation as by a miracle. (1942, pp. 128-9)

My plan would be to abandon ... regions, except the initial home region, and substitute focal points, from each of which the visualizing and rationalizing eye would sweep over gradually widening areas

[37] 'The streams of commodities over the face of the earth, considered as an element in human environments, present many analogies to the currents of the ocean or the winds of the air' (1895, p. 8).
[38] See also Fisher (1970), especially pp. 378-81.

until at last it embraced the entire surface of the world, and the region would be identical with the globe. Preparatory to that stage of thought would be a series of spherical studies each consisting of the projection upon the globe of a pattern depicting the features and/or processes of a single world activity, either physical or human. It would be the integrated complex of all those patterns which would be studied in the final stage of regions growing from focal points. (1943a, pp. 70–1)

The distributions of geographical data form global shapes which, combined, form the map of the world.

By the 'map of the world' Mackinder does not mean the physical or political map found in an atlas, but a mental map in which the various horizontal distributions and movements of global phenomena are vertically integrated in dynamic inter-action. A geographical education should ensure that its main lineaments were as familiar as the multiplication table:

The map of the world is a great achievement of human enterprise and accurate science. The philosophical geographer builds upon it. His methods and his aims are his own. To the agriculturalist it is primarily the chemical and physical constitution of a soil which matters, but to the geographer it is the shape which the space covered by that soil presents on the map. He correlates it with such another shape as that which shows the distribution of a particular type of farming, and seeks the reasons for any difference in the two shapes. (1928, p. 6)

[the aim of geography is] the mapping of the 'scheme of things entire' on the surface of the globe. (1942, p. 126)

They may be seen as six global spheres: lithosphere, hydrosphere, atmosphere, photosphere, biosphere, and psychosphere; these in combination form a complete conspectus of geography.

Mackinder was responsible for the terms 'lithosphere' and 'hydrosphere' taking their place alongside 'atmosphere' in English usage (Mill 1890, p. 182). Later he added further spheres to interact with the original three:

... geographers recognize five principal interpenetrating spheres—atmosphere, lithosphere, hydrosphere, biosphere, and psychosphere ... By their ever changing interaction these five spherical patterns constitute an orchestra rendering a new music of the spheres ... (1937, pp. 179–80)

At our Exeter meeting last year I ventured on the enumeration of six constituents of the planetary surface: Land, Water, Air, Light, Life and Mind. I now rename them in global terms: Lithosphere, Hydrosphere, Atmosphere, Photosphere, Biosphere, and Psychosphere. (1943a, p. 70)

Physical geographers have been obsessed with the lithosphere; but the atmosphere and the hydrosphere are more important geographically because their global circulations shape the lithosphere and are vital to the biosphere; indeed, the hydrosphere sets the limits of geography and gives it unity.

Surely we may find our first geographic unity in the hydrosphere ... May we then not ... say that geography studies the distribution of phenomena within the limits of the hydrosphere? That statement will hold both physical and human geography. (1928, p. 5)

What is it that really gives a unique interest to the surface of this earth? Surely not its dead features; there are mountains also on the moon ... Is it not the fluid envelopes, the water and the air, which by their circulations, their physical and chemical reactions, and their relation to life, impart to the earth's surface an activity almost akin to life itself? ... We will ... define the object of geographical study as extending to those parts of the lithosphere and of the atmosphere which are interpenetrated by the hydrosphere. (1931, pp. 4–6)

Mackinder consciously over-emphasized the hydrosphere because of the geomorphologists' almost exclusive preoccupation with the lithosphere. If one of the spheres was to predominate it should be that which bound the others together and which was the most significant to man.[39] Although the initial reaction was not favourable (Howarth 1951, p. 139; Hartshorne 1959, p. 24; Cantor 1960, pp. 224–6) it can now be said that, 'Today, in a very real sense, water is a unifying focus of study for geographers, drawn in increasing numbers from specialisms across the broad spectrum of the discipline' (Ward 1980, p. 130). More physical geographers have come to see the dangers of an almost wholly geomorphological study (e.g. Walton 1968)

[39] Sauer (1925, p. 33) had already pointed out that 'relief is only one category of the physical landscape and ordinarily not the most important one; it almost never supplies the complete basis of a cultural form.' But, 'We may say confidently that the resemblance or contrast between natural landscapes in the large is primarily a matter of climate. We may go farther and assert that under a given climate a distinctive landscape will develop in time, the climate ultimately cancelling the geognostic factor in many cases' (p. 39).

and have welcomed Mackinder's viewpoint as leading to a unified physical geography that could be of use to human geographers in particular and to mankind in general. Nevertheless, 'at the research level ... there are many more geomorphologists than there are both climatologists and biogeographers put together' (Doornkamp and Warren 1980, p. 95).

Man is part of the biosphere, in which his mobility gives rise to circulations comparable to those which agitate the atmosphere and hydrosphere.

Vegetation and soil interact so that they constitute together a single living skin to the Earth, which is of the very stuff of geography, the most intimate meeting ground of all the co-operating influences. We and the rest of the animals are mere parasites on that skin, but since we can move and bite we shape it at our will ... Man is part of his own environment, as cheesemites are part of the cheese. (1935, p. 9)

Mackinder constantly stressed the dynamic side of geography—the movement of air and water, and of man. In an early paper (1890) he distinguished between man settling, who seeks productive areas, and man travelling, who seeks lines of least resistance. Technological progress was opening up a whole new era of expansion for travelling man. The disposition of land and sea, of deserts and other natural barriers, should be looked at from the point of view of man circulating:

The pre-eminent characteristic, I take it, of our time is the marvellous development of human mobility. (1909a, p. 474)

But ideas constitute an independent force which grows in strength with improved technical knowledge and social organization; it is the psychosphere.

Mackinder was one of the first to see ideology as a potent geographical factor. Although man was physically part of the biosphere, he possessed other territorial drives than the mere need for food and shelter; ideas and ambitions were powerful forces which must find a place in a comprehensive human geography. The ideal geographer could not only 'visualize the play and the conflict of the fluids over and around the solid forms'; he could also 'visualize the movement of ideas and words as they are carried along the lines of least resistance' (1895, pp. 8–9).

Curiously it is in the psychosphere ... that our geographical revolution has produced its most immediate reactions. The imagination of mankind, massed by the new instantaneous mobility of thought ... has been panicked into rival ideologies, 'communist' to embrace all the world in a single community, and 'nationalist' to find safety in the self-sufficiency of each of a number of regional communities ... (1937, p. 180)

Now that all parts of the earth have been discovered and explored, the interplay of the forces of the psychosphere has become a closed system: their action in any part of the world is felt throughout the whole.

Mackinder (1887, p. 141; 1904, pp. 421–2) was the first to see that, now 'the expansion of Europe against almost negligible resistances' was over, the geopolitical world had become a closed system, and that future international crises would tend to be global rather than merely regional.

Geography draws upon both sciences and humanities for its data, seeing knowledge whole within areas.

This was geography's greatest weakness and yet its main strength. It could lead to the geographer becoming a 'jack of all trades' or to his becoming more interested in one of the contributory subjects than in a unified geography; on the other hand, it gave him the opportunity of reconstituting a reality which had been broken up into 'subjects'. The geographer's skill lay in his ability to select only what was pertinent to his synthesis. He was very definite that the study of a distribution unrelated to other kinds of geographical phenomena was not admissible:

Geography has bearings on many subjects, but it does not bodily include those subjects. Even the great Peschel includes in his 'Physische Erdkunde' a discussion on the barometer ... Such digressions are the cause of the often repeated charge that geographers are merely dabblers in all the sciences ... So far as the animals and plants in question form an appreciable factor in man's environment, so far their distribution is very pertinent. So far also as that distribution gives evidence of geographical changes, such as the separation of islands from continents or a retirement of the snow-line, so far it is also pertinent. But the study of the distribution of animals and plants in detail and as an aid to the understanding of the evolution of those beings, is in no sense part of geography. It is part of zoology or botany. (1887, p. 154)

... let us emphasize the fact that geography is not the science of all things. (1895, p. 11)

... the geographer ... brings to the inter-scientific frontier, his maps, ready made, and his trained faculty of thinking visually, but the technique from across the border almost invariably dominates. Consider the case of geomorphology: you cannot there go far in field research without a complete geological technique. The cases of geophysics and zoogeography are parallel. But with the alien technique there almost inevitably enters also the alien philosophy ... For these reasons I have spoken of geographical aspects of other subjects rather than special aspects of geography. (1935, p. 10)

The dependency on other disciplines proved a fatal weakness in the hands of Mackinder's successors: 'geography to-day appears to be an extensive field embracing a range of disparate disciplines' (Moss 1970, p. 29). Some geographers 'have a closer association at the research level with scientists in cognate disciplines than they do with colleagues in other branches of geography' (Doornkamp and Warren 1980, p. 100). Gregory (1978, p. 171) reaches the gloomy conclusion that it is 'high time to abandon the pretence of a separate existence for geography', since all that is intellectually worth while in it comes from other disciplines. And Slater (1977, p. 50) 'would argue that there is no such thing as geography in general' but only 'specific systems which have specific spatial structures'.

In its analysis of the distribution of phenomena and in their representation on the map, it is a science—the science of distribution; but it is not a science in the sense that physics and chemistry are, because the patterns formed by its distributions are unique.

At first Mackinder (1887) was prepared to see geography as a science, particularly in its mathematical, cartographic, and physical aspects: 'it is the science of distribution, the science, that is, which traces the arrangement of things in general on the earth's surface' (p. 160). The map-making stages of geography were scientific because they required mathematical exactitude and proof. In genetic geomorphology, which he initially accepted as part of geography, he had seen a law-making function:

... if I look at a headland projecting into the sea, I cannot help feeling that there must be some cause for the place which the headland holds, and for its shape, and I cannot help feeling from the analogy of the other sciences, that if I knew the cause and compared it with the causes of other things, I should be able to see that they were related, and so should be able to work out a law of considerable simplicity where apparently we have got irregularity of distribution. (1887, p. 161)

He later denied that geography could be nomothetic, a view not seriously challenged until the 1950s,[40] when the contrary opinion won support because it offered 'scientific' respectability to a profession of would-be scientists.

The physicist or chemist has before him myriads of repetitions of the same phenomena ... But the geographer seeks to decipher the pattern of a unique phenomenon, the surface of this globe. There can be for him no question of law in the physical sense, since there is no repetition of the pattern ... Both geographer and scientist proceed no doubt by analysis with a view to subsequent synthesis, but the synthesis of the strict scientist is of like with like, whereas that of the geographer is of unlikes. (1935, p. 8)

From the beginning Mackinder was attacked for his deductive approach. In the discussion of his 1887 paper, Canon Daniel was

astonished that Mr Mackinder should place geography in a category by itself. Why should it be treated any differently from any other inductive science? Was it to start with an hypothesis, with a succession of hypotheses, and then to account for the facts? Or was it not rather to start with the facts themselves, to collect them, to classify them, then to form hypotheses that would account for them, and then to verify the hypotheses? That was just what Mr Mackinder had not done. (*Proc. RGS* ix (1887), p. 168)

and Seeley, Professor of Geography at King's College, London, agreed. A few years later, H. R. Mill (1902), reviewing *Britain and the British Seas*, wrote—with perhaps a touch of sarcasm:

Of the two philosophical methods which might be employed in such a work, Mr Mackinder has apparently chosen the deductive ... It is by far the more attractive ..., for it allows a great definiteness of treatment and the citation of a minimum of data, while it gives to the reader the pleasure of discovering innumerable coincidences of fact with theory. The drawback is that the unanimous trend of facts thus

[40] By Schaefer in 'Exceptionalism in Geography' (1953).

detected has precisely the same logical force as the unanimous resolution of a political meeting to which the public is admitted by a
careful selection.

And Mackinder's successors, whether traditionalists or 'spatial
scientists' have mostly pursued inductive methods, in the belief
that they were more scientific. The philosopher Popper,[41] has
demonstrated the falsity of that belief. His view, as expressed
below, justifies the Mackinder approach:

> we must not look upon science as a 'body of knowledge', but rather as
> a system of hypotheses, that is to say a system of guesses or anticipations
> which in principle cannot be justified, but with which we work as long
> as they stand up to tests, and of which we are never justified in saying
> that we know that they are 'true' or 'more or less certain' or even
> 'probable'. (Popper 1959, p. 317)

Medawar (1969)[42] develops Popper's reasoning: 'At the very
heart of induction lies this innocent-sounding belief: that the
thought which leads to scientific discovery ... is logically ac-
countable and can be logically spelled out' (p. 24); inductivism
'fails altogether to explain how it comes about that the very
same processes of thought which lead us towards the truth lead
us so very much more often into error' (p. 31). It is the creative
brain, capable of forming daring hypotheses, that—as often as
not—stumbles upon scientific truth, perhaps through intuition
or even through sheer luck. Moss (1970), as a physical geographer, accepts these conclusions, asserting that a solution to
geographical problems 'can be achieved only in the context of
scientific deductive method' with which he associates 'the brilliant perceptions of Mackinder concerning the character and
use of geography'. From the human side Gregory (1978, p. 37)
adds that 'geography has had a long-standing penchant for ...
inductive procedures ... the quantitative revolution continued
... some would say strenthened—the hold of inductivism'. However, in the 1970s we meet 'a second generation of quantitative
geographers who have incorporated deductive mathematical
thinking ... rather than inductive statistics into the geographical ambit' (Cooke and Robson 1976, p. 82).

[41] Sir Karl Popper (1902–   ). Born in Vienna, he later came to England.
[42] Sir Peter Brian Medawar (1915–   ), Nobel Prize for Medicine 1960, Director of
the National Institute for Medical Research.

Because the test of relevance of its data is from a human standpoint, and because it applies human values, it cannot be wholly objective.

I believe that nine out of ten students who approach geography will necessarily approach it from the human standpoint. (1887, p. 162)

... I do not believe that a scientific analysis in human geography can ever give you more than assistance or can ever give you a complete explanation ... (1916, p. 274)

The 'new geography' of the 1960s, with its pseudo-scientific methods and positivist philosophy, rejected his view, but a reaction against positivism has made it acceptable to many today: 'it is over a decade since Pahl exposed the myth of a value-free geography' (Gregory 1978, p. 71).

In its explanatory descriptions of landscapes it is an art.

In 1895 Mackinder spoke of the geographer's 'almost artistic perception of land form', and eight years later he maintained (1903a) that 'there is as much art as science in geography'. After all, 'one of the chief ends of geography is description' (Mackinder 1909); and description that brought a landscape to life was no easy task: it was an art, and consequently geography was an art, 'the art of description' (*The Times*, 9 Jan. 1926). This idea of geography, though generally decried, was kept alive by a few brave spirits, notably E. W. Gilbert, but except for Mackinder's own work, there are few examples in English of geography as an art. One has instead to look to travellers and regional novelists for the art of painting landscapes in words (Gilbert 1955, p. 21).[43]

It is both science and art, and this enables it to build a bridge between the sciences and the humanities.

This bridge-building function was seen by Mackinder as the most valuable contribution geography could make. The classics were the basis of a common culture among educated people, but they could not take account of the scientific developments which were revolutionizing the world. Geography was better suited to the times. In urging the bridging of the gulf between the sciences and the humanities (1887) he anticipated C. P.

---

[43] For a philosophical discussion of the tradition of geography as 'an essentially artistic enterprise', see Gregory (1978, pp. 131-3)

Snow's 1959 Rede lecture, 'The Two Cultures and the Scientific Revolution', by over seventy years.[44]

Geography has its own philosophy: this justifies its claim to be an independent discipline.

... geography is a distinct standpoint from which to view, to analyse, and to grasp the facts of existence. (1895, p. 11)

I believe that geography contains in it elements of three things: elements that are essentially of science, elements that are essentially of art, elements that are essentially of philosophy. (1904a, p. 192)

... geography is not so much a science as a philosophy, an art, and a literature. (1927, p. 214)

[Geography is] a concrete philosophy, with both scientific and humanistic roots ... (1935, p. 11)

... it is a philosophy of Man's environment. (1942, p. 129)

For it asks the question 'Where?' with the object of posing the further question, 'Why there?'.

Physiography asks of a given feature, 'Why is it?' Topography, 'Where is it?' Physical geography, 'Why is it there?' Political[45] geography, 'How does it act on man in society, and how does he react on it?' Geology asks, 'What riddle of the past does it help to solve?' ... The first four subjects are the realm of the geographer. The questions come in sequence. You may stop short at any one of them, but ... you cannot with advantage answer a later one unless you have answered those which precede it. (1887, p. 147)

I have ventured to define geography ... by saying that it answers two questions. It answers the question Where? and it then proceeds to answer the question Why there? (1904a, p. 192)

From the very beginning Mackinder clarified his definition of geography and its distinctiveness from other subjects by posing the questions it asked. This made his approach consistent with the modern philosophy of science. Thus Moss (1970), quoting Popper,[46] maintains that the primary question is 'whether there is a distinct class of problems, demanding a particular kind of

---

[44] For the bridge character of geography, see also pp. 92–3 above.
[45] i.e. human.
[46] 'We are not students of some subject matter but students of problems.'

approach, which requires study and solution, which we may associate with the term *geographical*, or with the term *environmental*' (p. 22).

> *This question may be asked in a genetic or in a dynamic sense: it may mean 'how does it come to be there?', an historical question, or 'why is it there and not somewhere else?'—a geographical question inquiring into present phenomena and their interactions.*

So we are led to the great question of philosophical geography: 'Why there?' Now there are two orders of answer to the question 'Why there?'. If a man stand on the top of a mountain he is there because the rocks hold him up and also because he climbed there. The first answer is dynamic, the second is genetic. It is well to keep the distinction between these two great chapters of philosophical geography clear in the mind. (1928, p. 6)

From the dynamic point of view origin is immaterial. The Suez Canal is a strait. Relatively to navigation it performs the function of a strait. So with a harbour; it gives like shelter whether it be due to a coral reef or a breakwater. (1928, p. 7)

> *Although the genetic approach has a place in geography, particularly in geomorphology, the dynamic is the more geographical.*

Mackinder seemed at first satisfied that the genetic had a legitimate place alongside the dynamic, but when he saw it come to dominate both physical and historical geography, he found himself compelled to assert the superior claim of the dynamic, and to reject much genetic writing as history. He realized that it would be impracticable now to exclude morphogenetic geomorphology, but true physical geography considered the dynamic interaction of the lithosphere, atmosphere, and hydrosphere 'at a given moment of time'; and the true historical geography considered the dynamic interaction of geographical phenomena at a time in the past.

It was Peschel who asserted the claim of geography to include geomorphology, and so rendered possible a genetic, as opposed to a merely conventional classification of the features of relief. (1895, p. 6)

Now the genetic answer involves the consideration of process ... Pure geography is the study of the present, an analysis and imaginative recomposition of a dynamic system. But process of change is history, which we call geology in the one case just cited and just history in the other case. By common consent, however, the study of the process of denudation is included in physical geography ... (1928, p. 7)

There is however a true historical geography. It involves what the literary people call the historic present.[47] The historical geographer seeks to restore imaginatively the dynamic system of some past moment of time, say, the height of the Roman Empire ... (1928, p. 8)

Which is the prior—function or form? I admit that in my earlier writings I myself went often astray, attracted by the antithesis which Archibald Geikie drew ... between the laying down of the rocks and the shaping from those rocks of the existing surface. It seemed that the former was geology and the latter geography. (1931, p. 4)

The trained geographer may restore imaginatively the geographies of the past and so contribute to geology, archaeology and history; in a word he may study the historic present; but whether he study the present or past, he is primarily concerned with space, and with time only in the sense that everything has momentum. (1931, pp. 10–11)

It seems to me that there is a little danger that we should mix history with geography without seeing clearly what we are doing. Geology is a part of history, and I think we ought to remember all the time that geography is a description of things in the present. Geography should, as I see it, be a physiological and anatomical study rather than a study in development. As its name implies, it should be description, with causal relations in a dynamic rather than genetic sense. (1931b, p. 268)

This advice has been ignored. A widely-read text on the nature of geography (Wooldridge and East 1951) was significantly written by a genetic geomorphologist and a genetic historical geographer, and they averred that 'the best way, in general, of understanding anything is to understand how it has evolved or developed', whereas Mackinder had written: 'there is no need of geological history in order to appreciate the liberation of energy from coal in the process of combustion to-day'; and, 'to the merchant of to-day the origin of London ... is unimportant' (1931, p. 12). Darby (1953, p. 11) was able to write that geomorphology and historical geography were 'the basic elements of our discipline'. Genetic processes had come to

[47] Robinson and Patten (1980) have misunderstood M.'s use of the term 'historical present'. They write, 'To him historical geography meant a "study of the historical present", in other words, relict features in the present landscape' (p. 412).

dominate geography, lending themselves nicely to the mathematical techniques and nomothetic ambitions of the supposedly
scientific 'new' geography of the 1960s and after.[48]

Mackinder's views on historical geography were consistent
with a strong geographical tradition reaching back to Kant. On
this basis, Hartshorne (1939), although surprisingly ignorant of
Mackinder's arguments, had stated categorically: 'That historical geography is to be considered simply as the geography of
past periods is a view on which there is perhaps more agreement
among geographers than on almost any other question of definition . . .' (p. 185). Yet so successful were Clark in America and
Darby in Britain in urging that historical geography was the
history of landscape change (most of which in practice has
turned out to be economic or social history), that Hartshorne
(1959) abandoned his soundly-based case and capitulated to
the new fashion.

Moss (1970) has pointed to the results of the adoption of 'the
evolutionary-genetic method' in physical and human geography: 'more and more minute analysis' in the context of 'tracing
out historical relations'. But whereas there has been a move in
physical geography from the purely genetic and temporal to a
more dynamic and spatial approach, a process-dominated historical geography continues to flourish.[49] Many economists and
economic historians believe Mackinder's approach would be
more useful. Postan (1973) suggested that the 'weaving of some
historical facts into a cloth of an epoch may . . . do more for our
understanding of mankind than the spinning of facts with their
antecedents into evolutionary yarns'[50] (qu. in Coones 1979).

[48] For a succinct and penetrating critique of the genetic in historical geography, see
Coones (1979).
[49] Cooke and Robson (1976) reporting on British geography 1972-6 write, 'The
broadening interest in historical geography owes something to the developing interest
in structuralism which inevitably helps to undermine any latest anti-historicism within
geography . . . The emphasis on process was evident in the structure of *A New Historical
Geography of England* . . .'.
[50] He expressed a similar view in his review of H. C. Darby and I. B. Terrett (eds.),
The Domesday geography of Midland England (1954). E. L. Jones, an economist, reviewing
Darby (1973), wrote, 'If portrayal is the intention, and the internal evidence of even
the historical chapters suggests it is, this could surely have been done by a whole set of
"stills"—cross-sections alone. If the aim was to describe the changes as they unfolded,
the exercise must cease to be geography . . . and turn into narrative history', and describes it as 'taking much of its material and the bulk of its explanatory content from the
work of economic historians' (*Annals of the American Assoc. of Geog.*, lxiv (1974), pp. 460-1).

Geography must, however, take account of momentum from the past.

Mackinder used the term 'genetic' to imply not only a study of the origin and development of features, but also that momentum which comes from the past into the present. This *vis inertiae* he regarded as essential to geographical explanation:

Milford Haven, in the present state of things, offers far greater advantages than Liverpool for the American trade; yet it is improbable that Liverpool will have to give way to Milford Haven, at any rate in the immediate future. It is a case of *vis inertiae*. (1887, pp. 157–8)

The facts of human geography, like those of all other geography, are the resultant for the moment of the conflict of two elements, the dynamic and the genetic. Geographical advantages of past times permitted a distribution and movement of men which, by inertia, still tend to maintain themselves in the face of new geographical disadvantages. (1895, p. 8)

... as forest will often continue to clothe a surface when the conditions have passed which could reproduce forest, so by a parallel process of geographical inertia societies of men will often continue to reside in the accustomed localities when the causes which drew them together have ceased to act. (1902, p. 329)

In E. W. Gilbert's survey of Mackinder's geographical ideas entitled 'Seven Lamps of Geography' (1951), the lamps were the region, the homeland and the empire, world geography, the unity of geography, the map, applied geography, and the philosophy of geography. Twenty-five years later Stoddart (1976) wrote, 'Few of these ideas now have the attraction they had when Gilbert wrote, and such analysis, by tying Mackinder's achievement to a specific set of ideas, paradoxically throws his contribution into doubt.' It is possible, however, to see another seven lamps shining throughout his geographical work which are not subject to such an objection. These are expressed by seven of his favourite words: shape, pattern, visualization, imagination, outlook, mobility, and balance. Mackinder was fond of quoting Thring of Uppingham[51] as saying that geographers thought in shapes. *Shape* was a readily identifiable fact, such as the outline of a country or of a landform. It was also a geographer's function to identify *pattern* in geographical distributions;

[51] Edward Thring (1821–87), headmaster of Uppingham School from 1851.

but this needed training, and different geographers saw different patterns from different viewpoints. *Visualization* was the recreation in the mind's eye of actual landscapes from maps and other data, but *imagination*, while it included this facility, also implied the creative ability to frame hypotheses. *Outlook* was the realistic and comprehending view of the world which the ideal geographical education gave the student. *Mobility* stressed the dynamic aspect of geography—the necessity to consider the movement as well as the distribution of phenomena; it was, for instance, a reminder that 'man travelling' was as important, if not more so, than 'man settling'. *Balance* was the symmetry and equilibrium necessary for stability and well-being in nature.[52]

[52] See Honeybone (1954), 'Balance in Geography and Education'.

Chapter 6

Geopolitician

Through his geopolitical ideas, Mackinder became one of the most influential thinkers of modern times, helping to determine the course of history through his impact upon the external policies of Germany before the war and of the United States after it. Dickinson (1976) does not exaggerate when he writes that his concept of the 'Heartland' in the 'World Island' and its geostrategic implications 'may be soberly assessed to-day as one of the most influential in world affairs in the twentieth century' (p. 36). Most people who know of him, do so as the geopolitician responsible for this concept, yet he did not see himself as a geopolitician, a word which, along with 'geopolitics', he disliked. His main interests were the preservation of the Empire and democracy and the advancement of education and geography. His geopolitical statements were occasional excursions into the wider world to illustrate the value of the application of imagination and foresight to an interpretation of the interplay of history and geography. They form a quite small proportion of his work.

The term 'geopolitics' (*Geopolitik*) was introduced in 1899, by the Swedish political scientist Kjellen,[1] as a study of states as organisms engaged in a perpetual struggle for life and space, and whose development was subject to laws derived from the study of geography and history. Similar ideas had been developed by Ratzel.[2] A wider view is generally held of the subject today, especially in America, where it has been defined as 'the geographical facts regarded in terms of their political relevance

---

[1] Rudolf Kjellen (1864–1922), Professor of History and Government at the Universities of Uppsala and Göteborg; he predicted the decline of the maritime powers and the rise of continental states; his chief work was *Staten som Lifsform* (1916) (*Der Staat als Lebensform*, 1917).

[2] Friedrich Ratzel (1844–1904), Professor of Geography in the University of Leipzig. His *Politische Geographie* (1897) discussed the close and indissoluble relationship between state, nation, and the territory they occupied; he saw states as quasi-organisms which grew or decayed, and needed living space (*Lebensraum*).

in a global context' (Walters 1974, p. 7). Geopolitics as developed by Haushofer[3] in pre-war Germany became infamous because of its subservience to Nazi aims, but a modern German definition sees it as studying the links between the policies of states and geographical space (Jacobsen 1979). In the Soviet Union it has been defined as a 'bourgeois reactionary conception, which uses selectively interpreted facts of physical and economic geography for the formation and propagation of the aggressive policies of imperialist states' (Bol. Sov. Ents. 1971, vol. vi, p. 316).

Mackinder is usually included in studies of geopolitics along with Mahan,[4] Kjellen, Ratzel, and sometimes Spykman[5] and Seversky,[6] and it has been said that he 'has probably contributed more than anyone else to the popularity of geopolitics' (Aron 1966, p. 191). The earlier geopoliticians were trained in natural science and apply Darwinian theory to geography. They take a more or less organic view of the state, and see international affairs as a struggle for existence, with the fittest surviving (Neumann 1943, p. 286). Mackinder, although he hoped that mankind would rise above the 'mere fatalism' of the view that only those states would survive 'which adapted themselves best to their natural environment' (1919, p. 3), seems originally to have approached political geography within a Darwinian framework (Blouet 1975, p. 7). He wrote that, in his fourth year at Oxford he 'took up modern history with the idea of seeing how the theory of evolution would appear in human development', and he occasionally refers to the state as an organism (e.g. 1905, p. 140). Geopolitical writings are seldom

---

[3] General Karl Haushofer (1869-1946). After an army career, he became Professor of Geography in the University of Munich. He developed the ideas of Ratzel, Kjellen, and M. into a programme for the triumph of a German-dominated Eurasian alliance against Anglo-Saxon sea power. He launched the influential *Zeitschrift für Geopolitik* in 1924. He was appointed President of the German Academy by Hitler.

[4] Admiral Alfred Mahan (1840-1914), US Navy. In his *Influence of Sea Power in History 1660-1783* (1890) he maintained that sea power was the key to world mastery; in his *Problem of Asia* (1900) he analysed the advantages and disadvantages of land power based on the Eurasian land mass, and concluded that, on balance, it could be contained by an alliance of the maritime powers.

[5] Nicholas Spykman (1893-1943), Professor of International Relationships at Yale University. Like Mahan he believed the 'Rimland' of peripheral maritime states could successfully contain the Eurasian 'Heartland' power.

[6] Alexander de Seversky, US Air Force, in *Air Power, Key to Survival* (1950), was an advocate of reliance upon supremacy in the air.

politically neutral; they usually 'embody some element of argument justifying or attacking a particular state of affairs or proposing ways to change it' (Sprout 1964). Such lack of objectivity, while causing geopolitics to be labelled 'unscientific', does at least imply that its practitioners do not really accept the 'fatalism' of Darwinian theory; they clearly believe that the course of history is not predetermined but can be altered if statesmen will listen to and act upon their arguments. Despite their shortcomings, Sprout (1964) believes that 'geopolitical speculation and theorizing' have 'enriched our understanding of the international system'.

Mackinder's interest in the sea-power–land-power dichotomy, to the understanding of which he was to be the principal contributor, was foreshadowed by a sentence in his first geographical address to the Royal Geographical Society in 1887 (*aet.* 25): 'Now conquerors are of two kinds: land wolves and sea wolves.' But his first major geopolitical utterance was his paper, 'The Geographical Pivot of History', also delivered to the RGS on 25 January 1904 (*aet.* 42). The audience does not seem to have been large: one of those present 'looked with regret on some of the space which is unoccupied here'. The address opened with an example of his ability to perceive epoch-making change long before there was any general awareness of it. This was the ending of what he calls the 'Columbian age'—the age which had seen 'the expansion of Europe against almost negligible resistances'; it had succeeded an age in which 'Christendom was pent into a narrow region and threatened by external barbarism'. It was itself now about to be followed by a post-Columbian age, with the whole world 'a closed political system' in which, 'Every explosion of social forces, instead of being dissipated in a surrounding circuit of unknown space and barbaric chaos, will be sharply re-echoed from the far side of the globe, and weak elements in the political and economic organism of the world will be shattered in consequence' (p. 422). He then attempted to correlate geographical fact and historical event in a formula which, having been shown to be valid for the pre-Columbian and Columbian ages, might illuminate the likely evolution of the post-Columbian age. Before he could do this, he had to ask his audience to shed the belief that European history was the only history that mattered, and, instead 'to look upon Europe and European history as subordinate to Asia and Asiatic history' (p. 423). It has taken half a century or more for the primacy of European history to give way to world history, which must necessarily be very largely Eurasian history.[7]

Mackinder began the search for his formula with the physical geography of Russia, stressing the two great east–west trending belts of forest and steppe: while the Slavs took refuge in the forest a 'succession of horsemen rode across the steppe'. Another feature of Russian geography was that the rivers run mostly north and south, producing a rival mobility to that of the horsemen—that of the Viking boatmen who set up a north-south-trending Russian state athwart the great east–west vegetation zones. Both of these mobile forces 'hammered' Europe, the Vikings from the north, and the horsemen from the south and east; Europe acquired much of its character from its forced response.

Mackinder found the key to his formula in the interior or 'heart-land'[8] of the vast Eurasian land mass, the open part of which is the extensive area of steppe with its 'sparse ... population of horse-riding and camel-riding nomads' (p. 429). Pivoting around this 'heart-land' or 'pivot-area', arranged in an inner and an outer crescent, were the marginal coastlands, peninsulas, and islands which, in contrast to the 'pivot-area', often support dense populations. Europe was but one of these densely-peopled marginal areas, all of which 'sooner or later felt the expansive force of mobile power originating in the steppe' (p. 430). But the Europeans became 'ship-men' and were thus able to counter the mobility of the nomads; for 'mobility upon the ocean is the natural rival of horse and camel mobility in the

---

[7] As late as 1978, almost seventy-five years after M.'s paper, *The Times Atlas of World History* claimed credit for having 'broken away from this traditional Western view'— i.e. from Eurocentricity. Spengler (1926) was one of the first to follow M. in this respect: 'The ground of West Europe is treated as a steady pole, a unique patch chosen on the surface of the sphere for no better reason, it seems, than because we live on it—and great histories of millennial duration and mighty far-away cultures are made to revolve around this pole in all modesty' (p. 17).

[8] The word 'heart-land' appears thrice in the 1904 paper, on pp. 430, 431, and 434, as correctly observed by Gilbert (1951a, p. 10). Jones (1964, p. 376) can be forgiven for saying that it appears 'only once', as M. himself had stated this (1943, p. 596). Cohen (1964, p. 40) wrote, 'The term Heartland, incidentally was not actually introduced by Mackinder, but by James Fairgrieve in his 1915 work.' Doubtless Fairgrieve had seen it in M.'s 1904 paper.

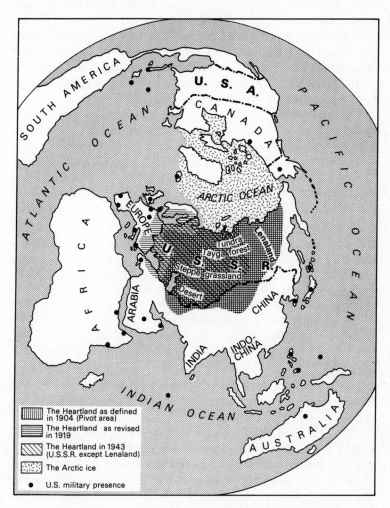

FIG. I. The Land Hemisphere showing Mackinder's Heartland

heart of a continent' (p. 432). Europe, by command of the sea, was able to dominate the marginal coastlands and encircle 'the Euro-Asiatic land power which had hitherto threatened her very existence' (p. 433). New Europes were created and 'Britain, Canada, the United States, South Africa, Australia and Japan are now a ring of outer and insular bases for sea-power and commerce, inaccessible to the land-power of Euro-Asia' (p. 433). Thus the centre–periphery antithesis becomes also a land-power–sea-power antithesis. (Fig. 1).

Having demonstrated that the dominant geostrategic feature of the Columbian age was the European control of the crescents surrounding the 'pivot-area', Mackinder mentions a striking coincidence: 'the Tudor century, which saw the expansion of Western Europe over the sea, also saw Russian power carried from Moscow through Siberia' (p. 433). From this he develops the theme of an historical opposition between East and West, rooted in both ideology and technology:

It is probably one of the most striking coincidences of history that the seaward and landward expansion of Europe should, in a sense, continue the ancient opposition between Roman and Greek ... The Teuton was civilized and Christianized by the Roman, the Slav in the main by the Greek. It is the Romano-Teuton who in later times embarked upon the ocean; it was the Graeco-Slav who rode over the steppes, conquering the Turanian. Thus the modern land-power differs from the sea-power but no less in the source of its ideals than in the material conditions of its mobility. (p. 433)

In the subsequent discussion this continuity was questioned, but Mackinder replied that he still thought it 'substantially correct' (p. 433 fn.).

The historical continuity of an East–West schism is beyond doubt. It found political expression in the division of the Roman Empire into western and eastern parts (395 AD) with rival capitals in Rome and Byzantium; this split fostered distinct Greek and Roman forms of Christianity. In 1054 the two branches of the Church parted company and before long they were vilifying each other; the last of the Crusades was fought, not against the infidel but against Constantinople. Russia had been converted to the Greek church, and after the destruction of the eastern Empire by the Turks, Moscow became the dynamic centre of the Orthodox religion. There was consciousness of the Byzantine heritage, as well as a touch of pride, in the sixteenth-century Russian abbot Filofei's prediction that Moscow would be the final centre of world civilization: 'for two Romes have fallen, and the third stands, and a fourth will not be'. This doctrine appealed to secular as well as religious Russians, and among all classes a new self-confidence grew, sometimes becoming an arrogant xenophobia. When the Holy Roman Emperor offered a crown to Grand Duke Ivan III, it was disdainfully refused: the Russian prince derived his power direct from God and recognized no earthly authority. Instead the imperial title of Caesar or Tsar was assumed and the Byzantine double eagle adopted as the state emblem.

Pride in a distinct civilization with ancient roots led to determined opposition to Westernization. This found an early expression in the seventeenth-century writings of Krizhanich, who did not think Russia should try to compete with the West in material culture: 'for they are incomparably better than us in all craftmanship'. Instead the Russians should concentrate on moral virtue in which they were superior to the heretical and decadent Westerners:

Let us compete in the temperate use of bedclothes ... let us not use two or three feather mattresses underneath and a third or fourth above, as the Germans do ... Let us not imitate too much the curious and painstaking cleanliness of the Germans,[9] who so often wash the floors of their houses, and where a guest may not spit or spew on to the floor. And if by chance he does so, straightway a servant wipes it up. Such men, in their voluptuousness and carnal cleanliness, attempt to make a heaven out of a mere earthly home. And yet, with all this epicureanism, cleanliness, splendour and fastidiousness, the Germans turn into the same dirt and dust as do other people. And therefore it should not be asked who has the cleanest floor or bedding, but who has the clearest conscience ... Cleanse your heart and not your floor. (qu. in Parker 1968, pp. 106–7)

Krizhanich gloried in the fact that Russia had 'never belonged to the empire of Rome', for 'the Russian realm is as high and glorious, and as powerful as the Roman was'.

So Mackinder was justified in adding to the opposition between central and peripheral location, and between land

---

[9] The word 'Germans' was often used to denote Western foreigners generally, the Germans being the Western people with whom the Russians had most contact.

power and sea power, a conflict of ideals, and in tracing this back to ancient times. And if, since he wrote, the opposition between the eastern and western forms of Christianity has been lessened by the decline in organized religion, its place has been taken by the divide between communism and capitalism. In this change also continuity can be argued: the Orthodox church stressed the brotherhood of man and glorified the Russian *mir* or commune; the Western churches gave prominence to individual salvation, and the advent of capitalism was assisted by the emergence of Protestant doctrine (Tawney 1938).

Mackinder had demonstrated that while the 'Rimland', as Spykman was later to term the peripheral oceanic world, was falling under European dominance, the 'heart-land' or 'pivot-area' came under the sway of the Russians with a quite different culture and outlook. The next step in the argument was that 'railways are now transmuting the conditions of land-power' and that 'the century will not be old before all Asia is covered with railways' (p. 434). These railways would allow the development of formidable economic power, for the 'spaces within the Russian Empire and Mongolia are so vast, and their potentialities in population, wheat, cotton, fuel, and metals so incalculably great, that it is inevitable that a vast economic world, more or less apart, will there develop inaccessible to oceanic commerce' (p. 434). Once again the Eurasian Heartland will make its power felt in the surrounding lands. And so, 'does not a certain persistence of geographical relationship become evident? Is not the pivot region of the world's politics that vast area of Euro-Asia which is inaccessible to ships, but in antiquity lay open to the horse-riding nomads, and is to-day about to be covered with a network of railways?' (p. 434).

It was not until the introduction of Stalin's first five-year plan in 1928 that the prediction began to come true, and although it would be an exaggeration to say that the Eurasian Heartland is 'covered' with railways, there has been an impressive and continued growth at a time when railways are in decline in most other parts of the world (Fig. 2). Since the Revolution the route length of the Soviet railway system has grown by 70,000 km, with almost all of this increase in Siberia and Central Asia; the 1970s alone saw the building of the line from Tyumen on the Trans-Siberian to the oilfield areas of Samotlar, and the

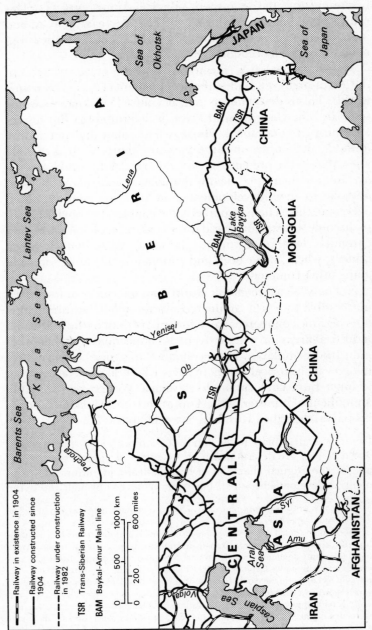

FIG. 2. Railways in Soviet Asia

beginning of the enormous Baykal–Amur project. This railway-building, aided during the last ten years by road and pipeline construction, has been the chief agent in the development of the Soviet economy.[10]

Mackinder says it is 'inevitable' that the great resources of the 'pivot-area' will lead to the development of a 'vast economic world'. This is determinism and, of course, Mackinder's whole thesis in 'The Geographical Pivot' is deterministic. But his determinism is conditional. He says that 'man and not nature initiates, but nature in large measure controls' (p. 422). He knew that in the presence of vast resources, man would *sooner or later* initiate their use;[11] he saw that inaccessibility was the main obstacle to their development, and that the railway would overcome this. These resources have enabled the Soviet Union to become the major world producer of coal, oil, iron ore, chromite, lead, manganese, platinum, mica, potash, steel, cement, wheat, sugar beet, and cotton, and a leading source of many other commodities.[12]

Not only 'a vast economic world', but one 'more or less apart, inaccessible to world commerce'. In no major industrial state does oceanic commerce play a lesser part than in the USSR; no industrial areas have fewer overseas connections than her great industrial complexes. This economic 'apartness' of Russia reinforces its historical distinctiveness which likewise arose from its inner-Eurasian location. Even such a 'Westernizer' as Witte, an influential minister of the Tsar at the time Mackinder wrote his paper, described Russia as 'a world apart':

Her independent place in the family of peoples and her special role in world history are determined both by her geographical position ... and by the original character of her political and cultural development; a development which has been achieved through the living

[10] In 1979 over 65 per cent (tonne-km) of Soviet overland freight was moved by rail, 22 per cent by pipe, 8 per cent by motor, and 5 per cent by waterway.

[11] It could be argued that the development of Siberia came about only because of the historical accident of Soviet organization, determination, and compulsion, and was not inevitable; but Communism merely brought forward a development that would have come eventually under Capitalism. *The Economist* of 6 Jan. 1973 wrote, 'The world prices of fuel and ores have only recently risen to levels which would justify the cost of exploration and extraction from the fastnesses of eastern and northern Russia.'

[12] e.g. natural gas, uranium, bauxite, cadmium, cobalt, gold, magnesium, mercury, molybdenum, nickel, silver, titanium, tungsten, vanadium, zinc, asbestos, diamonds, graphite, phosphates, salt, sulphur, etc.

interaction and harmonious combination of three elements that have manifested their full creative powers only in Russia.

These elements were orthodoxy, autocracy, and 'the Russian national spirit'. It was on these that Russian power had been founded, and it was therefore impossible for Russia 'to be fused with the West'. Such a Russia would carry civilization to the people of Asia, 'not under the standard of europeanization, but under her own special standard' (qu. in Sumner 1951, p. 3).

The conclusion of Mackinder's paper is that, in the post-Columbian age which he is anticipating,

Russia replaces the Mongol Empire. Her pressure on Finland, on Scandinavia, on Poland, on Turkey, on Persia, on India, and on China, replaces the centrifugal raids of the steppemen. In the world at large she occupies the central strategical position held by Germany in Europe. She can strike on all sides and be struck from all sides, save the north. The full development of her modern railway mobility is merely a matter of time. Nor is it likely that any possible social revolution will alter her essential relations to the great geographical limits of her existence. (p. 436)

The Russian revolution was a rejection of the Westernized elements of the old régime—the largely German tsardom, the French-speaking nobility, the bourgeois parliament, the 'European' capital of Petersburg,[13] foreign capitalism; it was in fact a return to the distinctive and separate Russia of the past; it reinforced the opposition between land and sea power, and between the central and peripheral areas of the world. Of course, in 1904, 'the pivot state, Russia', was 'not equivalent to the peripheral states', but what if she were to expand into 'the marginal lands of Euro-Asia', and use 'her vast continental resources for fleet-building'? 'The empire of the world would then be in sight' (p. 436). This state of affairs would be hastened by a German alliance; in fact, all kinds of combinations affecting the balance of power could occur, but in any event, 'from a geographical point of view, they are likely to rotate round the

---

[13] '... "Petersburg", says Dostoyevski, "is the most abstract and artificial city in the world ..." Everything that arose around it was felt by the true Russdom as lies and poison. A truly apocalyptic hatred was directed on Europe, and "Europe" was all that was not Russia. "The first condition of emancipation for the Russian soul", wrote Aksakev in 1813 to Dostoyevski, "is that it should hate Petersburg with all its might and all its soul". Moscow is holy, Petersburg satanic' (Spengler 1928, vol. ii, p. 193).

pivot state, which is always likely to be great, but with limited mobility as compared with the surrounding marginal and insular powers' (pp. 436-7).

Before concluding, Mackinder gave a formula for assessing power. It was the 'product, on the one hand of geographical conditions, both economic and strategic, and, on the other hand, of the relative number, virility, equipment, and organization of the competing peoples' (p. 437). This makes it clear that he does not see the course of history as determined by geographical conditions alone; favourable geographical conditions could be balanced by superior human resources and vice versa. But the implication is that, if to a strong strategic position and unmatched natural resources there were to be added a large, skilled, well-equipped, and highly-organized people, the danger to world freedom would be great. This could arise from the internal development of Russia,[14] or from her alliance with Germany; but it was not impossible that the Chinese, 'organized by the Japanese', should overthrow the Russian Empire and conquer its territory, constituting a real threat to the world, 'because they would add an oceanic frontage to the resources of the great continent, an advantage as yet denied to the Russian tenant of the pivot region' (p. 437).

In the English-speaking world Mackinder's paper lay forgotten in the pages of *The Geographical Journal* for thirty-five years. But on 26 August 1939, *The New Statesman*, commenting on the recently-announced Ribbentrop-Molotov pact between Germany and the USSR, wrote: 'the Russo-German agreement does not come as a complete surprise to those who have studied closely the ideas which have been shaping the policy of the Nazi leaders'. It went on to tell how Haushofer had taken his ideas from Mackinder, who in 1904, 'had set out for the first time ... his startling doctrine of the "pivot of history" ... the heartland of the Old World'. Through his assistant Hess, Haushofer had come into contact with the Nazi movement, and 'had been almost alone in visiting Adolf Hitler, when imprisoned in the little Bavarian fortress of Landshut on Lech'. The Nazis' policies

---

[14] It is sometimes said that M., in 1904, saw the development of the Heartland as coming only from German initiative or Sino-Japanese conquest. But the possibility of the building of a strong pivot-state by the Russians themselves is implicit in the paper itself and explicit in M.'s reply to the following discussion (p. 443).

had 'to a considerable extent been stolen from the intellectual arsenal of British Imperialism', for Mackinder had been a leading imperialist.

Haushofer had used Mackinder's 1904 paper as early as 1921, and continued to do so throughout the inter-war period. In 1937 he attributed his own thesis 'to the greatest of all geographical world views', referring to Mackinder's 'The Geographical Pivot of History'. 'Never', he exclaims, 'have I seen anything greater than these few pages of a geopolitical masterwork' (qu. in Weigert 1942, p. 116). In 1939 he remarked how fortunate it was that the British Foreign Office did not allow the Prime Minister or Foreign Secretary to learn of Mackinder's ideas (Gyorgy 1944, p. 167 fn). This recalls the words of a member of the audience in 1904—he regretted that some of the empty seats were 'not occupied by members of the Cabinet'. Throughout the 1939–45 war and after, the paper was widely read and regarded as 'uniquely prescient' (Graham 1965, p. 29); it was reprinted at least three times,[15] and its hypothesis 'became one of the most intensively debated geographical ideas of all time' (de Blij 1967, p. 132).

One reason why the paper had little impact in 1904, and would have been regarded by the Cabinet—had they heard it— as of little practical value, was that it was concerned with the future rather than the present. And the present had pressing problems of its own, the chief of which was how to contain Germany, not Russia. As for Germany allying herself with Russia, this was not very likely for France had already done so, and Britain was preparing to come to an understanding with her. The immediate danger was from German industrial competition and naval rearmament rather than from landpower in the remote fastnesses of Eurasia. Mackinder himself, in his every-day life as an academic engrossed with politics, also saw this as the real peril:

at the turn of the century, von Tirpitz began to build a German high seas fleet ... The German movement meant, I saw, that the nation already possessing the greatest organized land power and occupying the central strategical position in Europe was about to add to itself sea power strong enough to neutralize British sea power (1943, pp. 595–6).

[15] In Gilbert (1951); Pearce (1962); de Blij (1967).

In other words, the centre–versus–periphery model was still working on a continental or European scale. Just as it had been an expansionist France who had threatened her neighbours in eighteenth-century Europe, and against whom encircling alliances had been formed, so it was now Germany who, in the greater Europe formed by the addition of newly-westernized Russia, threatened aggression and was in turn threatened with encirclement. The 1904 paper's lesson was that, now the globe was a closed system, such continental situations would give way to a global one, with the heart-land in the centre, and the maginal lands and off-lying peninsulas, islands, and continents peripheral to it. Here it will be Russia who 'occupies the central strategic position held by Germany in Europe' (1904, p. 436).

Many of the criticisms later made of 'The Geographical Pivot of History' arise from a misunderstanding of the fact that Mackinder is writing about a coming *global* system, at a time when minds were still exercised over a *continental* system. His justification would therefore lie only in the future. Those who were satisfied with the actual disposition of power and wished to preserve it, would scarcely welcome his disturbing farsightedness, but to the Germans or Russians, groping amidst the pessimistic chaos of the early 1920s, his prognosis gave hope.

It has been said (Blouet 1973, p. 10) that Mackinder 'drew upon an extensive collective experience', and that some of his points had been anticipated or already debated by others, notably Seeley and Curzon.[16] Mahan (1900), whose views on the invincibility of sea power were widely accepted, had, as recently as 1900, drawn attention to 'the vast, uninterrupted mass of the Russian Empire' (p. 24), adding that it was not possible to interfere with its internal lines of communication, 'for the Russian centre cannot be broken' (p. 26). Russia must inevitably be dissatisfied with her shut-in position, and 'dissatisfaction takes the form of aggression—the word most in favour with those of us who dislike all forward movement in nations'. It would be in her interest 'not merely to reach the sea at more points, and more independently, but to acquire by possession or

---

[16] Sylvester (1968, pp. 55–6) suggests that he borrowed his ideas from Partsch (1903), whose book on Central Europe he had edited for his Regional Geography series. The evidence adduced is not convincing; it bears little relationship to the great themes of M.'s paper, and is not borne out by a reading of Partsch's book.

by control, the usufruct of other and extensive maritime regions' (p. 44). In a contest between the Eurasian land mass and the maritime powers he did not doubt, however, where the victory would lie. 'The empire of the sea is doubtless the empire of the world' (p. 53). Of course, Mackinder had read widely and his active brain drew upon a multitude of diverse sources for stimulation. But the coherent thesis that resulted was his alone.

It is often said that Mackinder's paper was a product of his concern for the British Empire and of his campaign to unite its members in the face of a growing threat from continental powers; that it was deeply rooted in the ideas, anxieties, and fallacies prevalent at the time; and that it could only have been written by an Englishman living at the beginning of the twentieth century. 'The Heartland concept was a product of its age', writes Blouet (1973), who points out (1976) that a few months before the paper was read, the Coefficients Dining Club, with Mackinder present, had debated the relative threat of German or Russian expansion; and 'so it was the desire to transmit the message—unify or be overtaken by the super-states—that constituted one of the major reasons for writing the 1904 statement' (Blouet 1976a, p. 229). He goes so far as to say (1976) that it was 'an intellectual justification' for his conversion to tariff reform. Troll (1952) describes 'The Geographical Pivot of History' as 'no objective conception', but conceived at a time of virulent Russophobia.

It can be argued, however, that the 1904 statement is a work of genius independent of the nationality of its author, free from the preoccupations of its time and from the stigmata of geopolitical propaganda. There is no internal evidence that it was a tract for the Empire cause, an anti-Russian campaign, or an anti-German crusade. It avoids emotive words; it does not warn that the situations it contemplates hold danger; nor does it urge that they should be forestalled; it is calm and dispassionate historico-geographical analysis. Here Mackinder has escaped from the day-to-day cares of a busy academic and political life, from wrestling with the problems of Empire and tariff reform, to indulge in an intellectual exercise, of a geopolitical nature certainly, but conceived from a wholly detached standpoint. This view is reinforced by his own account of his motives: 'My objective was to place on record a statement of values, adjusted to measured facts as known at that date, in the hope that other "outlookers" would, with due readjustments, register the changes of values at later dates, and so vindicate the study of philosophical geography' (1944, p. 132).

The paper's originality and brilliance lay in the way it related the fact of the world having become a closed system to technological changes in communications, with the balance of advantage oscillating between land power and sea power, between centre and periphery. It thus reduced the complex interplay of historical event and geographical fact to an astonishing simplicity. This had little to do with the nationality, politics, or environment of its author. It could as well have been written by a German or a Russian or a Frenchman. Admittedly, it had a certain topicality at the time it was delivered. Mackinder said later that it was the contrast between Britain supplying her forces in South Africa by ship and Russia supplying hers in Manchuria by rail, that had suggested the idea of the Heartland. Yet he traced it back to the day in 1870 when he had read the news of the Prussian victory at Sedan on the post-office door at Gainsborough. In short, 'it had a background of many years of observation and thought' (1943), and these were its parents rather than imperialism and fear. Far from being a 'product of its time' it was too far ahead of its time to be placed in the context of its time.

A year after 'The Geographical Pivot of History' Mackinder published a lecture he had given to the Compatriots dining club entitled 'Man Power as a Measure of National and Imperial Strength' (1905). This was avowedly a propagandist pamphlet, but his remarks on the nature of sea power were none the less valid and far-sighted. A special characteristic of sea power was that it could be maintained with relatively few men, thus enabling a small island to rule the waves. There were two ways in which it could be exercised in particular waters—either by keeping a fleet there or by preventing the control of their shores by a hostile power; the Indian Ocean exemplified the second alternative—we ruled that sea but kept 'no more than a police fleet there'. Britain would not, however, be able to go on maintaining her power so cheaply now that countries with greater resources were challenging her.

Meanwhile the Russo-Japanese war had ended in victory for

sea power, confirming the widespread belief that land power would never seriously challenge it. The Russian defeat led to a decade of social and political troubles culminating in the chaos of war and revolution in 1914–17. Yet during that decade Mackinder's Eurasian Heartland was transformed. By means of new railways the population of Siberia and Russian Central Asia rose from twelve to twenty million; new towns were growing up 'with American rapidity' (Nansen 1914); the 'new world apart' which Mackinder had foreseen was already developing. But British politicians, Mackinder included, were more concerned with the rapid industrial, commercial, military, and naval growth of Germany which was also phenomenal during these years.

The 1914–18 war came before German sea power had 'become strong enough to neutralize British sea power'. It eventually resolved itself into a struggle between land power using submarines and sea power using blockade; the sea powers had also to commit large forces to the conflict on land. The issue was for a time in doubt because submarines threatened to cut the essential supplies of the maritime powers. In the event, however, Germany was defeated and plunged into revolutionary chaos; the war had already produced revolution in Russia. The treaty of Brest–Litovsk (1917) would have enabled Germany—had she been victorious in the West—to dominate the weakened Russian state, and so command the Eurasian Heartland. But this was not to be; the two land powers which had caused the British Empire such anxiety seemed unlikely ever again to threaten the victorious Western allies, whose representatives met in 1919 to settle the terms of peace.

It was now that Mackinder published his *Democratic Ideals and Reality*,[17] urging the peace-makers to take account of geographical realities if they were to make a lasting peace: he warned that the issue between sea power and land power had not been finally resolved and that the duel between Teuton and Slav was yet to be fought out. Ruthless organizers would emerge from the present confusion in both Germany and Russia, and unless effective preventive measures were taken, another terrible war would be fought between them for mastery in eastern Europe.

[17] It was published by Constable in London and, almost simultaneously, by Henry Holt in New York (1919).

Whoever ruled there would have the key to the great Heartland, with its strategic advantages and its vast economic potential. Such a power would command the World Island and, by adding sea power to supremacy on land, would have the empire of the world within its grasp. This could be prevented by using the great and irresistible power of the present victors to see that super-states did not arise, but that the old continental empires were broken up into autonomous, economically-balanced and viable nations. This was especially necessary in eastern Europe in order to separate the great Teutonic and Slavic giants, and to keep them from gaining overweening size and power.

Mackinder's 1919 book was not, as his 1904 paper had been, purely an intellectual exercise in historical and political geography, but a work written to warn statesmen of the need to take a specific course of action if dire consequences were to be averted. It applied the 1904 concept of the pivot-area to the compelling circumstances of a real crisis—but only Mackinder could see that the situation remained critical. Victory had lulled both statesmen and public into the belief that 'the war to end war' had succeeded in its object. The crisis lay in the unresolved relationship between Germany and Russia. Whether it developed into alliance, or war between them with the conquest of the one by the other, the end would imperil freedom. Hence the urgency to set free and keep free those lesser nations situated so unhappily between the two.

The geopolitical argument in *Democratic Ideals and Reality* centres round the great geographical reality—the distribution of land and sea, with the massing of most of the land in one great 'World Island' dominated by the interior 'Heartland'; this offered immense possibilities to land power as opposed to the sea power lodged in and exercised over the circumferential margins and off-lying peninsulas and islands—some of the latter of continental size, but off-lying islands none the less. It adopts the historical analysis and the geostrategic logic of 'The Geographical Pivot of History' although it enlarges the westward extent of the Heartland in accordance with the practical experience of the war, replacing the earlier physical criterion with a strategic one. It also lays stress upon man-power—the number, capability, and efficiency of the population, its equipment, and—above all—its organization. It is organization that makes

a nation a 'going concern': man-power in the hands of a capable
and ruthless organizer, when located in a strategically advantageous territory such as the Heartland, and aided by such
technological advances as the railway, the motor vehicle, and
the aeroplane, would constitute a very real threat indeed.
Mackinder reverted to this theme at a public lecture: everything
seemed to be on the side of the organizer of a monolithic state in
his assault upon the freedom of man, notably the advances in
communication, and this, in association with geographical advantage, made a dangerous combination: 'the tremendous control of Moscow ... was possible because they had to deal with a
plain with one system of society right through. He dreaded all
organization on the world scale' (*The Times*, 7 Oct. 1921).

A selection of some of the more significant, penetrating, or
far-sighted geopolitical passages from *Democratic Ideals and
Reality* is given below:

We have been fighting lately ... a straight duel between land-power
and sea-power, and sea-power has been laying siege to land-power.
We have conquered, but had Germany conquered she would have
established her sea-power on a wider base than any in history, and in
fact on the widest possible base. (p. 81)

The joint continent of Europe, Asia, and Africa, is now effectively,
and not merely theoretically, an island ... let us call it the World-
Island. (p. 81)

The surrender of the German fleet in the Firth of Forth is a dazzling
event, but in all soberness, if we would take the long view, must we
not still reckon with the possibility that a large part of the Great
Continent might some day be united under a single sway, and that an
invincible sea-power might be based upon it? (pp. 91–2)

The Heartland is the region to which, under modern conditions, sea-
power can be refused access. (p. 141)

We have defeated the danger on this occasion, but the facts of geography remain, and offer ever-increasing strategical opportunities to
land-power as against sea-power. (p. 143)

... we have come to the conclusion that the World-Island and the
Heartland are the final Geographical Realities in regard to sea-power
and land-power, and that East Europe is essentially a part of the
Heartland. But there remains to be considered the Economic Reality
of man-power. We have seen that the question of base, not only secure,

but also productive, is vital to sea-power . . . Russia was the first tenant of the Heartland with a really menacing man-power. (pp. 179–80)

If we accept anything less than a complete solution . . . we shall merely have gained a respite, and our descendants will find themselves under the necessity of marshalling their power afresh for the siege of the Heartland. (p. 200)

Even with revolution in Germany let us not be too sure in regard to its ultimate effect . . . The end of the present disorder may only be a new ruthless organization, and ruthless organizers do not stop when they have attained the objects which they at first set before them. (p. 201)

It is a vital necessity that there should be a tier of independent states between Germany and Russia. The Russians are, and for one, if not two, generations must remain, hopelessly incapable of resisting German penetration on any basis but that of a military autocracy, unless they be shielded from direct attack . . . Autocratic rule . . . is almost inevitable if she (Russia) is to depend on her own strength to cope with the Germans. (pp. 205–6)

The Westerners are the Victors, and they alone are able to prevent the whole world from having to pass through the cycle so often repeated in the case of individual nations—Idealism, Disorder, Famine, Tyranny. (p. 233)

The diagnoses and prognoses contained in *Democratic Ideals and Reality* 'attracted little attention in the Anglo-Saxon world where they were treated as a fanciful exercise of the academic imagination and were soon forgotten' (Amery 1953, vol. i, p. 229). There were few reviews, even in geographical periodicals. The Royal Geographical Society's *Geographical Journal* did not consider it worth notice; the *Scottish Geographical Magazine* published a lengthy rambling review by Chisholm (1919) who was more intent on giving his own views than on discussing Mackinder's book.[18] The best review was in the American Geographical Society's *Geographical Review* (Teggart 1919): this, after noting that 'new ideas are never wholly welcome guests', and agreeing with the author that 'we cannot hope to safeguard our

---

[18] H. R. Mill (1951, p. 85) gives a telling comparison between Chisholm and M. 'The former was profoundly learned, laborious, accurate, and meticulous in definition and the safe-guarding of every detail. Mackinder was brilliant, brushing aside all irrelevancies, sketching the broad outlines of the science with a masterly hand, and by his gifts of generalization and exposition often suggesting new lines of research to the more pedestrian votaries of geography.'

democratic "ideals" without a grasp of the realities of geography and economics', praised him as 'one who has the courage to enlist erudition as a guide to action'. A learned analysis of the work followed, with the writer arguing that Russia, and not Germany, was the villain; the Europeans, instead of fighting among themselves, should have united 'in opposition to the power of the Heartland'. Had a 'United States of Europe' been formed in the 1880s, 'we should not have had the recent exhibition of Western Europe accepting an alliance with the Heartland enemy to destroy its own system of defense against that power'. Russia, 'as in a mist, lies portentous in the background ...' Another American critic (Dryer 1920) took Mackinder to task for calling America a 'satellite' of the World Island, but in 1922 the book was described (Joerg 1922, p. 434) as 'a fruitful application of the geographical viewpoint to political questions'. Outside of the geographical world, the *Times Literary Supplement* (8 May 1919) gave a rather sarcastic notice, the gist of which was that a geographer should leave history and politics alone.

Mackinder in *Democratic Ideals and Reality* insisted that 'we must see to it that East Europe, like West Europe, is divided into self-contained nations' (p. 203); his proposals for such a division are somewhat similar to those adopted at the Paris Peace Conference which met on 18 January 1919. The motive was different, however. The Conference was primarily activated by the principle of self-determination and by retribution for the enemy, Mackinder by the 'vital necessity' that there should be a tier of independent states between Germany and Russia to keep them apart. He was still more concerned with danger from Germany than from Russia, or he would have advocated an independent Ukraine; he recognizes its distinctiveness by naming it on his map (1919, p. 207) in similar lettering to that given to the states to be newly independent, but fails to mark it off from Russia by a boundary. He believed that German domination would prove to be 'a chastisement of scorpions as compared to the whips of Russia' (ibid., p. 179). But as the civil war in Russia progressed, he became more and more aware of the nature, aims, and efficiency of the Bolsheviks, and began to fear that he may have been mistaken on this point.

Mackinder made the bold and imaginative suggestion that

the question of Polish access to the sea should be settled, not by a corridor, which would be vexatious and leave Germany in contact with Russia in East Prussia, but by a transfer of population:

Why should we not contemplate an exchange of peoples as between Prussia west of the Vistula and Polish Posen? ... Rights of way over other people's property usually become inconvenient and lead to disputes. Would it not pay Humanity to bear the cost of a radical remedy in this case, a remedy made just and even generous towards individuals in every respect? Each proprietor should be given the option of exchanging his property and retaining his nationality or of retaining his property and changing his nationality. But if he selects the latter alternative there must be no reservation of special rights in respect of schools and other social privileges ... Why should we not use our modern powers of transport and organization to achieve the same happy conditions of affairs—justly and generously. The reasons for doing so in this particular instance are far reaching; a Polish Posen would bite a very threatening bay into the Eastern frontier of Germany, and a German East Prussia would be a stepping-stone for German penetration into Russia. (1919, pp. 209–10)

The *Times Literary Supplement*, in the notice referred to above, commented: 'He does not ask whether the Poles of Posen would wish to be turned into East Prussia, or the Germans of East Prussia would agree to be swept into Posen. If not they must be compelled to obey. This was the method chosen by the Kings of Assyria to settle their race questions. The fate of Nineveh hardly proves that it answered.' Could this writer have foreseen that Mackinder's suggestion would have removed the immediate *casus belli* of the next war, a war after which the peoples concerned were indeed to be 'swept' from one homeland to another, not 'justly and generously' but with the most harrowing cruelty, he might have regarded it more sympathetically.

An opportunity was soon to occur which, had circumstances proved more propitious, would have enabled him to play a prominent part in realizing his plan for the *cordon sanitaire* in eastern Europe. There was a group in the Government, led by Churchill, who were eager to aid the Whites and prevent the Bolshevik domination of Russia, and in January 1919 the supply of British arms to Denikin began. The British Government saw the need to give political direction as well as military aid, and on 29 July it was decided to send a representative to South Russia. Nothing was done, however, until Curzon became Foreign Secretary in October 1919; he at once sent for his fellow-geographer,[19] Mackinder, and offered him the post of High Commissioner to South Russia. Mackinder accepted, and from the first took the position very seriously, so much so that he was reproved by Curzon for recruiting too large a staff (FO 1920). There was a long delay before he was actually able to go, and by then the ground had been cut from under his feet by Lloyd George's publicly announced determination to end military assistance to Russia and by the defeat and retreat of Denikin. Nevertheless, Mackinder left England on 4 December for Paris where he saw members of the *emigré* All-Russia Council. Leaving Paris on 10 December with his assistant, Brigadier Keyes, he arrived in Warsaw on 13 December and there had interviews with the President, Pilsudsky, and the Prime Minister, Paderewski. The Poles wanted support for a march on Moscow to end the Bolshevik menace, but Mackinder asked them to support Denikin instead. He left Warsaw on the 17th, and his slow progress through eastern Europe continued, with pauses for further diplomatic activity at Bucharest, Sofia, and Constantinople, which he did not reach until 28 December. Finally, on New Year's Day 1920—the day his knighthood was announced—he arrived in southern Russia at Novorossiysk, but it was not until 10 January that he was able to meet Denikin and the head of the British military mission, General Holman. He strove to persuade Denikin to collaborate with the Poles and recognize the border states, but the White general was reluctant to incur the opprobrium that such an action would bring from the Russian people.[20] Mackinder soon saw that the situation was so desperate that it could only be remedied by a well-thought-out plan of action involving all the groups opposed to the Bolsheviks, and decided to return to England to submit such a plan. He left Novorossiysk on 16 January and completed his report to the Government at Marseilles on the 21st.

In this he concluded that the Bolsheviks' success had not yet gone so far that their army 'could not be overthrown with ease

---

[19] For Curzon as a geographer, see Goudie (1980).
[20] Nevertheless an agreement was reached along these lines. M.'s story is confirmed by Denikin (1930, p. 340).

by a properly organized and sustained military effort on quite a moderate scale, but if that effort be not made within the next few months there is undoubtedly great risk that such a weapon may be forged as may become a danger to the world' (Mackinder 1920, p. 777). The Poles were planning their own attack on Bolshevism, but this would rally support to the Communists. The Poles should only go to Moscow 'in alliance with Russians', and so it was 'of the first importance to keep in being the only Russian government in Europe outside the Bolshevik area'. The report goes on to give a penetrating analysis of the causes of Denikin's failure, notably his forfeiture of popular support through his own exactions and the atrocities of his Cossacks, and shows in detail how Mackinder would remedy the situation:

My belief is that, owing to the nature of the produce in this country—wheat, coal, sugar and hides—a single season would suffice to set the economic life going again, and I am inclined to think that it would not require much more than such a limited military advance as I have indicated, and such an economic organization as I have sketched, to establish a contrast as it were between Heaven and Hell, which would result in the sudden collapse of the Bolshevik tyranny. (ibid., p. 782)

This rich land, the Ukraine, would form part of a federal system, but such an idea should not be spoken of publicly, as any hint of its separation would alienate Denikin's supporters. He goes on to warn that 'it is only by strong immediate measures, taken before the thawing of the Volga ice, that the advance of Bolshevism, sweeping forward like a prairie fire, can be limited'. The British government should organize among the border states an anti-Bolshevik League of Governments and support it with administrative aid and economic assistance; the military involvement would, however, be minimal, and there would be no need for the direct participation of British troops. He realized that 'the hostility of certain classes of our own electorate' would be a difficulty in the way of adopting his plan, but he felt 'the time has come when the truth should be carried home to them'. They must be made to realize that, 'whatever the communistic ideals originally characteristic of Bolshevism, there is to-day a growing threat from Moscow of a state of affairs which will render this world a very unsafe place for democracies' (ibid. p. 785). He continued:

It is true that no man can say for certain what would be the course of events if you allowed Bolshevism to enjoy its present triumph, but explore the future as you will on that assumption and I can see no peace for the world. Whether the future of Russia be anarchy, or tyranny, or servitude to the German matters not; none of these conditions can co-exist with democracy in the world to-day. (ibid., p. 786)

Mackinder's bold and imaginative proposals were discussed in the Cabinet on 29 January, when he was present for part of the meeting. But the minutes state that they 'did not meet with any support' (Cab. 23/20, 1920, pp. 60-1). It was concluded that:

There can be no question of making active war on the Bolsheviks, for the reason that we have neither the men, the money, nor the credit, and public opinion is altogether opposed to such a course.

The Border States surrounding Russia must themselves take the full responsibility for deciding as between peace and war. Not the slightest encouragement, however, should be given them to pursue the policy of war, because if we were to give that advice we should incur responsibilities which we could not discharge. (ibid., p. 68)

It was further decided that Britain would be prepared to negotiate with the Bolsheviks when they can show 'that they represent the governing authority of the areas for which they claim to speak', and a hint to this effect was to be given 'in a public speech' (ibid.).

The die was cast. There was to be no anti-Bolshevik alliance—not even Churchill had supported Mackinder, who resigned his High Commission.[21] Blouet (1976a, p. 235) sums up the outcome justly:

The analysis made by Mackinder was not incorrect; indeed, in the context of the cold war it was highly accurate, but the political realities of the time in a democracy made it impossible to act upon his viewpoint. The country as a whole was tired of intervention in foreign disputes. The practical politicians, men looking to the next election, had difficulty seeing the value of analysis based on a 25-year view of events.

So 'Britain withdrew and with her went the support which many potentially autonomous regions, like the Ukraine, had

[21] For further discussion of M.'s South Russian expedition, see Blouet (1976a) and Ullman (1968, 1972).

been hoping for.' A disappointed man, Mackinder 'clearly felt that a chance had been missed to forestall the emergence of a Heartland power', but 'perhaps in the context of the times, and given the nature of democracies, it was just not possible to exploit the opportunity ... In the end Mackinder's reality foundered upon democratic ideals' (ibid., pp. 235–6).

After the failure of *Democratic Ideals and Reality* to attract attention and the rejection of his plans for the organization of a league of newly independent states in eastern Europe and western Russia, Mackinder withdrew from the general geopolitical field, contenting himself with the problems of Empire and the philosophy of geography. We know little of his feelings as the story of the inter-war years unfolded along the lines he had foreshadowed. The refusal of the United States to support the League of Nations undermined the alliance of maritime democracies which he had envisaged, and condemned the newly independent states of eastern Europe to a short life. The Treaty of Rapallo (1922) between defeated and humiliated Germany and unrecognized and ostracized Russia was significant to the Heartland concept. Strausz-Hupé (1942) commented:

What Mackinder feared was a slow and peaceful penetration of Russia by the efficient Germans during the years of economic prostration following the Russian Revolution ... the Rapallo Agreement of 1922 was a more sagacious step towards the ultimate goal of really controlling the Heartland than the Blitzkrieg tactics of the Nazis, which promised at best little more than mastery of a scorched earth ... the foundation of a constructive policy aiming at the control of the Heartland was laid by the very German democracy which Hitler so despises. (pp. 148–9)

The sequence of events which Mackinder (1919, pp. 19–21) so dramatically described as inexorably following from the disruption of democratic society by revolutionary zealots, resulting in 'the supreme rule of the organizer', came about in Russia, Italy, Germany, and Spain, as well as in some of the 'border states' created at Versailles. Germany recovered as he had forecast. Soviet economic development was carried boldly into the Heartland: Novosibirsk, capital of Siberia, over a thousand miles from the nearest sea—and that a frozen one—was but a hutted village when 'The Geographical Pivot' was delivered in 1904; by the outbreak of war in 1941 it had grown to a city of half a million. Mackinder wrote of 'the new map of Scythia', adding that it would 'be at our peril that we neglect to take account of it' (1935a, p. vi). It was this Soviet industrial development in and beyond the Urals that enabled the USSR to survive the German onslaught.

The co-operation between Russia and Germany envisaged in the Treaty of Rapallo had perished with Hitler's hostility to Bolshevism. But the influential Haushofer, with Mackinder's theories in mind, continued to urge the formation of a Eurasian bloc embracing Germany, Russia, and Japan, and he regarded the Nazi–Soviet pact of 26 August 1939, which led to the dissolution of the 'third tier' of states, with the utmost satisfaction. The policy had originated with Mackinder, but

Where does world history say that one may not learn from the enemy? *Fas est ab hoste docere* . . . Russia and Germany both lost the war because they fought on opposite sides. It took . . . a much longer time than Sir Halford Mackinder had expected, for the Germans and Russians to find that out. (Haushofer, qu. in Kruszewski 1954, p. 14)

In June 1941, however, the policy of conquest displaced that of co-operation; in either case the aim was access to the resources of the Heartland and a labour supply wherewith to work them; without these German success was not possible. It has been said that 'the validity of Haushofer's theories is unaffected by the manner in which Germany secures domination of the "Heartland"', and that although 'he would personally have preferred "amalgamation" to conquest . . . he greeted the declaration of war upon Russia as enthusiastically as . . . [he] had hailed the Russo–German pact' (Strausz-Hupé 1942, pp. 79–81).

By now Haushofer and Mackinder had become household names in the United States where geopolitics had become all the rage. Alerted by the article in the *New Statesman* of 26 August 1939,[22] scholars and journalists alike hastened to read the works of Mackinder. There they discovered that much that had happened, including the titanic collision between Teuton and Slav, had been foretold by the English geographer, and that the importance of the Eurasian Heartland, both in motivating and in deciding such a struggle, had been outlined as far back as 1904: 'maps illustrating Mackinder's Heartland conception

[22] See pp. 158–9 above.

began to appear in American publications, and Americans became aware of the importance of global thinking' (Kruszewski 1954, p. 14); 'the ideas of Mackinder burgeoned into significance in the turmoil of the Second World War and overnight became imperatives for armchair strategists' (Weigert 1949, p. 80). *Democratic Ideals and Reality* was republished in 1942 to meet the American demand, the author commenting wryly, 'my book returns as a ghost revisiting a world in which it lived without much honour' (Weigert 1942, pp. 135–6). As a result millions of Americans became 'acutely aware of the strategic realities of the world in which they live' (Gyorgy 1944, p. 282).

The American journal *Foreign Affairs* asked Mackinder to 'carry further' some of the themes which he had dealt with in his past writings, and in particular to consider whether his strategical concept of a Heartland had 'lost any of its significance under the conditions of modern warfare' (Mackinder 1943, p. 595). His reply, published in July 1943, as 'The Round World and the Winning of the Peace' is often described as his 'third statement' of the Heartland idea. However, it was not a spontaneous essay, but written on the insistence of others; he was now 82 years old, and writing in the midst of the confusion of a great war.

After detailing some of the economic developments that had enriched the Heartland, he concluded:

... if the Soviet Union emerges from this war as the conqueror of Germany, she must rank as the greatest land Power on the globe. Moreover, she will be the Power in the strategically strongest defensive position. The Heartland is the greatest natural fortress on earth. For the first time in history it is manned by a garrison sufficient both in number and quality. (p. 601)

His concept of the Heartland was 'more valid and useful to-day than it was either twenty or forty years ago' (p. 603). The German problem had receded, for there was now 'within this vast natural fortress a garrison adequate to deny entry to the German invader'. The problem of securing the maritime world of the democracies remained, and for this he proposed a North Atlantic alliance to provide a 'bridgehead in France, a moated aerodrome in Britain, and a reserve of trained manpower, agriculture and industries in the eastern United States and Canada'

(p. 604). His interest in an Atlantic alliance goes back to a much earlier time (Mackinder 1905, pp. 139–40), and in 1924 he had written that 'Western Europe and North America now constitute for many purposes a single community of nations'. In 1942 he had told the Geographical Association that:

Such an association might have avoided this second World War, and ought to have done so if the triple alliance of the United States, Great Britain and France, negotiated after Versailles had not been abandoned before it became operative. None of the great democracies had at that time fully learnt its lesson, but in the present tragedy let us hope that all of them will have come to a higher wisdom. (Mackinder 1942, p. 130)

The 1939–45 war disposed of the idea of Central Europe. The United States, displacing Great Britain, emerged as the leading maritime power and her influence extended over western Europe, and in fact, over the whole of the peripheral maritime world; the Soviet Union, displacing Germany, was now clearly the dominant land power, extending her influence over eastern Europe, and in possession of the Heartland of the World Island. The partition of a weakened Europe was followed by the dissolution of the European empires, exposing many parts of the 'inner' and 'outer crescents' either to American penetration by sea or Soviet pressure by land, creating a peripheral zone of instability. Such was the changed world upon which Mackinder closed his eyes in March 1947. But the great geographical realities remained: land power versus sea power, heartland versus rimland, centre versus periphery, an individualistic Western philosophy versus a collective Eastern doctrine rooted in a communal past. Mackinder died but his ideas lived on.

Chapter 7

Mackinder and the Course of Events

Although the Anglo-Saxon world did not awake to the importance of Mackinder's geopolitical ideas until 1939 and after, they had already been powerfully effective abroad, and especially in Germany. In 1944, on the occasion of receiving the Charles P. Daly medal, he said:

I have been criticized in certain quarters as having helped to lay the foundation of Nazi militarism. It has, I am told, been rumoured that I inspired Haushofer, who inspired Hess, who in turn suggested to Hitler while he was writing 'Mein Kampf' certain geo-political ideas which are said to have originated with me. Those are three links in a chain, but of the second and third I know nothing. This, however, I do know from the evidence of his own pen that whatever Haushofer adapted from me he took from an address I gave before the Royal Geographical Society just forty years ago, long before there was any question of a Nazi Party. (Mackinder 1944)

There is no doubt about the first link in the chain, the flow of ideas from Mackinder to Haushofer. This was made abundantly clear by Haushofer himself in many of his publications;[1] and both under interrogation by the US Army (23 Aug. 1945) and in his *Apologie der deutschen Geopolitik* his defence was that his doctrines were derived from Mackinder's 'Geographical Pivot of History' (Jacobsen 1979a, vol. i, pp. 333–42, 639–46). The link was first revealed to the English-speaking world in the *New Statesman* of 26 August 1939 and soon generally recognized: 'from Mackinder he borrowed the root-idea which was to energize German geopolitical thought' (Walsh 1943, p. 18); 'Haushofer accepted and expanded the great Englishman's theory' (Neumann 1943, p. 280); 'Haushofer's passages on the Heartland are so worded that the reader cannot doubt how strong was the psychological attraction for Haushofer of Mackinder's ideas' (Strausz-Hupé 1942, p. 155).

The attraction of Mackinder's theory was that, properly util-

[1] e.g. 1924, *passim*; 1936, pp. 50–1.

ized, it could lead to German domination of the Eurasian land mass and the destruction of British sea power (Weigert 1942, p. 157; Gyorgy 1944, p. 238). Its lesson was clear: Germany must pursue one aim—to dominate the Heartland, both for its strategic advantages and for its rich resources; then and then only could she match the Anglo-Saxon powers; all other policies, such as recovery of Alsace–Lorraine, colonial adventure, or naval challenge were wasteful and mistaken diversions.[2] Mackinder, looking back to the 1914–18 war, had written (1919, pp. 193–4):

Had Germany elected to stand on the defensive on her short frontier towards France, and had she thrown her main strength against Russia, it is not improbable that the world would be nominally at peace today, but overshadowed by a German East Europe in command of all the Heartland. The British and American insular peoples would not have realized the strategical danger until it was too late.

There were, however, two paths to the main goal: alliance with peaceful penetration, or conquest and exploitation. Haushofer and his school consistently advocated the former; one colleague asked: 'Does she (Germany) want to be a satellite of the Anglo-Saxon powers and their super-capitalism?' and answered, 'Germany and Russia have been friends for centuries; their economic structures are complementary; they must stand together' (Weigert 1943, p. 404). This recalls Bismarck's advice: 'keep the peace with Russia—then there will never be war'. For war would no longer be necessary.

Haushofer followed Mackinder in paying only slight attention to the real or latent power of the United States. Both were preoccupied with the British Empire. It has been suggested that this was because of their use of Mercator maps, but American power did not loom so large in the years of isolation and before the 1941–5 war as it does today. Both could argue that they were subsuming American power in the sea power that land power would challenge: Mackinder had talked of an Atlantic alliance and Haushofer refers to the Anglo-Saxon or the Anglo-American powers; and, as regards sea power, the rise of America has been balanced by the decline of Britain and the

[2] '... the Eurasian supra-continental policy offers possibilities that are found in none of the other combinations one can envisage' (Haushofer 1925, p. 87).

loss of her Empire. Haushofer sagely noted that 'Great Britain seeks and obtains, in the wars she wages for the preservation of her empire, the help of the U.S. But by accepting such help she mortgages her empire to the very power that has the strongest geopolitical interest in liquidating it' (qu. in Strausz-Hupé 1942, p. 67).

Haushofer was a talented man who had distinguished himself both militarily and academically. Like Mackinder, whom he is said to have strikingly resembled in appearance,[3] he showed remarkable insight and made some astute predictions as to the future. He was intensely patriotic and nationalistic, characteristics shared with most Germans of the era and attributable to the recent defeat and humiliation of a people only newly unified; but he never joined the Nazi party. He was scrupulous in acknowledging his debt to other scholars—Ratzel, Kjellen, Mahan, Curzon, Fairgrieve, and above all Mackinder, whom he praised as the most outstanding geopolitical thinker of all time.

Haushofer joined the army in 1887 at the age of 18, and in 1908 went on a two-year military mission to Japan, soon making himself an authority on that country; he became convinced that she would one day become a foremost world power. In 1914 he was awarded a doctorate *cum summa laude* in geography, geology, and history by the University of Munich, becoming the only German army officer to be so qualified. He served throughout the war, and retired in 1919 (*aet.* 50) to become Lecturer in Geography at Munich; two years later he was appointed Professor. From 1934 to 1937 he was President of the German Academy, an appointment in the gift of the Führer. The German-Soviet pact of August 1939 was the culmination of his geopolitical work, but when the war began to take a disastrous course under Hitler's personal and bizarre leadership, he became increasingly disillusioned. His son Albrecht was shot by the SS for complicity in the July 1944 conspiracy, and he himself committed suicide early in 1946.

Haushofer was well placed in Munich, the headquarters of the National Socialist movement. His pupils took up important

[3] Troll (1952): '... der ihm sowohl im Denken wie in der Physiognomie auffallend ähnlich war' (p. 178), but the many photographs of Haushofer in Jacobssen (1979a) show little resemblance, other than that they both have moustaches!

posts in the Party, in the civil service, in journalism, and in the professions. This resulted in 'the wide and profound impact of his teachings upon the German mind and the powerful influence of his many followers on national policy' (Strausz-Hupé 1942, p. 77), and enabled him to make 'very important contributions to internal propaganda' (Hartshorne 1964, p. 55). A German study (Jacobsen 1979) concludes that he 'prepared the ground spiritually for the rise of the National-Socialist system and, for a time (i.e. until 1939) vindicated the foreign policy of the Nazis. He thus contributed to the credibility of the Nationalist-Socialist government.' He also 'had a strong hold on the men who did the brain work in the German army ... Haushofer's plans actually became an integral part of the global strategy of the German General Staff—until the dreamer of Berchtesgarten took over himself, and substituted intuition for calculation' (Weigert 1942, pp. 70–1).[4]

There is then no doubt of the link between Mackinder and Haushofer, and of the great significance of that link because of Haushofer's influential position in Germany. What of the links between Haushofer and the leaders of the National Socialist party and Hitler himself? There is no direct evidence to prove that Hitler consciously adopted Haushofer's ideas, and in one important respect he differed fundamentally; for Hitler often seemed to favour an alliance with England against Russia, whereas Haushofer looked for a Eurasian bloc to challenge the Anglo-Saxons.[5] However, the circumstantial evidence for considerable influence by Haushofer is strong: Haushofer was the foremost German geostrategist; he had convincing credentials and was working in the headquarters town of the National Socialist movement; Hitler personally appointed him to the presidency of the German Academy; Rudolf Hess, one of the most important men in the Party had been Haushofer's aide

[4] M. spoke in 1944 of 'Dr Hans Weigert, a German of distinguished and cultivated mind, who for the sake of his wife and child, fled with them from his Fatherland' to America in 1939, 'because his freedom was threatened by the Nazis on account of his adhesion to the persecuted Pastor Niemüller.' Weigert became the leading American political geographer of the immediate post-war years.

[5] 'I confess openly that in the pre-war times already I held it better had Germany, at the sacrifice of senseless colonial policy and at the sacrifice of the merchant and naval fleet, stood in alliance with England against Russia.' qu. by Weigert (1942, p. 150) from *Mein Kampf* (ed. Reynal & Hitchcock), p. 962.

and assistant, and was his personal friend;[6] here and there in his writings Haushofer suggests that his advice is listened to by the country's leaders; Hess introduced him to Hitler when the latter was confined to the Landsberg fortress after the abortive *putsch* of 1923, and Haushofer then visited Hitler regularly to discuss geopolitical matters; Hitler was writing *Mein Kampf* at the time, and certain passages read as though they could have been written by a Haushofer—or even by a Mackinder; Hitler, even allowing for his intuition, had to learn about the real world— he was not initially an educated man, and here was a university professor, learned in the subject matter of the book he was writing, and ready at hand with just the kind of suggestions he wanted to hear; and finally, Hitler did in fact give priority to an eastern policy, placing access to the Heartland and its riches in the forefront of his strategy.

As all this became known to the world outside, some exaggerated conclusions were drawn, mainly by sensation-seeking journalists. Weigert (1942, p. 9) tells how the *Readers Digest* reported that Haushofer and his Munich men, 'with their ideas, their charts, maps, statistics, information and plans have dictated Hitler's moves from the beginning ... Haushofer's Institute is no mere instrument for Hitler's use. It is the other way round. Dr Haushofer and his men dominate Hitler's thinking.' Col. H. Beukema, who instructed at West Point, and who had lived in Germany, said 'history will rate Karl Haushofer, prophet of German geopolitics, more important than Adolf Hitler' (*Time*, 19 Jan. 1942). It is perhaps in reaction against such statements that attempts have been made to minimize the importance of Haushofer, usually by those geographers who also belittle Mackinder's influence (e.g. Crone 1948, pp. 106–7; 1951, p. 45; Hartshorne 1964, pp. 54–5; Pounds 1963, p. 409). Crone, referring to a Mackinder–Haushofer–Hitler chain, claims that 'the erroneousness of this conjunction was pointed out by Strausz-Hupé as early as 1942'. Strausz-Hupé is indeed a foremost authority on German geopolitics,[7] and he does say

---

[6] They corresponded regularly throughout the inter-war period. In a letter to Haushofer dated 26 August 1939, Hess apologizes for not coming in person to bring the Führer's greetings on his 70th birthday.

[7] Robert Strausz-Hupé (1903–), political scientist. Born in Vienna; went to the US 1923; served as US Ambassador to Ceylon, Belgium, Sweden, and NATO; Professor of Political Science, Univ. of Pennsylvania.

that 'there is no reason to believe that Hitler consulted Haushofer when making his momentous decisions' (1942, p. 79), but he continues, 'He did not need to. *Geopolitik* is Nazi foreign policy'—in other words, Hitler had already swallowed Haushofer's ideas, hook, line, and sinker! Later he writes that 'Haushofer made Mackinder's theory the cornerstone of *Geopolitik*' on which 'rests the official doctrine of Nazi expansionism' (p. 168).[8]

In fact, most informed writers believe that Haushofer's geopolitics had some effect on Hitler, though they may differ on how much:

Mackinder's Heartland theory had a great influence in Nazi Germany and a marginal impact on Hitler himself. (Walters 1974, p. 7)

The distinctive idea in the national socialist theory of imperialism was supplied by an English geographer, Sir Halford J. Mackinder ... Substantially this was the theory of German politics that Hitler outlined in Mein Kampf ... The national socialists will 'terminate the endless German drive to the south and west of Europe, and direct our gaze towards the lands in the east ...' (Sabine 1973, p. 832)

Haushofer's conversations and visits persuaded Hitler to accept certain fundamental geopolitical ideas which found their way into *Mein Kampf*. (Gyorgy 1944, p. 181)

Le grand succés de Haushofer fût de convaincre de l'utilité pratique de ses idées les dirigeants du parti national-socialiste, Rudolf Hess, puis Adolf Hitler. Il devait devenir auprès du gouvernement hitlérien et pour sa politique générale un conseiller précieux et écouté ... Ainsi toutes les formules de Mackinder, élaborées par un grand patriote pour servir son pays, étaient mises à profit pour les grands desseins d'un autre et en fait surtout contre le pays de Mackinder. (Gottmann 1952, pp. 57–8)

A few of the more striking passages from *Mein Kampf* will indicate that several of the concepts and some of the program of geopolitics appear to have influenced Hitler profoundly. (Whittlesey 1943, p. 408)

Hess ... brought Hitler into personal contact with his teacher, Karl Haushofer, who had taken the ... 'geopolitics' expounded by Sir Halford Mackinder, and shaped it into a philosophy of imperialist expansion. (Fest 1974, p. 217)

The basic incontestable truth is that Haushofer, directly in some

---

[8] Crone was misled by Troll (1947, p. 21); Troll (1949) repeated his misattribution to Strausz-Hupé.

instances, indirectly in others, co-ordinated, integrated, and rationalized the whole field of comparative geography for the use of the Führer—and in a manner particularly attractive to a mentality such as Hitler's. (Walsh 1943, p. 22)

Mackinder, through Haushofer, made a tremendous impact on Hitler's mental processes. (Earle qu. by Gyorgy, p. 167, fn. 11)

The above extracts come from political scientists, students of international affairs, and political geographers with a special interest in geopolitics. A distinguished historian and authority on Hitler, Trevor-Roper[9] (1953, pp. xxx–xxxii), believed that Hitler's thinking 'finally crystallized' in his months in prison in 1923–4; he had recently met Hess, 'a devoted disciple who now shared his all and with whom he must often have discussed, and in discussion formulated, his ideas'; Hess was 'the friend and enthusiastic follower' of Haushofer, who 'had taken up and was now popularizing in Germany those doctrines of Eurasian land-power which derived from Mackinder, and advanced as the basis of Russo–German agreement, were soon found applicable to a very different purpose, the conquest of the East'. He concluded: 'That Hess was a channel whereby Haushofer's geopolitical ideas were conveyed to Hitler's mind, there to be transformed into the doctrine of Eastern *Lebensraum*, seems to me almost certain.'

That Mackinder's work was ignored in Britain while seized upon in Germany is indicative of a different status of geography in the two countries. Geographical knowledge—an understanding of the features of the land and their economic and military significance—was an essential to survival for the Germans, placed in the middle of Europe, exposed on all sides to invasion, and with a long history of struggle on the west and to the east. The national territory could not be taken for granted; it had to be fought for. And if the state were to grow, to find land for its growing population, materials for its expanding industry, or markets for its thriving commerce, it could not expand overseas as the maritime powers had done—it must wrest land from its neighbours. Austria and the other marches of eastern Germany had originated as the defensive outposts of Europe; western Germany had suffered the French expansionism of the seven-

[9] Regius Professor of Modern History at Oxford, 1957–80; now Lord Dacre of Glanton.

teenth and eighteenth centuries. Strategic thinking was second nature to the German educated classes and was based on geography. Universal military service and compulsory schooling had, as Mackinder (1919, pp. 26-9) pointed out, spread this geographically-based strategic mentality thoughout the nation: 'every educated German is a geographer in a sense that is true of very few Englishmen or Americans'.

Very few indeed! And this was the root cause of many of Mackinder's failures. 'In this country', he wrote (ibid., p. 20),

we value the moral side of education, and it is perhaps intuitively that we have neglected materialistic geography. Before the War not a few teachers within my knowledge objected to geography as a subject on the ground that it tended to promote Imperialism, just as they objected to physical drill because it tended to militarism!

'Democracy', he added (p. 30), 'refuses to think strategically unless and until compelled to do so for purposes of defence.' As a young man he had heard the President of Section E of the British Association for the Advancement of Science[10] at Manchester in 1887 say:

Of all persons who require a knowledge of geography stand first those who are most concerned with the government of our empire, and yet they have for the most part been brought up at schools where the mental training for geography is most defective. Our statesmen as a rule have neither theoretical teaching nor practical experience in the science, and it is perhaps not too much to say that ... the people are continually perceiving, with regard to matters of everyday life and practical experience that their law-givers are more ignorant than themselves. (Warren 1887, p. 268)

He went on to give examples of the damage done by ignorance of geography in imperial administration and policy. The situation was not much better when Dillon (1919, pp. 53-6) wrote scathingly of the ignorance of the Anglo-Saxon delegates— Lloyd George in particular—to the Paris Peace Conference: 'in matters of geography ... they were helplessly at sea, and the stories told of certain of their efforts to keep their heads above water while maintaining a simulacrum of dignity would have been amusing were the issues less momentous'. He gives many amusing examples. In the inter-war years, 'British habits of

---

[10] Sir Charles Warren (1840-1927), general, surveyor, and archaeologist.

mind were far more receptive of the political nature of communism and later of fascism' than of the geographical and strategical realities that underlay the international situation, and 'the Czechoslovakian bastion, the centre-piece of Mackinder's proposed "Third Tier", was allowed by a British Prime Minister who knew little geography to be eliminated by a Germany which was saturated in it' (Fisher 1968, p. 3). Sprout (1963, p. 190) speaks of the 'resistance in the English-speaking countries to bringing geographical concepts and tools to the study of international politics'. Haushofer, wondering at the failure of British statesmen to see what Mackinder saw, commented: 'the costs of geographical ignorance are immensely high' (qu. in Weigert 1942, p. 117).

The pre-war influence of Mackinder's work was not confined to Germany, but reached the governing circles of Japan, Italy, and the USSR (Weigert 1942, p. 177; Gyorgy 1944, p. 167 fn.; Pearce 1962). In the USSR his writings have had an influence upon naval policy in particular: Dombrovsky, the Soviet chief of naval staff in the 1920s, advised that 'one should think about the foreign writings and consider the weight of the heartland in the naval defence of the motherland'. Another early Soviet naval writer, Zof, concludes that 'one must consider these statements of Mackinder for the defensive structure of the new navy' (Pauly 1974, pp. 4–5).[11]

By an interesting transplantation of ideas, the study of geopolitics, which had flourished in pre-war Germany, took root in the United States in the 1940s,[12] and may now be described as primarily an American science (Herold 1974). In America, as in Germany, geopolitical thinking has dominated the strategic policies of the State, and once again it is upon Mackinder's ideas that they have been based. No sooner had Germany been defeated and the invading armies from the two great extra-European powers met in the centre of Europe, than Mackinder's warning of 1919, ignored at the time but now become a familiar jingle, began to sound like a tocsin:

Who rules East Europe commands the Heartland:
Who rules the Heartland commands the World Island:

[11] Pauly's work shows that neglect of the Heartland thesis in the USSR has not been so complete as Kristof (1976) believes.

[12] 'Geopolitics has migrated from Germany to America' (Bowman 1942, p. 652).

Who rules the World Island commands the World.
(Mackinder 1919, p. 194)

Spykman (1947, p. 7) urged that geopolitics was 'appropriately named for a type of analysis and a body of data which are indispensable to the process of reaching intelligent decisions on certain aspects of foreign policy'; he had read Mackinder and was urging that the United States should organize and reinforce the 'rimland' in order to imprison the 'heartland' within its bounds, and some detected a Haushofer-like approach (e.g. Gottmann 1952, p. 62; Kristof 1960, p. 21 fn. 14). Whittlesey (1943) wrote that geopolitics 'invariably turns out to be a design for the practice of American power politics'. Doubtless the rapid elevation of the United States to a position of supreme power had much to do with the entrenchment of geopolitics there.

In Britain, in sharp contrast, there was no explosion of geopolitical writing, and Weigert (1974, p. 177) refers to those 'especially in Britain' who minimize the influence of Mackinder, and argue 'that the West would have reacted in much the same way regardless of Mackinder's writings'. Such a view is refuted by the wording of a memorandum which the British Foreign Secretary, Ernest Bevin, placed before the Cabinet on 3 March 1948. This proves that Mackinder's influence had reached the highest level, even in Britain. For in it he stated that the USSR

is actively preparing to extend its hold over the remaining part of continental Europe and, subsequently over the Middle East and no doubt the bulk of the Far East as well. In other words, physical control of the whole World Island is what the Politburo is aiming at—no less a thing than that.
(CAB. 129/25, 1948, p. 48)

The post-war course of events will next be surveyed within the framework of Mackinder's ideas, a course of events which these ideas played their part in determining. This will be done by considering five geopolitical or geostrategic aspects of the post-war world: the land-power–sea-power relationship; the American 'containment' policy—and the Soviet reaction to it; the competition for the allegiance of the marginal lands; Middle Eastern instability and the oil crisis; and finally, the significance of China.

Mackinder had argued that, once the world had become a closed political system, the ultimate geographical reality would make itself felt. This was the massing of most of the land surface of the globe in a 'World Island' with continental and insular satellites out in the surrounding oceans. Sea power based in this outer area would guarantee access to and control of the marginal lands of the World Island, until the Heartland was developed to such a degree that its strategic position could be used to bring pressure upon the margins from the inside. Railways and other means of land transport would aid such development. Land power could defeat sea power in two ways: by depriving it of its ports and bases by landward attack, or by coming on to the seas with an invincible navy. He did not predict victory for either side.[13] In the Pre-Columbian age land power had been strong and mobile, yet Western Europe survived. The Post-Columbian age would see the resurgence of Eurasian land power. But the West could still survive, if it remained watchful and resourceful.

It was along such lines as these that history had moved. The 1939-45 war had transformed the international situation: Europe ceased to contain great imperial powers of the first rank and was partitioned between the spheres of influence of the two extra-European states which had invaded it from either side, one by land and one by sea. Geostrategy was now global instead of continental, since each superpower owed its influence to a global rather than a continental situation. The continental opposition between Britain and Germany had given way to the global confrontation of the United States, the largest and most powerful of the 'island' states of the 'outer crescent', with the Soviet Union, the first power to command—with unsurpassed military strength—the Heartland of the World Island. Mackinder's land–sea dichotomy emerged not only unscathed but reinforced:[14] 'The pattern of political power after the Second World War seems to bear out Mackinder's prophecy. A Russian state of continental proportions stands in opposition to the

[13] M.'s stand is thus more flexible and adaptable to changed circumstances than Ratzel's, which predicted ultimate victory for land power, or Mahan's, which was confident of the triumph of sea power (Alexander 1957, pp. 8–9).

[14] The existence of the land-sea/centre-periphery dichotomy is often concealed by misuse of words. Thus 'East-West rivalry' is a term commonly met, where West may include Japan, Taiwan, South Korea, Singapore, Thailand, and possibly even China!

Western sea powers who in turn try to keep Russia out of the oceanic borderlands' (Cochran 1972, p. 31). Who better able to confirm this than President Nixon? His use of the word 'heartland' is further proof of the continued force of Mackinder's ideas in the formation of American attitudes:

The United States is an 'island' country and therefore a sea power; the Soviet Union situated in the center of the Eurasian heartland, is basically a land power. As a land power, the U.S.S.R. can reasonably be expected to maintain superior ground forces along its long borders with potential adversaries. As an island sea power, dependent on ocean-going commerce and on sea lines of communication with our allies, the United States must insist on decisive superiority on the waterways of the world. (Nixon 1980, p. 193)

In East Germany Heyden (1958, p. 235) quotes Schmitt (1955) as saying that the tensions of today's *Welt-Dualismus* cannot be properly understood without Mackinder's 'global reality'—the opposition between the continental and the maritime worlds.

Cohen (1963, pp. 64-5) gives a modern form to Mackinder's hypothesis:

There are, strictly speaking, only two geostrategic regions today:
1) The Trade-Dependent Maritime World, and 2) The Eurasian Continental World.
The core of the Trade-Dependent Maritime World is the Maritime Ring of the United States; that of the Eurasian Continental World is the Russian Industrialized Triangle.
The United States is thrusting its development energies toward its coastal rims, intensifying connections with other parts of the Maritime World. The Soviet Union's development thrust is landward, with its major direction into the Eurasian Heartland.

The United States is heavily dependent upon sea communications for raw materials from the marginal lands. Since 1950 its ocean-borne trade has risen by over five times, while its domestic freight has only doubled. Thirty-one sea routes have been designated 'essential' by the United States government and are subject to special protective legislation (EUSFTR 1969). Therefore America 'must keep the freedom of the seas in order that, in Mackinder's terms, the vast population of the Inner Crescent may be free to interact economically with the United States' (Whebell 1970, p. 633). When the Heartland of the World

Island was a barbarous void, such economic organization or exploitation of an accessible maritime world under the protection of invincible naval power was the key to undisputed world empire, and Sir Walter Raleigh's dictum (qu. in Malin 1964): 'whosoever commands the trade of the world commands the riches of the world and consequently the world itself' held true.[15] But many of America's suppliers of vital material have now to take account of Soviet land power to their rear.

Systematic development of the Soviet Heartland began in 1928 with the first five-year plan and has continued ever since; even the 1941–5 war, which devastated western Russia, led to accelerated activity in the safer lands to the east. Gradually the immense resources of Siberia and Central Asia were harnessed to an expanding industrial base, upon which military power has been erected. Soon the USSR was mining more coal and more iron ore than USA; in 1964 it passed America in the production of cement, in 1971 of steel, and in 1974 of petroleum. The extensive building of railways, roads, airports, pipelines, and electricity transmission lines has also greatly increased the Heartland's economic potential and strategic importance. Its compact and continuous territory is strengthened by internal lines of communication; military forces may be moved swiftly to points on the Rimland, comparing favourably with the slow, open, and exposed delivery of power by sea. The whole is organized in one single and unified political system, contrasting with the loose and discrete nature of maritime and marginal associations of states. Contiguous territories, even when nationally or ethnically diverse, are more easily welded together than scattered rimland dependencies linked only by marine communication.

A fact to be considered in appraising the validity of Mackinder's theory, is that the development of the Heartland is by no means complete. A frontier is still being pushed eastwards, uncovering vast new resources, but requiring immense quantities of scarce capital and rare skills. Nor is the internal trans-

---

[15] Spykman (1944, p. 44) was preferring Raleigh's view when he argued that the Rimland, because of its greater development, resources, accumulated wealth and concentrated population, was the key to world power. He reversed M.'s warning to read:

Who controls the Rimland rules Eurasia;
Who rules Eurasia controls the destinies of the World.

portation network yet adequate, and even if it were a further stage is necessary before penetration and control of the Rimland can be achieved—the building of transport links with the margins: 'It is quite conceivable', writes Meinig (1956, p. 567),

that the heartland could become once more the nexus of trade routes with and among the rimland regions, and that the Soviet Union could gradually build a pattern of economic interdependence with all her bordering nations. In this manner, without the use of military force or political penetration, she could achieve a measure of domination over most of Eurasia . . . It would mark, in short, the capture of the rimland and its complete reorientation from an outward maritime zone to an inward continental periphery.

Noteworthy in this respect are the growing use of the Trans-Siberian railway for Euro-Japanese trade, and the gas pipelines to eastern Europe, Austria, Italy, and West Germany. To the growing advantages of land power must be added what some see as a weakening of surface naval power; thus Cohen (1971, pp. 330–4) does not think surface vessels, commercial or naval, can survive attack from modern submarines.

Although the Heartland has immense resources, it has powerful 'anti-resources' which slow down its development. The northerly latitudes and interior continental position cause long and severe winters, with high heating and lighting costs, while the harsh conditions lower labour productivity; snow and ice complicate transport. Agriculture is confined to a perilously short season. The harsh and costly physical conditions of the Soviet realm impose a lower standard of living and a harder life upon its peoples compared with more benign lands. This, by making for political instability, could undermine the highly centralized power upon which the advantages of continental position largely depend. The bureaucratic centralization necessary for the administration of a great land empire tends to stifle the initiative and enterprise essential for wealth creation. Some sectors of the economy are notoriously backward technologically. The country is unable to support the huge demands for military expenditure which her protection and superpower position require without exacting further sacrifices from her

---

[16] This point was made by Chancellor Schmidt of West Germany in an interview broadcast on BBC television on 1 Dec. 1980.

peoples.[16] The rapid increase of her Asian population, which will soon reduce the Slavic element to a minority, may also threaten stability.

The alternative threat to that of land power denying sea power its bases by seizing them from the rear, was for it to build its own navy and challenge the sea power on the oceans. Mackinder had insisted that full development of the industrial base and the securing of an outlet to the open sea should precede any such challenge, but the USSR has gone ahead without either. Mackinder would have recalled his reference (1919, pp. 198-9) to the 'short cut' by which Germany had hoped to defeat British sea power by challenging it directly on the seas instead of concentrating first on mastery of the Heartland.

Russia's decision to build up her naval strength has been seen as a reaction to her impotence in the face of the American blockade of Cuba, and also as widening the range of conventional alternatives to the nuclear option. She has always yearned for the free access to the ocean enjoyed by other great nations.[17] A thousand years of Russian history can be interpreted as that of a land-locked state struggling to break out from claustrophobic isolation. Where she has succeeded in reaching seas they have been but ice-impeded antechambers to the open ocean, entered and left only on the sufferance of the states controlling the straits. Admiral Mahan (1900, p. 56) said that Russia's interests 'may be condensed into access to the sea as extensive and free as possible'. The autarkic policy rigorously pursued throughout the Soviet period has lessened the commercial need for Soviet sea power, and defensive and strategic motives must be uppermost. The fact remains that a large Soviet navy on the oceans, which cannot enter or leave its home seas except through channels dominated by hostile bases, is a defiance of geography. For not only do 'her ships still have no clear and easy access to the high seas', but 'her surface and sub-surface fleets must move over tremendous distances around the "rim-lands" . . . past coasts held by other powers', and 'her fleets must be distant, scattered and divided, with no easy means of shifting vessels from sea to sea or of reinforcing one fleet with another'

---

[17] This has been questioned (e.g. by Morrison 1952, Meinig 1956), but the evidence in support is formidable, the arguments against refutable.

(Baldwin 1955, p. 59).[18] The Soviet navy has adapted itself technically to geographical constraints: it

does not in fact need much shore-based support to maintain a forward presence. By providing logistic support at sea, by careful servicing of equipment and by maintaining remarkably low operating tempos, the needs of deployed combatants for shore-based support have been kept to a minimum. This was demonstrated in 1977, during the Ogaden war. (IISS 1980, p. 23)

The 1979 strength of the US Navy was 524,200 personnel, 180 major combat vessels, and 80 attack submarines, 73 of them nuclear-powered; and of the Soviet Navy, 433,000 personnel, 275 major combat vessels, and 179 attack submarines, 41 of which were nuclear-powered. But the United States, which has to rely upon sea power to carry its air power to critical points on the Rimland, has 13 aircraft carriers of about 90,000 tons each, 3 of them nuclear powered. The USSR did not begin to build carriers until the 1970s, and in 1979 had two 43,000 ton vessels (IISS 1979). An expert assessment (IISS 1980, p. 24) states that the Soviet navy 'has vastly increased its capacity for the forward projection of power, but considerable constraints of geography and operational capability still limit its overall flexibility'; and though now 'a powerful force in absolute terms it does not yet match the West's greatly superior capacity for operating in distant waters'.

The functions of the two navies are quite different. The purpose of the US fleet is to protect American sea-borne trade, to transport American airpower to Rimland crisis points, and to maintain command of the seas so that supplies too bulky to move by air can be safely ferried thither. The Soviet navy's job in war time would be to destroy American commerce at sea, to cut America's links with her Rimland allies and dependencies, and to defend from seaborne attack her own allies and dependencies. A function common to both fleets is to reassure friends and impress neutrals by 'showing the flag', and also to carry submarine-borne nuclear weapons.

[18] General Hackett (1978, p. 91), looking forward to 1985, writes, 'The attempt to turn the Eurasian landmass into a base for world-wide naval operations had suffered the inescapable setbacks of geography and temperament.'

The policy of containment or encirclement of the USSR was evolved as a direct response to the threat seen to arise from Soviet domination of the Heartland. Cohen (1963, p. 40) asserted that 'most Western strategists continue to view the world as initially described by Mackinder'; Hooson (1964, p. 117) saw Mackinder's ghost stalking 'the corridors of the Pentagon'; and according to Walters (1974, p. 22) 'the Heartland theory stands as the first premise in Western military thought'. Eastern bloc writers also ascribe the American policy of encircling the Soviet Union with hostile groupings to the doctrines of Mackinder (Schöller 1959, p. 95; Semjonov 1955, p. 177).

The containment policy, although anticipated by Spykman, was first formulated by Kennan,[19] early in 1947: 'the main element of any United States policy toward the Soviet Union must be that of a long-term patient but firm and vigilant containment of Russian expansive tendencies'. Such a policy would be 'designed to confront the Russians with unalterable counter force at every point where they show signs of encroaching upon the interests of a peaceful and stable world' (Kennan 1947, p. 575, 581).[20] Kennan denied that his statement had anything to do with Mackinder, but as Fisher (1971, p. 297) observes, 'anyone familiar with the writings of either Mackinder or Spykman must inevitably have been reminded by these remarks of the geopolitical concept of an expansionist Heartland power probing the weak spots of the surrounding Rimland'. Walters (1974, p. 178) quotes this passage from Kennan: 'our problem is to prevent the gathering together of the military–industrial potential of the entire Eurasian land mass under a single power threatening the interests of the insular and mainland portions of the globe', and comments, with reason, that these words could have been taken 'straight out of Mackinder's Heartland theory'. He notes that Kennan admitted to having been greatly influenced by Earle's *Makers of Modern Strategy* which owed much to Mackinder.

[19] George Kennan (1904–   ), American historian and US State Department authority on foreign affairs.

[20] It became, in effect, the official policy of the USA—with the enunciation of the Truman doctrine on 12 March 1947. The simultaneous Marshall plan bound the recipient states to American policy in return for aid, and sustained the activity of the American economy.

Not only those who formulated policy but also those whose job it was to carry it out showed familiarity with Mackinder's doctrine; in 1951, for instance, the Chairman of the American Joint Chiefs of Staff, General Bradley, said that 'If the Soviet Union ever controls the Eurasian land mass, then the Soviet satellite imperialism may have the broad base upon which to build the military power to rule the world' (qu. in Walters 1974, pp. 23–4).

Containment of the Heartland power was successfully applied in the immediate post-war years to Persia, Greece, Turkey, and Malaya, although it had to concede Soviet domination in eastern Europe. Chambers (1963, p. 685) comments: 'It is interesting to note that while the greater part of the Intermediate Europe approachable by land passed under Soviet domination, those areas escaped—notably Yugoslavia and the Greek peninsula—that could be succoured from the sea.' The containment policy found expression in the NATO, CENTO, and SEATO alliances, and in many unilateral pacts with Rimland states. Normally the stationing of American armed forces and the building of American military bases followed, thus creating 'the American perimeter of defense'. The policy led to the forced restitution of the *status quo* in Korea by war (1950–2). It lay behind the rearmament of Germany and Japan. It culminated in the Vietnamese war (1965–73), the long-drawn-out agony of which brought it into discredit: 'The end of the global policy of containment came with Vietnam', according to a high Pentagon official, who explained: 'The public and Congress got fed up with the war; the trouble is they got fed up with the policy too' (*Newsweek*, 21 Jan. 1980, p. 23) Geopolitics went out of fashion. So that, whereas 'Kennedy and Nixon were used to thinking and talking geopolitically', Carter formed his world view 'when geopolitics was in some disrepute ... and came to the presidency thinking not about the power of armies and political systems, but about the power of moral principles' (*Time*, 21 Jan. 1980, p. 14). The Soviet intervention in Afghanistan revived the policy of containment and the interest in geopolitics. 'Back to Maps' was *Time*'s headline, and the weekly remarked that the influential Brzezinski[21] was a 'well-established, if somewhat controversial geostrategist' (21 Jan. 1980,

[21] National Security Adviser to President Carter.

p. 14). Reagan immediately and vigorously reasserted the containment policy.

The policy—and by implication the Heartland theory from which it derives—has attracted much criticism. The threat from the Heartland is said to have been greatly exaggerated, and the Cold War therefore unnecessary. Several factors had reinforced Mackinder's warnings in the American mind—the German failure to conquer the Heartland power, the shutting out of the 'free world' by the 'iron curtain', the emotional hold of anti-communism, and the establishment of Communist governments in Eastern Europe and China. After the signing of the Sino-Soviet treaty of alliance (1950), 'the Mackinder nightmare' assumed the 'most menacing of all possible shapes' (Fisher 1965, p. 298). An imminent attack on western Europe was feared. In point of fact the Soviet Union presented no such threat; it had suffered twenty to thirty million deaths in a war that had devastated its most productive regions, and it needed all its available manpower and capital resources for reconstruction; that accomplished, any diversion of resources into military adventures could only be at the expense of its economic development, an essential prerequisite if it was ultimately to fulfil the role Mackinder had predicted. Any Soviet aggression could have been immediately halted by use of the atom bomb, which the USSR did not have until 1949. In so far as a threat lay in Soviet military power, it could be argued that it was a response to rather than the cause of American policy. The 'free world' had 'become the victim of a myth ... the myth that stems from Mackinder's earlier writings' (Cohen 1963, p. 58).

De Gaulle tried to convince Dulles in 1958 that there was no real Soviet threat to Europe. Communism only flourished in bad economic conditions, but the European countries were now fully recovered and prospering. 'As for attempting to impose by force the totalitarian yoke on three hundred million recalcitrant foreigners, what would be the point of trying, since the Soviets have such difficulty in doing so with a third as many satellite subjects.' Because of Chinese ambitions, 'it was towards Asia, rather than to Europe that they would turn their attention, provided the West did not threaten them' (de Gaulle 1970, p. 213).

The containment policy has also been criticized for its inflexibility, automatically demanding American intervention at any point on the circumference of the World Island where the Soviets might intervene or appear to gain influence; and as involving the 'domino' theory,[22] in its presupposition that any one accessible marginal state should be supported lest in its fall its neighbours should be toppled, and so on. As a result 'those who have accepted the Heartland–Rimland thesis' have 'driven themselves into a frenzy of effort to plug all possible leaks in the Rimland dyke, regardless of the risks involved ... or the chances of success' (Cohen 1963, p. 59). Or as Walters (1974, p. 191) writes: any 'dictator who wanted funds from the U.S. treasury could receive them by aping the true anti-communist faith'.

Finally there is the moral objection. This was put, long ago, by Mahan (1900, p. 45), and applies perhaps to most geopolitical arguments:

It is a mistake, and a deplorable mistake, when recognizing conditions of conflicting interests ... to see in them only grounds for opposition and hostility. States that are more fortunate in the extent of their sea board, and in physical conditions which facilitate the circulation of the life-blood of trade throughout their organization, owe at the least candour, if not sympathy to the fetters under which Russia labours in her narrow sea-front, in her vast and difficult interior, and in a climate of extreme rigor.

Containment is the peripheral sea power's name for what in the central land power is called encirclement. And encirclement is intended to prevent aggression, actual or potential. Both encirclement and aggression are bred of the fear which arises from the geographical–geometrical opposition of land and sea, centre and circumference. The histories of most European nations abound in attempts to organize alliances to resist the unifying policy of a powerful central region; likewise in Europe peripheral alliances on a continental scale were organized against France and then Germany. Once a strong land power

---

[22] M. (1934, p. 521) had stated the 'domino' theory but he used ninepins! 'The wider defence of India begins in France and ends in Japan ... right round the world ... there went a chain of Powers like a row of ninepins—knock down one and you knock the next and the next.' Perhaps therefore, Fryer (1974, p. 481) was not wholly correct in his well-intentioned defence of M. from Bunge's accusation of responsibility for the domino theory (though probably correct in describing M. as a better geographer than Bunge).

controlled the central part or Heartland of the World Island, the dichotomy had reached a global stage. Although tension would have developed in any case, Mackinder's contribution was to forewarn and explain what was happening, and alert the world to a new situation. As a result the United States 'adopted a global policy of defence, thus repudiating conflicting defense theories which were either continental or Western Hemisphere in character' (Weigert *et al.* 1957, p. 279).

It is difficult to apportion blame or distinguish cause and effect in the encirclement–aggression situation. The policy of containment was a reaction to Soviet activity in eastern Europe, Greece, Turkey, and elsewhere in the immediate post-war years, but this activity may have been the natural defensive reaction of a state that had just suffered a devastating invasion. The further probing at weak or unstable spots around the Rimland may well have been a riposte to the system of hostile alliances and the ring of military bases by which the Heartland state was surrounded.[23] Soviet and East European writers blame Mackinder for this policy of encirclement: 'the encirclement of the USSR by means of a system of hostile alliances and strategic bases rests upon the English geographer Mackinder's doctrine of "the Heartland of the earth and its marginal regions"' (Schöller 1959, p. 95). 'The ring of American steel around Russia' is the graphic title of a feature in the *Guardian* (14 March 1977). From the Soviet point of view, the adjacent territories which it controls are a defensive shield or 'strategic periphery': 'emphasis on the strategic periphery was a reflection of renewed fears of encirclement' (IISS 1979).

This open hostility between the two superpowers, expressed in intrigue and counter-intrigue in the less stable countries of the Rimland, and in an arms race of exorbitant cost, was known as the Cold War, a conflict in which the Heartland theory was obviously a factor. During the Khrushchev period (1955–64) there was a call from the Russian side for 'peaceful co-existence', and under Presidents Nixon and Ford (1969–76) the Cold War gave way to relaxation of tension or *détente*. The SALT I treaty was agreed and ratified. Acts of provocation declined,

---

[23] 'Well, he started it, you know,' says Ermyntrude of a war begun by the Inca of Perusalem (the Kaiser?) in Shaw's play of that name, but the Inca replies, 'Madam be just. When the hunters surround the lion the lion will spring.'

consultation and co-operation increased, and a commercial relationship based on the exchange of minerals for grain and advanced technology was begun. Plans for Western participation in Siberian devlopment were mooted. Soviet trade with America, negligible in the 1950s and 1960s, jumped from 183.6 million rubles in 1971 to a peak of 2,205.5 million rubles in 1976 (Vnesh. Torg. 1971, 1976). With increased Soviet and Cuban activity in Africa, and with Carter's emphasis on human rights in the USSR, *détente* declined. His adviser Brzezinski followed an avowed anti-Soviet policy. The SALT II treaty, though signed in Vienna (1979), was not ratified by the US Senate. Polish-born Brzezinski believed in a peripheral world organized by the United States in 'regional clusters'. These clusters were to be formed round Rimland states specially selected for their economic potential and military strength, e.g. Mexico, Brazil, Nigeria, India, and 'very much' China. He was not prepared to concede parity to the Soviet Union but insisted that the United States must 'maintain a military posture second to none' (*Fortune*, 23 April 1979, pp. 71–5). Reagan proclaimed a similar policy.

Although the Soviet intervention in Afghanistan signalled the resumption of the Cold War and brought geopolitics, the Heartland theory, and the containment policy to the fore again, informed American opinion acknowledged that *détente* was already a lost cause: 'one reason for the Soviet incursion was Moscow's belief that détente was already moribund' (*Fortune*, 25 Feb. 1980).

Because of the frozen Arctic wastes that border the northern coastline of the USSR, Mackinder regarded the World Island as essentially the World Promontory, throwing out into the ocean the great peninsulas of Europe, Africa, Arabia, India, and Indo-China. The post-war period can be seen in his terms as a competition between the Heartland power, ensconced within the Promontory, and the leading power of the Outer Crescent, for the allegiance of the Inner Crescent—Spykman's Rimland (Cohen 1963, p. 48; Whebell 1970, p. 633). The need of the United States to control those areas is the more compelling, because of her dependence on them for minerals, markets, and bases. In 1954 a special presidential commission had reported that the United States could no longer depend for sustained growth

on the resources and markets of its own territories, but must, for its economic well-being, become involved increasingly with distant resources and markets. This has proved particularly true of investments, as more and more American firms are seeking overseas outlets for their retained profits. (Whebell 1970, p. 634)

She is now wholly or almost wholly dependent on overseas countries for asbestos, bauxite, chromite, cobalt, graphite, gold, lead, manganese, mercury, nickel, tin, and zinc;[24] she is heavily dependent on imports of copper, iron, petroleum, and natural gas. For these widening and deepening deficiencies she draws upon almost seventy different countries, in most of which the prospecting, mining, and transport is carried out by American companies. This dependence on foreign states for minerals and fuels grows ever more serious. And although a certain proportion comes overland from Mexico and Canada, an ever increasing volume is sea-borne.

The United States could take an isolated stance when her resources were relatively abundant and complete, when her industrial and social needs were relatively limited and simple, and when the Royal Navy held the seas. Today she has little choice but to organize and protect, if not to exploit and dominate the accessible maritime world; she must therefore be to some degree an imperialist power. She must have guaranteed access to the primary produce and to the markets of the periphery of the World Island. She also draws upon that periphery for much of the brain power upon which her advanced technology depends.[25] Her policy of encirclement of the Soviet Union is possible only because she has been allowed to maintain bases and station forces in Rimland states. In return she contributes vast sums in military and economic aid. Many Rimland nations are penetrated by her powerful multinational corpora-

[24] and many others; those named are listed by the US Defense Production Act as 'strategical and critical materials' and stockpiled.
[25] Brains are attracted to America by scholarships, fellowships, and grants. The beneficiaries, instead of returning to their homelands with the benefits of the training they have received, often decide to remain in the US.

tions which play an influential role in their economic, social, and political life.

For Fairgrieve (1915, p. 333) the Rimland was, because of its intermediate position, the 'crush zone', while to Cohen (1968, p. 67) it was a 'shatter belt' occupied by states 'caught between the conflicting interests of the great powers'. Meinig (1956) stressed the importance of not allowing a single generalizing term such as Rimland to disguise the manifold differences among the marginal states: it is a discrete and discontinuous ring of countries with widely differing histories and cultures, economies and political systems; this complexity makes the American task of attempting to unify it very difficult. Many Rimland states are more moved by feuds with their neighbours than by fear of the Heartland power, as tensions between Greece and Turkey, India and Pakistan, Iran and Iraq, Israel and Syria, etc. testify. Pakistan probably joined the SEATO and CENTO groupings more to strengthen herself against India than from fear of the Soviet Union (Fisher 1971, p. 302). American support of Pakistan in 1965 alienated India and brought that country close to the Soviet Union. In the Afghanistan crisis of 1980 Mrs Ghandi condemned the United States 'for provoking trouble in the area and pushing the Soviet Union into its invasion'; she also rejected a proposal for a South Asia Security Plan—one of Brzezinski's 'regional clusters' (*World Business Weekly*, 16 June 1980, p. 21).

Where economic development and foreign influence have unsettled traditional society, political instability gives an opportunity for the Heartland power to undermine American-sponsored rulers, although the opposite is also true. Much destabilization arose from the withdrawal of European control: 'around the maritime margin of Asia there is no longer a strong structure of British, Dutch, French and Japanese imperial power' (Latimore 1953). Meinig (1956, p. 569) lamented that the Americans 'are in the unenviable situation of being the successor alien power seeking to hold on to the steadily shrinking maritime rimland. Already we must rest principally upon the insular fringe—Japan, Okinawa, Formosa, the Philippines.' Some countries with pride in a glorious past do not take kindly to imperial patronage: France expelled American troops and withdrew from active participation in NATO in order to assert her national sovereignty. Many states believe it prudent to follow a policy of neutrality between the superpowers.

Another difficulty for the United States is that the national character appears to require a moral stance: 'the outward attitude towards communism and Russia was cloaked in the mantle of a crusade of goodness against evil' (Walters 1974, p. 23). It has been said of the Americans that 'they have gone too far in clothing the skeleton of *Realpolitik* in the robes of saintliness' (Davidson 1979).[26] They pose as the champions of 'freedom', 'democracy', 'decency', and of 'human rights' generally; yet in order to obtain the kind of stability needed for Rimland control the United States supports military dictatorships which suppress human rights with American arms. This not only provides the USSR with powerful propaganda, but develops anti-American feeling in the countries concerned. An interesting aspect of the *détente* period was that the United States gave greater reality to its moral policy: for example, military aid was cut off from Turkey, though a vital Rimland state, because of her action in Cyprus. With the resumption of the Cold War in 1980, however, the supply of arms was renewed, and a military coup, replacing the unruly Turkish democracy, followed hard upon. The first act of this new dictatorship was to abolish the right to strike, the assertion of which the United States was at the same time applauding in Poland. The fall of Batista in Cuba (1958) and of the Shah in Iran (1978) demonstrated the risks in this policy, and led to caution in supporting Zia in Pakistan (1980). 'Too visible a military connection with the West, and in particular the United States, might weaken domestically uncertain regimes, rather than strengthen them' (IISS 1980, p. 9).

The United States finds her strongest allies at both ends of the World Promontory—Western Europe and Japan. Britain has been her most complaisant friend, willingly playing the role of offshore offensive base which Mackinder had long ago forecast for her. Despite the inevitable destruction that this would invite in war time, she accepts what Nixon in 1953 called 'her destiny to be an air-strip for the United States air-forces' (*The*

[26] This does at least give the option of substituting indignation for action, and not only in the US. In Britain Prof. E. G. R. Taylor (1947, p. 292) said, with reference to M., 'We are at the moment witnessing that pressure of the heartland on the periphery of which he spoke. The curious thing to my mind is that our politicians are attempting to counter geographical realities by moral indignation.'

Times, 21 Aug. 1968). France, on the other hand, abandoned this obsequious stance on the coming to power of de Gaulle, who asserted her national dignity and independence. He was not willing to accept Mackinder's role for France—that of bridgehead to the continent for America; nor was he willing to accept Mackinder's—and the Americans'—view of the danger from the Eurasian land mass; he was certainly not willing for France to become part of a 'crush zone' or 'shatter belt'. The USA and the USSR would not attack each other with nuclear weapons except as a last resort, said de Gaulle (1970, p. 213), but what was to stop them dropping their bombs on Europe? Although remaining formally a member of the Atlantic alliance, he withdrew from military participation in NATO, expelled American forces from France, and equipped France with strategic forces under her own sole control (ibid.).

Mackinder recognized that Germany was the key to the Heartland-Oceanic Periphery balance; her alliance with the Heartland power would make for an irresistible combination; her conquest of it would give her world empire. Expanded into *Mitteleuropa* she might be strong enough to achieve this conquest. But the idea of Central Europe had a fatal geographical flaw. It lay athwart the boundary between Maritime Europe, with its oceanic interests, and the Eurasian Heartland, with its continental outlook (Fig. 3). There was thus 'no space for a Central Europe' in Mackinder's concept (Sinnhuber 1954, p. 16).[27] The true German dualism was not so much between a Prussia expanded along the North European Plain in conflict with the Slavs and an Austria developed along the Danube as a bulwark against the Turks. It was between the commercially—and

---

[27] M.'s disciple, Fairgrieve (1915, pp. 331-2) described Central Europe thus: 'Central Europe, unorganized and broken into small and antagonistic communities, essentially belongs to the crush zone, but organized and powerful, is in a very different position. In touch with the sea and tempted on to the ocean Germany is one of the sea powers, while her situation on the western and most populous margin of the great heartland makes her, at any rate, a possible centre from which that heartland might be organized.'

Haushofer (1936, pp. 12-13) attributed the first modern delineation of *Mitteleuropa* to M. because he asked Partsch to write a book on such a region for his 'Regions of the World' series. A German-dominated area in central Europe was then a fact, even though it lay astride a fundamental geographical divide. That this divide ultimately triumphed and produced two Germanies supports M.'s belief in the *eventual* likelihood of the geographical factor asserting itself.

For more on Central Europe, see Meyer (1946).

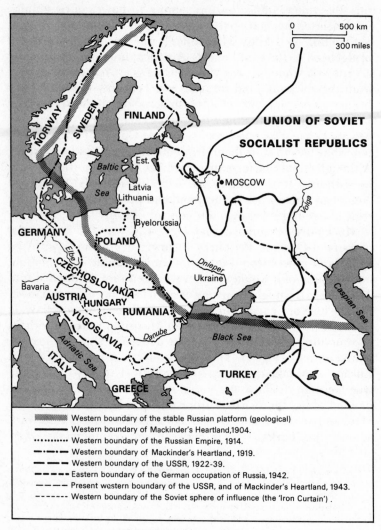

Fɪɢ. 3. Some boundaries in Eastern Europe

industrially-minded west and the territorially-motivated east; the divergent interests of the two had caused Germany to fight on two fronts and to lose the 1914-18 war. The partition of Germany into two states after the 1939-45 war, one within the Eurasian orbit, the other within the Atlantic sphere, was a natural consequence of defeat: 'Mackinder's boundary that divided the Heartland from Maritime Europe was given political status shortly after World War II' (Cohen 1963, p. 81).

West Germany shows some of the dualism that marked the policies of the old Germany. As she became strong enough to assert a degree of independence from America, she developed her own *Ostpolitik*, supporting *détente*, and forging close economic links with the East. She has become Russia's leading capitalist trading partner, supplying technologically-advanced equipment in return for natural gas and other minerals. The central political problem of the Federal Republic is to reconcile the *Ostpolitik* with her position in the Atlantic alliance (Kaiser 1979). It is made easier, however, by the pursuit of a similar policy by France. Their economic co-operation with the Soviet Union lessens the impact of American high-technology embargoes.

The Heartland power, because of its economic self-sufficiency, based upon an abundant and almost complete range of mineral wealth, does not need the Rimland states for exploitation and trade in the same way as the United States. From its point of view, a benevolent neutrality, such as Finland and India display, is ideal, for this prevents the United States from using their territories as part of its 'perimeter of defense'. It is infinitely preferable to incurring the cost and unpopularity of the relationship which it has perforce to thrust upon the countries of eastern Europe and Afghanistan for strategic reasons.

Each side has gains and losses to chalk up in the Rimland stakes. The greatest gain of all was the accession to the Communists of China in 1949, rounding off their domination of the Heartland and at the same time adding the warm water front that Mackinder feared; but the transformation of China from friend and ally into a virulent and vituperative foe by the refusal of nuclear technology (1959) was a catastrophic loss to the Soviets, even though the United States was to look this gift horse in the mouth for nearly twenty years. Other swings of fortune are relatively insignificant, though important in themselves, e.g. the Soviet gain of Cuba in 1959 which proved more lasting than friendship with Egypt, begun in the Suez crisis of 1956, but lost to America twenty years later. Africa has seen many such vacillations.

Mackinder considered the Middle East—and Suez in particular—the most vital part of the whole 'Inner Crescent', and so it has turned out to be today; but not so much for the reasons he envisaged—the crossroads of three continents, as because of its vast petroleum reserves. Their strategic importance is heightened by the United States now having to import half the oil she uses. In 1974 the Soviet Union displaced America as the world's foremost oil-producing country; however, the American CIA has predicted that by the mid-1980s Soviet production will be falling off, and that the USSR will then turn her attention to the Middle East. If this should prove to be so, here will be a real and practical test of sea power versus land power, and so of the Heartland theory. An American observer (Meyer 1980, p. 88) believes that the Soviet Union is now well-placed to obtain Middle-Eastern oil 'without sending the Soviet army too much further than it has already gone':

As the Mafia godfather in any U.S. city well knows, when the threat of force is credible, the use of force is rarely necessary. This axiom is especially valid when those who will be threatened have a shaky grip on their own domains. And, unfortunately, the one characteristic common to most oil-exporting nations is political instability. It should be possible for the Russians to use this instability as a lever with which to extract—to extort that is—as much oil as they might need without triggering a war.

Land power could, in any case, act with elements of surprise and speed which sea power could not easily match. A coming Soviet shortage of oil is, however, by no means certain, and this is not the first time that it has been predicted and has failed to materialize.

For the United States there are two strategic problems: the protection of the petroleum source and the guarding of the supply routes. Had the oil for western Europe and America continued to pass through Suez the canal would have retained the importance that Mackinder attributed to it. With the use of giant tankers unable to pass through the canal, however, it is control of the Gulf of Oman, the Arabian Sea, and the Indian Ocean that now matters. No longer does the maritime power hold these seas indisputably as in the period of British supremacy; naval facilities around their shores are enjoyed by the USA and the USSR, both of which maintain naval forces in the Indian Ocean. But the large American base on Diego Garcia, along with the proffered Kenyan and Somalian facilities, should enable the United States to command the Indian Ocean. The relatively modest Soviet naval presence seems mainly concerned to 'show the flag', and has been weakened by the loss of use of the Somalian port of Berbera; it has no permanent naval base to compare with Diego Garcia. After the intervention in Afghanistan, US naval forces in the Indian Ocean were increased to form a virtual 'fifth fleet'. But it remains doubtful whether oil tankers could successfully make their way to America in war time in the face of submarine and air attack.

To guarantee the source of supply means the ability to preserve the oil fields for Western use. After the Afghan incident Carter declared that the United States would regard 'an attempt by any outside force to gain control of the Persian Gulf region' as an 'assault on its vital interests', and that 'such an assault will be repelled by any means necessary, including military force'. America has allies in the region prepared to offer base facilities, notably Israel, Egypt, and strategically-placed Oman; she already has the air and sea bases of Bahrain. But most Arab rulers would be chary of openly supporting America, the patron of Israel, and, 'Compromise over the Palestinian issue would do more to strengthen Gulf stability than even the most effective and credible display of military force ...' (IISS 1980, p. 10). An Arab ambassador to Washington is quoted as saying, 'if only the U.S. used its influence and leverage with Israel to solve the Palestinian problem, you Americans would be welcome everywhere' (*Fortune*, 25 Feb. 1980).

The Soviet incursion into Afghanistan brought the land power closer to the oil fields and within fighter-aircraft range of the Arabian Sea. This could be viewed as a defensive move to preserve Soviet influence in a border state that had already entered the Communist orbit in 1978, or as an expansionist move intended to further designs on the oil fields. For the latter purpose direct intervention in Iran would have been more advantageous, although, of course, more perilous. As Mahan (1900, pp. 56–7) remarked eighty years ago, 'progress through Persia would not only approach the gulf, but if successful would turn—would outflank—the mountains of Afghanistan, avoiding the difficulties presented by the severe features of that country and by the character of its inhabitants'. Iran is in revolutionary chaos and Pakistan held tenuously together by a military regime. Saudi Arabia's position is crucial, and notwithstanding her anti-communism and sympathies for the West, she might consider it prudent to come to terms with the land power. She had

already been worried by U.S. inability or unwillingness to prevent Somalia's defeat in the war with Ethiopia and her Cuban and Soviet allies, and by the establishment in 1978 of a Marxist, pro-Soviet regime in Afghanistan. Now, it seemed to her, Washington had failed two more crucial tests: it had been unable to secure an acceptable Israeli-Arab settlement, and it could not maintain a friendly regime in power in Iran. (IISS 1980, p. 26)

The national aspirations of the Kurds who desire to see a Kurdistan built from the lands they inhabit in Turkey, Iran, Syria, and Iraq, is another disturbing factor: these lands adjoin the Soviet Union and Soviet support for their cause would give her pretext for intervention in the region (Whebell 1970, p. 634).

Perhaps the greatest test of the Heartland theory is the emergence of China as an independent force. Is China a Heartland state? Mackinder saw her as part of his 'inner or marginal crescent', i.e. as part of Spykman's Rimland. Seen on a political map, the USSR and China seem to share the Heartland between them. But maps of population and development show that China proper is maritime rather than continental and, therefore, part of the world periphery. China's western continental areas are empty, except where they border upon developing Soviet regions. Here the peoples are non-Chinese and have more in common with those across the border in the USSR. Many of them do not take kindly to Chinese rule. The successful

Communist movement which in 1949 broke China's close as-
sociation with the United States and the maritime world, allying
her with Russia for a decade, led some to take a contrary view.
Thus Cohen (1968, p. 68), after stating that the Maritime
Geostrategic Region is formed binodally around the United
States and Western Europe, adds, 'the Continental Geostrategic
Region also has two nodes, the Soviet Industrial Triangle and
North China'. Many Anglo-American political geographers
thought the Sino-Soviet alliance had proved Mackinder wrong
(Hall 1955, Weigert *et al.* 1957, Jackson 1962, Cohen 1963).
Jackson (p. 12) added that China 'will not be in a position to
challenge Soviet leadership or to carry out an independent state
policy for many decades to come'. In fact, within a single
decade, China had broken away to adopt a policy of unbridled
hostility to Russia, as Kennan had said she would. The split was
occasioned by China's attitude to nuclear war, as expressed by
Mao to Khrushchev in 1957, which appears to have shocked
and alarmed the Russians; it decided them to deny China's
request (1959) for assistance in making her own nuclear
weapons (Fisher 1971, p. 305). The historical background of
Russian imperialism towards China, the fact that the Soviet
Union held territory that had once been Chinese, and the
resentment of a proud people at a position of dependency, were
also factors in the quarrel.

For over a decade after the Sino-Soviet break the United
States refused to recognize the People's Republic as the legitimate China, a policy born of disappointment at losing the
friendship of a country she had done so much for during and
after the war, and of bitterness engendered by the Korean
conflict. Not until the early 1970s did Nixon and Kissinger
explore the possibility of *détente* with China, and not until the end
of the decade did Carter and Brzezinski consider playing 'the
China card' against the Soviet Union. After the Afghan crisis of
1980 the card was played. Defense Secretary Brown suggested
in Peking that the US and China should seek 'complementary
actions' to counter Soviet expansionism; he announced that
China would be granted 'most favoured nation' status and
provided with some military technology, both denied to the
Soviet Union (*Time*, 20 Jan. 1980). This fateful decision allotted
to a willing China full Rimland status in the hostile encirclement

of the USSR. Vice-Premier Deng Xiaoping used his 1979 American visit to denounce Soviet expansionism, to stress the identity of interest and view between Washington and Peking, and to call publicly for a Sino-American-Japanese alliance (IISS 1980, p. 29). Restrained use of China's hostility to Russia had been proposed by those who regard it as a preferable alternative to all-out containment, e.g. Walters (1974).[28]

Mackinder's Heartland theory warns that *ultimately*, the tenant of the Heartland would be in a strong position to dominate the World Island and therefore the World. But there are three conditions to be fulfilled: one is that this tenant should have sufficiently developed the great resources of Eurasia; another is that he should have full command of the Heartland; and the third is that he should be the unchallengeable holder of the tenancy. At one time Mackinder feared that Germany might meet these conditions, or a Russia in partnership with Germany. If he were alive now, he would probably point out that none of these essentials has yet been met, and that the policy of containment has been wrongly based on the assumption that they have. Despite much progress, the Heartland remains a largely undeveloped region. Unlike the United States, which enjoyed unimpeded freedom from outside interference and an unlimited supply of labour and capital from Europe when it was pushing its frontier westward, the Soviets have had to shoulder an immense defence burden and to rely almost wholly on domestic labour and capital.[29] The arms race has been a potent weapon in delaying the development of the Heartland. With a GNP estimated (IISS 1979a) at only a quarter that of the USA, the USSR supports a defence burden as great or greater. Yet she has to match the armament, not only of America, but of all the hostile encircling groupings and states, including China. In 1979-80 the military expenditure of NATO, Japan, and China alone amounted to 267 billion US dollars, while that of the Warsaw Pact, on the highest (CIA) estimate,

---

[28] Ex-President Nixon writes (1980, p. 135): 'At our U.S.-Soviet summit meetings, Brezhnev repeatedly warned me against the Chinese threat, and described the Chinese leaders as brutal and barbaric in their treatment of their own people; he urged that "we Europeans" should unite to contain the potential great threat from China.'

[29] The 1941-5 war meant a loss of ten years—those of destruction and those of reconstruction.

was 168 billion dollars.[30] Yet NATO expenditure was greatly increased in 1981 on the grounds of excessive Soviet outlay on arms.

As for full command of the Heartland, there is within the region an amalgam of races and nationalities whose loyalty may vary greatly. The development of the Heartland's resources has not gone far enough to enable the great and growing burden of defence to be borne without holding down these peoples' expectations. The non-Slavonic populations are increasing so fast, that Russians now form little over half the total, and by the end of the century will be a shrinking minority.[31] With regard to the third requisite, who is to say that the Russians are unchallengeably the tenants of the Heartland? The last sentence of Mackinder's 1904 paper, 'The Geographical Pivot of History', may yet prove to be the most portentous of all his statements:

Were the Chinese ... organised by the Japanese, to overthrow the Russian Empire and conquer its territory, they might constitute the yellow peril to the world's freedom just because they would add an oceanic frontage to the resources of the great continent, an advantage as yet denied to the Russian tenant of the pivot region.

Japanese relations with China had been damaged by the Japanese invasion and by the anti-capitalist stance of previous Chinese communist administrations, but in 1972 they were 'normalized', and trade between the two began to grow. In February 1978 a bilateral trade agreement paved the way for large-scale commercial exchanges and on 12 August a Friendship Treaty was signed, including an 'anti-hegemonist' clause and therefore 'openly anti-Soviet' (*Soviet News*, 15 Aug. 1978). In 1979 the Japanese undertook the modernization of the Chinese railway system, the first of a series of arrangements for the exchange of Japanese technology for Chinese minerals (*Financial Times*, 8 Feb. 1979). It would have been greatly in the Soviet interest to have forestalled this with their own compre-

---

[30] IISS (1979a). Details are (bn. of dollars): USA 122.7, Canada 3.8, Western Europe in NATO 80.39, Japan 10.08, China *c*.50; USSR *c*.148, Eastern Europe in Warsaw Pact 12.28. Soviet and Chinese defence expenditure cannot be estimated with any reliability; the GNP also cannot be accurately assessed.

[31] General Sir John Hackett believes that 'the Soviet Union and the Warsaw Pact would have fallen apart by the end of the century' (*Sunday Times*, 12 Oct. 1980).

hensive arrangement with Japan, but although there have been some co-operative ventures, a major overall programme was prevented by the dispute over the Kurile Islands; yet while Japan participates in the encirclement of the USSR, that country cannot afford to give them up for strategic reasons. China has meanwhile urged Japan to re-arm against the Soviet Union by doubling its military budget (*Economist*, 10 May 1980). Mackinder's 1904 warning that the Chinese 'organized by the Japanese' might conquer the Heartland, was re-echoed by Nansen (1914, p. 374), Fairgrieve (1915, p. 332), and Chisholm (1919, p. 251). Fairgrieve warned that, 'like Germany, and to an even greater extent than Germany, China is in a position to dominate the heartland with little possibility of interference from others'. Nixon (1980, p. 127) believes that China 'could emerge during the twenty-first century as the strongest power on earth'.

She certainly makes no bones of her bitter anti-Soviet attitude, and does all she can to incite anti-Soviet feeling, not only in Asia, Africa, America, and western Europe, but even in eastern Europe. She lays claim to large areas of Soviet Heartland territory. Russia is disturbed to learn that large sums are to be spent in commemorating Ghengiz Khan as a national hero of Communist China (BBC 1980), for the traumatic Mongol conquest is deeply imbedded in the Russian folk-memory (Stepun 1962). This deep-seated fear of the East was re-awakened in 1957 when the two countries were still allies. Mao Tsetung then boasted that China's vast population would enable her to survive nuclear war. According to Brezhnev, 'with appalling airiness and cynicism he spoke of the possible destruction of half of mankind in the event of atomic war' (*Soviet News*, 10 June 1969). Such a war could totally eliminate the populations of Europe, North America, and the Soviet Union, while leaving China with numbers adequate for her needs and for the recolonization of Siberia and Soviet Central Asia. Furthermore, China's vast population could eventually enable her to field armies equivalent in size to the whole Soviet population—she can already call upon para-military organizations with a strength of up to two hundred million. Once she has the industrial capacity to arm this huge potential army, only nuclear weapons could deter her from invading Soviet Asia. Once she

had reached nuclear parity with the Soviet Union her conventional superiority would be irresistible, and the command of the
Heartland would be hers. Concern about China is not limited
to Russia. Whatever her present intentions, her other neighbours will always fear that 'the most fundamental of human
pressures, for more land for more people, will reassert itself, in
one way or another, at their expense' (Fisher 1971, p. 308).

This surely is what would most worry a Mackinder, who
would urge caution before embarking on a policy of co-operating with China to weaken the Soviet Union, if only by imposing
upon her an arms burden beyond her capacity to bear. He
would see a tragic irony in the fact that his own Heartland
theory had played a major part in bringing about this state of
affairs. With his love of historical generalization he might recall
earlier failures to readjust the balance of power in time, leading
to unnecessary conflict: how England continued to support
France against Spain in the seventeenth century long after the
latter had ceased to be a menace, thus aiding the aggrandise-
ment of France; how in the nineteenth century fear of France,
unnecessarily prolonged, aided the rise of Prussia; and how
insistence upon the unconditional surrender and utter destruction of Germany had brought Russia to the fore, necessitating
the urgent and costly rebuilding and re-arming of a Germany
recently annihilated with so much suffering. Would not the next
and final act be for the West to call in the aid of China to destroy
the Soviet Union, thus leading to an unchallengeable Chinese
domination of the Heartland and of the World Island?[32]

Grounds for believing this are to be seen in his belief in
keeping the balance of power; in his 1943 paper he clearly
foresaw that this balance could be between the Atlantic alliance
and the Soviet Union on the one side, and China and the rest of
Monsoon Asia on the other:

a thousand million people of ancient oriental civilization inhabit the
Monsoon lands of India and China ... They will then balance that

[32] 'English policy until late in the (seventeenth) century was vitiated by two cardinal
mistakes: overestimation of the power of Spain and underestimation of the power of
France' (Deane Jones 1931, p. 235). In the 1860s, when Prussia was consolidating her
position, 'fears of France still determined the policy of Great Britain' (Woodward 1938,
p. 312). Mackinder wrote, 'In 1870 Britain did not support France against Prussia ...
should we not, perhaps, be justified in asking whether we did not fail to back the right
horse?' (1919, p. 177).

other thousand million who live between the Missouri and the Yenisei. A balanced globe of human beings. And happy, because balanced and thus free.

This concluding sentence has been ridiculed as being too 'neat'—and Mackinder was 82 when he wrote it. Yet, seen as an alternative to an alliance against the Soviet Union that would lead to Chinese domination, in turn, of Heartland, World Island, and World, it may make sense. The last words, 'balanced and thus free', in particular, take on a new meaning. It has been said that Mackinder himself abandoned the Heartland theory in this paper; in a way this may be true, but it could be argued that he was demonstrating its flexibility and adaptability. If this is so, Whebell's (1971) conclusion that 'Mackinder's world view is as up to date as tomorrow' would apply equally well to 1981.[33]

[33] It is interesting to note that Abdel-Malek (1977, p. 304) sees 'the shape of the new world balance of power' in the year 2000 as consisting of 'a western-European power block, led by the U.S.S.R.', an Asian-Oriental power bloc, led by China, in alliance with the Arab world, and a 'Western-American power bloc, essentially made up of and dominated by the U.S.A.'.

Chapter 8

Criticisms of the Heartland Theory

Although the Heartland theory, first enunciated in 1904, lay neglected by English-speaking writers until the 1939–45 war, it then became 'one of the most intensively debated geographical ideas of all time' (de Blij 1967). It has been said (Cohen 1963) that 'seldom have one man's theories been so exposed to critical examination as have those of Mackinder'; that, 'despite being repeatedly challenged ... they are still allowed to form a basis for argument. The ghost seems never to be completely laid' (Blacksell 1977); and, 'On several occasions the Heartland thesis has been systematically dismantled only to rise Phoenix-like for further punishment' (Muir 1975). It has been accepted, sometimes enthusiastically, sometimes with reservations, by many geographers, historians, and political scientists, some of whom have elaborated it into geopolitical systems of their own (notably Spykman[1] 1944, Meinig 1956, and Cohen 1963). It has, however, attracted much criticism, mainly from political geographers. Examples of generally critical views are Cressey (1945), Fawcett (1947), East (1950), East and Moodie (1956), Alexander (1957), Weigert *et al.* (1957), Pounds (1963), Learmonth (1971), Walters (1974), and Muir (1975). It has been roundly condemned by Hall (1955), Malin (1959), de Blij (1967), and Bunge (1973). Malin wrote, 'It would be difficult to find an essay of comparable length and reputation that is more indefensible in terminology and ideas than Mackinder's "The Geographical Pivot of History".'

About a hundred different criticisms have been levelled at the Heartland theory. Often the critic has misinterpreted or misunderstood what Mackinder wrote; commonly, he appears to have read very little of Mackinder, or is merely repeating the allegations of others. In this chapter criticisms have been classified in groups and examined in the light of what Mackinder

---

[1] Although always referred to as by Spykman, the work was actually written, after his death in 1943, by his research assistant, H. R. Nicholl.

wrote and of the actual course of events. The most numerous group includes those that may be characterized as 'geostrategic'. Some have denied geography any significant place in power politics. L. S. Amery (1904), after the reading of 'The Geographical Pivot of History', asserted that, in the coming air age, 'a great deal of this geographical distribution must lose its importance', and that it would not matter whether the successful powers were 'in the centre of a continent or on an island' provided they were strong and resourceful. Over half a century later, Malin (1959, p. 340) insisted that 'the idea that geographical position is the basis of power' was discredited and must be abandoned. Spykman (1944), however, had written that 'the geographical location of a state in the world is of basic importance', and later Hooson (1964, p. 117) claimed that 'the most fundamental of all the elements of national power is sheer location on the globe'.

Seen from the land-locked position of the USSR, encircled by contiguous or closely-adjoining states, many of which host American bases, and with no free outlet to the open ocean, it must be difficult to accept that it does not matter whether one is 'in the centre of a continent or on an island'. Nor could the United States, with no immediate neighbours except Canada and Mexico, and with two wide ocean-fronting coasts, to and from which its essential overseas commerce and military supplies are carried, take such a view. Nor is it borne out by the conversation reported between Nixon and Khrushchev when they met in Moscow in 1959: Nixon said that whether missiles could best be launched from land or sea 'depended on the strategic situation of the nation involved', and Khrushchev replied that the USSR would concentrate on the destruction of the ports and navy of the enemy, 'because the Soviet Union's potential enemy would be highly dependent on sea communications' (Mazo and Hess 1968, pp. 194–5). In his 1980 book Nixon reaffirmed the strategic contrast between the United States as an 'island' country and 'a sea power', and the Soviet Union 'situated in the centre of the Eurasian heartland' and 'basically a land power' (p. 193).

The strategic armament of the two superpowers illustrates the importance of geographical position. Aircraft carriers play an overwhelming part in American strategy, a negligible one in that of the Soviet Union.[2] Intercontinental ballistic missiles, being independent of the land–sea or centre–periphery anti-theses, are comparable in number. But as the USA has few neighbours and the USSR many, with several of them in the enemy camp, there is a striking contrast in the number of intermediate- and medium-range ballistic missiles and of long-range and medium-range bombers. The USA does not deploy IRBMs and MRBMs—it has no need to deter Canada or Mex-ico, but the Soviet Union has over seven hundred. The Ameri-can bomber force is almost wholly long range; the Soviet, over three-quarters medium range (IISS 1979).

Many criticisms concern the nature of the Heartland, one of them the uncertainty of its boundaries (Teggart 1919, Chisholm 1919, Gyorgy 1944, Meinig 1956, Kristof 1976). For Gyorgy, generally sympathetic to the Heartland theory, this is 'the main criticism'; and he comments that 'this extremely vague outline of so vital a geographical area seems unacceptable' (p. 168, fn. 15). In 'The Geographical Pivot of History' it is that part of Eurasia which has 'no available waterways to the ocean' (p. 431), in other words, the regions of internal and Arctic drainage, including the Volga basin. At first, *Democratic Ideals and Reality* uses the same definition:

Taken together, the regions of Arctic and Continental drainage measure nearly half of Asia and a quarter of Europe and form a great continuous patch in the north and centre of the continent. That whole patch, extending right across from the icy, flat shore of Siberia to the torrid, steep coasts of Baluchistan and Persia, has been inaccessible to navigation from the ocean ... Let us call this great region the Heart-land of the Continent. (p. 96)

And so it is shown upon his map (pp. 100–1); but later in the same book he extends what is wholly a physically-determined area westwards on strategic grounds and in the light of recent history:

We defined the Heartland originally in accordance with river drain-age; but does not history ... show that for the purposes of strategical thought it should be given a somewhat wider extension? Regarded from the point of view of human mobility, and of the different modes of mobility, it is evident that since land-power can to-day close the

[2] America's thirteen carriers have a combined tonnage of over a million; Russia's two, of only eighty-six thousand (IISS 1979a).

Black Sea, the whole basin of that sea must be regarded as of the Heartland. Only the Bavarian Danube ... may be treated as lying outside. (pp. 139-40)

Furthermore, 'The Baltic is a sea which can now be "closed" by land-power', so it too must be added. And therefore:

The Heartland is the region to which, under modern conditions, sea-power can be refused access, though the western part of it lies without the region of Arctic and Continental drainage. There is one striking physical circumstance which knits it graphically together; the whole of it, even to the brink of the Persian Mountains overlooking torrid Mesopotamia, lies under snow in the winter time ... At mid-winter, as seen from the moon, a vast white shield would reveal the Heartland in its largest meaning.[3] (p. 141)

The new boundary was more realistic geologically, geographically, historically, and culturally, for it corresponds more closely with the divide between the real Europe, fragmented and varied, and the monolithic continental uniformity of the Eurasian land mass eastwards (Parker 1960). It is the same divide that deprived the concept of Central Europe of geographical validity[4] (Fig. 3).

In 'The Round World and the Winning of the Peace' (1943) Mackinder maintains that 'the concept does not admit of precise definition on the map for the reason that it is based on three separate assumptions of physical geography which, while reinforcing one another, are not exactly coincident'. In elaborating this he goes on to give his most complete description of the Heartland, and at the same time justifies his imprecision:

First of all, we have in this region by far the widest lowland plain on the face of the globe. Secondly, there flow across that plain some great navigable rivers; certain of them go north to the Arctic Sea and are inaccessible from the ocean because it is encumbered by ice, while others flow into inland waters such as the Caspian, which have no exit to the ocean. Thirdly, there is here a grassland zone which, until within the last century and a half, presented ideal conditions for the development of high mobility by camel and horse-riding nomads. Of the three features mentioned, the river basins are the easiest to present cartographically; the water divide which delimits the whole group of

[3] Sylvester (1968) gives this sentence to illustrate his criticism that, 'The straining for generalization was sometimes a bit humorous'.

[4] See above p. 201.

Arctic and 'continental' rivers into a single unit does isolate neatly on the map a vast coherent area which is the Heartland according to that particular criterion. The mere exclusion of sea mobility and sea power, however, is a negative if important differential; it was the plain and the grassland belt which offered the positive conditions conducive to the other type of mobility, that proper to the prairie. As for the grassland, it traverses the whole breadth of the plain but does not cover its entire surface. Notwithstanding these apparent discrepancies, the Heartland provides a sufficient physical basis for strategical thinking. To go further and to simplify geography artificially would be misleading. (pp. 597–8)

He then points out that 'it is sufficiently accurate to say that the territory of the USSR is equivalent to the Heartland', but immediately makes a big exception—the huge far-eastern part of the Soviet Union beyond the Yenisei river, which he calls Lena Land. He does not explain this exclusion, other than to say that it is 'a generally rugged country of mountains, plateaux and valleys, covered almost from end to end with coniferous forests' and that its 'rich natural resources ... are as yet practically untouched'. The true and final Heartland is left, meeting Mackinder's liking for balanced neatness: 'West of the Yenisei lies what I have described as Heartland Russia, a plain extending 2,500 miles north and south, and 2,500 miles east and west' (p. 599).

Mackinder was always more concerned with the heart of a matter than with its precise definition,[5] with generalizations than with detailed analysis, with cores rather than with boundaries. He would have agreed with those who criticized the preoccupation of regional geographers with the limits of their regions, believing in useful patterns of essential characteristics without being overly concerned with the sharpness of their edges. Teggart (1919) wrote that 'if new terms are to be invented, they should not be applied at the very outset to quite different entities'. And it does seem a serious drawback, in a book in which he is concerned with East Europe as the gateway to the Heartland, for the Heartland to both exclude (1919, p.

[5] In a letter to Weigert he wrote, 'The desire for a precise definition of the Heartland is futile—as it is a strategical concept on the map' (Weigert 1942, p. 253). His attitude to precise definition may be gathered from his remark that 'in this country we define nothing if we can help it' (1935b, p. 502).

96) and include (ibid., p. 141) most of it. In 1943 it is excluded again in so far as the Heartland is considered to be roughly coterminous with the territory of the USSR (Figs. 1, 3).

Some criticisms deal with the geographical nature of the Heartland. Mackinder 'overestimates the advantages of his Heartland' (Cressey 1945), which is really unfit to be a seat of world power; it is an area of difficulty for human occupation (Fawcett 1947); its climate is unfavourable (Huntington 1943, Cressey 1945); it cannot support a large agricultural population (Mills 1956); it cannot therefore become economically strong enough (Spykman 1944, Fawcett 1947, East and Moodie 1956, Moodie n.d., Kristof 1976). Much of this criticism is valid in itself. The Heartland region does have a formidable array of 'anti-resources' which make its exploitation and settlement exceedingly difficult and expensive; and despite the herculean efforts of the Soviet peoples since 1928, its development is only sporadic and far from complete. Its economy is still unable to support an arms race with the United States and her associated allies without serious domestic economic, social, and political strains. But because so much of the world's mineral wealth is stored there, and because technology can to some degree overcome the 'anti-resources' (though at a cost), it is inevitable that, *sooner or later*, whoever commands the Heartland will be able to build an unrivalled industrial base for military power. This inevitability was stated by Mackinder in 1904.

Strategically, the Heartland theory does not require the industrialization and settlement of the whole of the region; it does not therefore so much matter if large areas of it are geographically unsuited to be the seats of power. The Heartland yields its power to the state which commands it, and it can be commanded from outside or from within. In 1919 Mackinder expected that command to be exercised from eastern Europe, whether by Germans or Russians. To command the Heartland strategically it is sufficient to be able to move forces within it and across it to various points on its perimeter.

The next set of objections are to the strategic importance of the Heartland: it has been greatly overemphasized (Spykman 1944, Alexander 1957); mere control of it is without significance (Huntington 1943); whoever rules the Heartland does not in fact command any marginal regions by virtue of that rule

(Fawcett 1947); its qualities of space and distance are no longer advantages (East and Moodie 1956, Hooson 1964); they are in fact more of a liability than an asset (Potter and Nimitz 1960); it is no longer secure (Hall 1955, Pounds 1963, Learmonth 1971, Muir 1975)—and it is getting weaker (Mills 1956); its centrality makes it a vulnerable target for attack from all round the Rimland (Cohen 1963); it is particularly vulnerable from attack across the Arctic (East 1950, Hall 1955, East and Moodie 1956, Mills 1956, Weigert *et al.* 1957, Jackson 1962, Müller-Wille 1966, Walters 1974).

Allegations that the Heartland is no longer secure depend heavily upon developments in weapon technology, dealt with under technological criticisms. Generally the insecurity is attributed to the ability of the outer powers to concentrate a barrage of airborne bombs and ballistic missiles upon the centre, and especially to the presence of missile-launching submarines in the Arctic Sea. These developments have, it is said, destroyed the protection given by such physical features as mountains, swamps, deserts, and frozen seas, and also by distance and sheer vastness. Yet, a conflict might after all be fought only by 'conventional' means, thus restoring the validity of 'conventional' defensive features, and it may still be true that 'big states have infinitely more chances for survival than small ones' (Strausz-Hupé 1942, p. 191).

Many criticisms deal with Mackinder's Inner Crescent (Spykman's Rimland) and his Outer Crescent (Spykman's Offshore Islands). Their general tenor is that he failed to understand their nature or appreciate their strategic importance, and Spykman (1944) and Cressey (1945) held that the Rimland is more important than the Heartland. Parts of the Rimland are, of course, more favoured physically, better developed economically, and more densely peopled than most, if not all, of the Heartland, and there may be some truth in Spykman's rejoinder to Mackinder that, 'Who controls the rimland rules Eurasia.' But the question remains, which is the more likely to control the Rimland, sea power based in the outer maritime continents and islands, or land power based centrally in Eurasia? East Germany, Poland, and Czechoslovakia are more favoured, better developed, more advanced, and more populous[6] than the Soviet

---

[6] In the true sense of the word, i.e. more densely peopled per unit of area.

Union, and even enjoy a higher standard of living; but this has not prevented their absorption within the Soviet orbit. The relative wealth of Rimland and Heartland is but one of many factors determining the strategic relations between them. The real test is whether, at any single point on the Rimland, land power or sea power can bring preponderant force to bear. The United States would have been in no stronger position to succour Afghanistan had that country been as rich as Switzerland. Cohen (1963) points out that 'the inadequacy of Spykman's doctrine is today most clearly apparent from the fact that no Rimland power is capable of organizing all of the Rimland because of the vulnerability of the Rimland to both the Heartland and the Offshore Powers' (p. 46).

The relationship between eastern Europe and the Heartland is confused by the fact that in 1919 Mackinder added eastern Europe to the Heartland (Fig. 3). The criticism that the real power of the Soviet empire lies in eastern Europe rather than in the Heartland (Fawcett 1947) results from this confusion, but one does not have to reside in the Heartland to command it and to make use of its economic resources and strategic advantages; it could have been commanded from Berlin as well as from Moscow. The next criticism is the reverse of the last, objecting that the Heartland is now commanded, not from eastern Europe but from Moscow. In 1919, when Mackinder wrote 'he who rules East Europe commands the Heartland', he was preoccupied with the fear of a revived Germany using eastern Europe as an entry into the Heartland; he was concerned, therefore, to alert statesmen to this possibility. Perhaps the warning would have been more accurately phrased had it said 'any outside[7] power ruling East Europe commands the Heartland'. That this view was endorsed by the Russians was shown by their own determination to rule eastern Europe. So, although it is true, as Hall says, that 'the first line of the famous three-line warning is now reversed: Who rules the Heartland commands East Europe', this is not so much a criticism as a confirmation of Mackinder's basic idea.

Pounds (1965) complains that 'Mackinder would have us believe' that the German invasions of Russia 'were made possible only by the open nature of the terrain in European Russia'

[7] i.e. external to the Heartland.

(pp. 400-1), and suggests that the determining factor was 'rather the contrasting technical levels of the opposing forces'. This criticism is quite unjustified. The open way into Russia was a threat in 1914 *because* of German technical superiority: 'Germany knew the weakness of Russia; there was no illusion of the "steam roller" for her' (Mackinder 1919, p. 198); in the immediate post-1914-18-war period the Russians would be 'helplessly incapable of resisting German penetration' (ibid., p. 205).

Hall's (1955) criticism that China does not owe her Heartland position to organization by Japan, as Mackinder suggested it might, but to her close alliance with the USSR, has been destroyed by events; in the 1980s Japan is in fact helping to 'organize' a China which insistently claims a larger share of the Heartland. Hall also claimed that a German-Russian alliance would be dangerous irrespective of the Heartland. Such an alliance would of course be awesome in any circumstances; but the strength of any such coalition would inevitably rest largely upon Heartland resources. That Mackinder was wrong to believe that the German domination of the Heartland would be 'a chastisement of scorpions as compared with the whips of Russia' was the view of an early reviewer of *Democratic Ideals and Reality*. Teggart (1919) feared that the destruction of the German and Austrian empires in the 1914-18 war had removed the protective marches that Europe had set up against the East; post-war concern should be rather to restore this protection than to guard against its reconstruction. This was a widespread view among conservatives in the inter-war years.

Almost as soon as he had sat down after reading his 1904 paper, Mackinder was taken to task for his use of a Mercator projection for his world map;[8] but Haushofer (1924) praised 'the Mercator map in Mackinder's audacious 1904 survey' because, by placing 'America on the eastern as well as the western side of the map', it became possible to 'consider both the Atlantic-Eurasian and the Pacific realms as wholes' (p. 69). For most critics, however, the placing of the western hemisphere on the outer edge of the world was at fault and particularly inappropriate to the air age, as was the use of Mercator (Weigert 1943, Cressey 1945, Crone 1951, Weigert *et al.* 1957, Pounds 1963, Hooson 1964). This had led him to believe that North

[8] By H. Spenser Wilkinson (1853-1937), journalist and military historian.

America was a mere satellite of the Old World; he failed therefore to appreciate the great power of the United States or to see in it another heartland, comparable to if not stronger than the Eurasian one (Dryer 1920, Cressey 1945, Weigert 1942, Hall 1955, Celérier 1955, Malin 1959, Hooson 1962, de Blij 1967, Muir 1975); nor, it is said, did he understand the crucial strategic value of the Arctic Ocean as a new Mediterranean lying between these two opposing heartlands (Weigert 1949, Hooson 1962). Although his critics are seldom unanimous, often refuting each other's criticism, they are mostly agreed on these points, well expressed below:

It is perhaps not incidental that the logic of Mackinder's Heartland seems to reveal itself best on a Mercator World map ... Here the Heartland lives up to its name ... However, we find it difficult, if not impossible, to visualize this relation of the Heartland to a surrounding inner and outer crescent if we exchange the Mercator map for the globe or any azimuthal-equidistant map. The concept of North America as part of a chain of insular powers distant from the Heartland now becomes a geographical myth. In terms of air geography the Heartland and North America appear in destiny-laden proximity. As viewed over the top of the world, the Heartland assumes a location different from that which Mackinder assigned to it, plotting it from Britain. (Weigert *et al.* 1957, p. 217)

For 'seen from North America, and in terms of new communications reaching out from many points in the far-flung "perimeter of defense" line, inaccessibility and vastness no longer conceal the Heartland from us' (ibid.).

The map does, of course, look different when the globe is regarded from above, and the geographical relationships shown are more accurate. But are they more realistic? How many people, including people of power and influence, actually take such a polar view? Although the earth is spherical, it rotates from west to east; the sun draws the torrid zone from west to east across its middle, neglecting the frigid zones around the poles; but between the torrid and frigid zones, in the northern hemisphere, it allows a more temperate west-east belt where great populous and productive industrial areas have grown up. It is natural and useful that this favoured belt should be seen in terms of the traditional rectangular map, old-fashioned though it may be. There is now a brief season of hazardous navigation along the Arctic coast of the USSR, but it is negligible as a factor in world commerce, while in war time it would be Soviet-controlled. For all practical purposes the World Island is still essentially a great promontory reaching out south-west, south, and south-east from the Heartland, rather than a circum-navigable island. Whether portrayed on a Mercator or a polar projection the Heartland has a Rimland on all sides except the north, and so this Rimland remains an Inner Crescent rather than a circle; the Outer Crescent also remains a crescent of islands large and small, for the vast Pacific places an enormous gap between North America and Australia.

True, the relationship between North America and the Heartland does appear transformed, for a polar-type projection makes it clear that only the narrow Bering Strait separates them. But their developed ecumenes remain separated by vast expanses of waste. It is mainly for air transport and missile-launching submarines that the difference between the two view-points is fundamental. But Mackinder was aware of the impor-tance of the Arctic for air transport a quarter-century and more before his critics began to accuse him of being misled by his maps, having pointed out (1924, p. 281) that the shortest route between parts of North America and northern Eurasia 'will be by way of the North Pole'.

Walters (1974) has stressed the damage done to the Heart-land theory by missile-launching submarines operating in the Arctic. This, he argues, converts the World Promontory into a *real* World Island, i.e. one that can be circumnavigated. The Heartland then ceases to be a 'heart' land, having a northern coastline accessible to sea power (p. 132). This is logical and persuasive, but the threat from the missile-launching submarine lies more in its missile than in its exercise of sea power. Missiles could also be launched from the Rimland, and the answer that applies to the nuclear-weapons criticism generally would apply here. But in so far as Walters is thinking of naval submarines used to raid, attack, or put forces and material ashore on the long northern coast of the USSR, his logic is irresistible. He continues, 'if the undersea ship can be developed into a viable commercial ship, the Arctic Ocean will be of vast importance for the future ... the shortest route between the most industrial-ized nations of the world' (p. 142). Perhaps it is a big 'if'.

Mackinder was not impressed by the argument that the Heart-land was now open to attack on its frozen northern side. 'It is true', he wrote (1943, p. 600), 'that the Arctic shore is no longer inaccessible in the absolute sense that held until a few years ago ... but a hostile invasion across the vast area of circum-polar ice and over the Tundra mosses and the Targa (*sic*) forests of northern Siberia seems almost impossible in the face of Soviet land-based air-defence.' It was the North Atlantic rather than the Arctic that aroused Mackinder's interest, and he saw more significance in possibilities of west–east co-operation between the nations of its two shores than in the confrontation of two superpowers across the Northern Ocean. With his love of 'balance', he refers (1943, p. 601) to the peace being held by 'land-power to the east, in the Heartland, and sea-power to the west, in the North Atlantic basin'. This is his 'second geograph-ical concept':

that of the Midland Ocean—the North Atlantic—and its dependent seas and river basins. Without laboring the details of that concept let me picture it again in its three elements—a bridgehead in France, a moated aerodrome in Britain, and a reserve of trained manpower, agriculture and industries in the eastern United States and Canada. So far as war-potential goes, both the United States and Canada are Atlantic countries, and ... both the bridgehead and the moated aerodrome are essential to amphibious power. (ibid., p. 604)

Critics have concentrated on his neglect of the United States and the second heartland they see there, believing that this is his Achilles heel. Hooson (1962) writes that 'a very important phenomenon, which had oddly escaped him, was that the twen-tieth was becoming increasingly the American century', and Mackinder's work generally suggests a blinkered outlook in this respect. Yet he was one of the first to warn—at the very start of the century—that it would be the age of the great continental powers. That he seldom singled out the United States for men-tion was because he concentrated on those countries from which he expected danger, and he regarded the United States as a great fellow democracy which would almost inevitably be on the same side as Britain in any conflict. In any case, Mackinder's work was done before the United States appeared on the world stage as an active great power, whereas most of his critics wrote in the full flush of the early and unchallenged exercise of that power.

Americans have resented the reference to their continent as a satellite of the World Island. An early critic of *Democratic Ideals and Reality* (Dryer 1920) speaks of 'the strain to which such a view subjects the imagination and the map'. Mackinder was using the word 'satellite' in its astronomical sense of a smaller body outside a larger one, and thinking of the smaller area and population, and of the insularity, of the continents and islands of the Outer Crescent; but the pejorative sense of an attendant fawning upon a great personage is still current, so the choice of word was unfortunate. The blame cannot be laid—as it usually is—to his use of Mercator's projection, for the Americas and Australia appear more as satellites (astronomical sense) on an azimuthal projection. Irrespective of the map used, it was the globe he saw with his mind's eye.

To recognize the importance of America is not, however, to accept it as a second heartland. Cressey (1945) wrote: 'If there is anywhere a world citadel or Heartland, it may well lie in North America rather than Eurasia' (p. 245), although the idea is usually attributed to Hall (1955) who, ten years later, wrote: 'We are justified ... in speaking of an Anglo-American heartland ... set in the midst of the oceans rather than in the centre of a great land mass' (p. 122). It is a matter of semantics: Mackinder was using 'heart' in the sense of 'the innermost or central part of anything' (*OED* def. 17), and presumably the world or the land hemisphere can have only one central part. To speak of both the USA and the USSR as heartlands is to deprive the word of its chief value in geopolitics, which is to bring out the contrast between a country lying landlocked and ringed round by a host of other states, and a nation set between two great oceans to which it has open access and on which it depends for its industrial life blood (Fig. 1).

It is difficult to follow Malin (1959) when he attacks Mackinder for 'casting the United States in the role of a sea power'; according to one of Mackinder's most insistent critics (Hall 1955): 'The United States has been a maritime nation from its inception' (p. 122). East (1950) questioned whether Mackinder had appreciated the defensibility of Africa against the landmass power, but the course of events has shown Soviet power to have been exercised effectively in more than one part of Africa. He also claims that Mackinder did not realize what was involved in controlling Monsoon Asia. Walters (1974, p. 116) alleged that 'the overall importance of the Middle East has been exaggerated by the Heartland theory'. Pounds (1963), following Meinig (1956) claims that 'it was implicit in Mackinder's thesis that the islands and island groups which lie beyond the coast of Eurasia are necessarily maritime in their interests', but as Gottmann (1952) points out, he knew very well 'that it was not enough to occupy an insular position, however advantageously situated, in order to rule the seas and grow wealthy from commerce' (p. 43).

Because Mackinder used the basins of rivers flowing to the open oceans to define lands accessible to sea power, he has been criticized for implying that he saw sea power as being literally exerted along rivers: 'he assumed that maritime states could move their forces up rivers ... but would be unable to cross divides, however low' (Jones 1964); 'he overestimated the ability of sea power to penetrate and control rivers (exposed by the plight of the Amethyst on the Yangtse river during the Chinese communist revolution)' (Muir 1975, p. 195). Mackinder used river basins because their conformation naturally leads their lines of communication to coastal sea ports, normally at or near the mouths of rivers. Such coastal regions would generally be accessible to and penetrable by maritime states, and although there will be anomalies, such a criterion is 'the easiest to present cartographically' as it isolates the Heartland 'neatly on the map' (Mackinder 1943, p. 598).

Some critics believe economic and technological factors to be of greater import than geostrategic considerations. The earliest of these was Amery (1904) who, after Mackinder had delivered 'The Geographical Pivot of History', claimed that it was a nation's industrial base and technological skill that would be decisive in any power struggle: 'those people who have the industrial power and the power of invention will be able to defeat all the others'. Amery's view is echoed by Weigert *et al.* (1957), Potter and Nimitz (1960), Jones (1964), and Sprout (1964). Weigert *et al.* wrote 'the USSR has become a world

power not so much because of its location in the "closed heartland of Eurasia" as because of a profound and far-reaching
social revolution which made the development of Amery's industrial power the paramount object of policy' (p. 450).

East (1950) and Crone (1951) also suggested that economic
rather than geostrategic factors were decisive. East commented
that 'Mackinder was little concerned here with either man-
power or wealth, actual and potential', relying instead on 'geographical position, physical remoteness from the world oceans,
natural security from attack ... and space' (p. 81). While it is
true that his primary concern was to draw attention to the
significance of these, he also insisted that a developed economic
potential was a *sine qua non*. There is evidence of this in his 1904
paper, and, replying to Amery afterwards, he said, 'with regard
to the basis of sea power in industrial wealth, I entirely agree.
What I suggest is that great industrial wealth in Siberia and
European Russia and a conquest of some of the marginal regions
would give the basis for a fleet necessary to found the world
empire' (p. 443). It is difficult to understand how anyone who
had read *Democratic Ideals* could really believe that he was 'little
concerned with manpower or wealth', and many who have
criticized him in other respects acknowledge his awareness of
the economic factor: Gyorgy (1944, pp. 167-8) says that Mackinder 'firmly believes in the military, economic, and political
superiority of the central heartland'; Potter and Nimitz (1960,
p. 489), summarizing the Heartland theory, write, 'Once it [the
Heartland] has achieved adequate communications and a high
level of economic development, the center of the great land
mass will be in the position to exert the greatest power.'

Mackinder would no more have claimed that the Soviet
Union had become a superpower solely because of its location
in the Heartland than he would have argued that Britain became a great sea-power only because of its location on an island;
indeed, he pointed out the fallacy of such an argument.[9] His
case was that, should the Heartland be possessed by 'a garrison
sufficient both in number and quality', they would build there
a power which would be able to exploit the advantages of its
geographical position. He took a balanced view, allowing
weight to the many forces at work. This was summarized in a

[9] '... mere insularity gives no indefeasible right to marine sovereignty' (1902, p. 358).

single sentence: 'The actual balance of political power at any given time is . . . the product, on the one hand, of the geographic conditions, both economic and strategic, and on the other hand, of the relative number, virility, equipment, and organization of the competing peoples' (Mackinder 1904, p. 437). Often the supposed inadequacy of Mackinder's argument is in the eye of the critic rather than in what he himself actually said or wrote.

To command the Heartland economically means the ability to transport its primary produce to the manufacturing centres of the commanding state or region, i.e. an efficient and pervasive transportation system. For Mackinder this was to be originally the railway (1904), and later, railways supplemented by airways (1919). It has been objected, however, that its railways are inadequate (East 1950, Hall 1955, Weigert *et al.* 1957, Muir 1975), and that, in any case, 'he overestimates the role which railroads can play in a vast continental country' (Kristof 1976). If the strategic or economic command of the Heartland had been impeded by lack of railways, these criticisms would be valid; but railway building has been more extensive than is generally realized (Fig. 2), and is supplemented, not only by airways, but by roadways, pipelines, and electrical transmission lines. Although Mackinder's words (1904, p. 434), 'the century will not be old before all Asia is covered with railways' have not been wholly justified, it is quite untrue to say that 'the strategical railways which Mackinder invoked . . . never materialized' (Muir 1975, p. 195). The Heartland transport system is by no means complete but neither is the economic development which it serves. The two advance *pari passu*. Strategically, large Soviet forces have been moved to and supplied at such Rimland areas as the North Chinese border and Afghanistan.

Kristof (1976) does not like Mackinder's emphasis on the importance of communications in opening up the Heartland, regarding it as a peculiarly English attitude:

Some of Mackinder's ideas and, in this writer's opinion, mistakes concerning the Heartland may be related to his English environment both cultural and geographic. Essentially, he saw the vast Eurasiatic land mass through the prism of a commercial society. Only so can we explain why he thought that the establishment of communications, the building of railroads was the main problem. Commerce is primarily concerned with moving goods, not with production. (p. 13)

But communications are surely essential to any form of development including production; internal communications are as necessary to a land empire as external communications are to an island sea power.

It is widely averred that Mackinder's thesis has been rendered obsolete by the modern technology of weapons and transport (East 1950, Hall 1955, Sprout 1963 and 1964, de Blij 1967, Muir 1975, Padelford *et al.* 1976, Blacksell 1977). De Blij writes of his 'inability to recognize the role of changing technology (p. 134); Hall argues that superiority is no longer a long-term attribute of sea power, land power, or air power, but an ever-changing battle of wits between the technologies of offence and defence (p. 125). Actually, the Heartland theory is based on a long-range view of changing technology in relation to geographical conditions, and Mackinder (1909a) was well aware that 'the value of a natural fortress alters . . . as the range of weapons grows'.

It is often said that he failed to see the importance of the aeroplane (Amery 1904, Bowman 1942, Cressey 1945, East 1950, Weigert *et al.* 1957, Malin 1959, Hooson 1964, Crone 1967, Muir 1975, Blacksell 1977). Many have remarked that Amery, within minutes of Mackinder expounding his formula, forecast that it would be upset by air power. Strausz-Hupé (1942) commented, 'A commendable feat of prophecy this, considering that the Wright Brothers had invented the airplane only one year before!' Slessor (1954) pleaded: 'do not let us be distracted by geopolitical talk about Heartlands, which was all very well in Mackinder's day but ceased to be relevant with the advent of the long-range bomber' (p. 31). Pounds (1963) wrote that Mackinder's 1904 paper 'was presented at the beginning of the air age and yet failed to take account of this new form of mobility' (p. 399); and that in 1943, 'at a time when bombers were reducing many of Europe's cities to ruins and nullifying the effectiveness of capital ships, Mackinder could nevertheless write that air power was capable of "effecting few permanent changes in the strategical conditions"' (pp. 401–2). However, Mackinder believed that air power would make little difference to the balance between land power and sea power, although it would operate more to the disadvantage of sea power (1919, pp. 142–3). The evidence from the 1939–45 war justified Mackinder completely. Despite extensive loss of life and damage to buildings, 'strategic bombing was largely a waste of effort ... German war production increased throughout the war' (Walters 1974, p. 66). This conclusion was confirmed in Vietnam. Perhaps the most striking achievements of air power in 1939–45 were the damage done to convoys *en route* to the Soviet Union, and the destruction of British and American battleships by Japanese air attack. Both were blows delivered at sea power.

In 1945 the critics were given a powerful new round of ammunition with the dropping of the first atomic bombs: 'The existence of the new bombs challenges Mackinder's views' (East and Moodie 1956, p. 445); 'nuclear weapons make obsolete his emphasis on the Heartland as secure from naval attack' (Learmonth 1971, p. 7). Sprout (1963) is the most explicit: 'When it becomes possible to fire ballistic rockets armed with nuclear explosives from nearly any point on the earth's surface ... then we shall have reached the end of the line for geopolitical hypotheses based upon the layout and configuration of lands and seas' (p. 196). Much the same point is made by Hall (1955), Hooson (1962) and Pounds (1963); but later Hooson conceded that 'it would be wrong to imagine that the missile age has in some way neutralized the strategic advantages or disadvantages of particular areas or nations' for, 'Clearly, countries with a large area or dispersed population, and also an interior "fortress" unusually far away from hostile bases are even today relatively less vulnerable' (p. 119). Others cautiously take the view that strategic nuclear weapons may not be used between superpowers possessed of second-strike capability; such a 'balance of terror' or nuclear stalemate leaves the field open to conventional weapons and strategy, and the Heartland theory therefore intact (Pearce 1962, Jones 1964, Müller-Wille 1966, Herold 1974).

Whether or not nuclear weapons invalidate the Heartland theory, Walters (1974) blames Mackinder for the West's reliance upon them: 'If the Soviet Union had a superior geopolitical position, then the "need" for nuclear arms was axiomatic' (p. 19). The Heartland 'came to be looked upon as a great fortress or castle ... The Iron Curtain, cutting off any information from the world beyond, seemed dreadfully ominous. The silent castle, epitomized by the Kremlin itself and by the Heartland, loomed overpoweringly in the dark recesses of the mind' (p. 43).

Walters (ibid.) argued that Mackinder wrongly assumed that sea power had reached a pleateau in its development, whereas it was just as capable of technological advance as land power, and he gives the example of the missile-launching submarine. The assumption 'that an increase in the efficiency of land mobility would automatically award an advantage to the attack in warfare' was no longer valid. This recalls Jones's (1964) observation that 'most transport systems work both ways ... In 1940 the Germans pushed the British off the continent. In 1945 the armies of the maritime powers swept into Germany along *Autobahnen* built to serve German troops.'

Mackinder claimed (1900b, p. 153) that commercially the railway gave land power an advantage over maritime states using shipping, four years before his first enunciation of the Heartland theory:

We are beginning to see the trans-continental railway; and although at the present time, it is held that the railway cannot carry goods as cheaply as the steamer, we must bear in mind the many lessons of the past, the many falsifications of predictions, the constant tendency to cheapening where there is sufficient incentive ... the railway has a significant advantage over the steamer, in that it is possible to avoid even the breaking of bulk which is involved in taking goods from the factory down to the ship,

and thus was of great advantage to Germany in her relations with the rest of central Europe. Many will not concede this, insisting that shipping still has a cost advantage (e.g. Cressey 1945, Jones 1964, Kristof 1976). Walters (1974) sees a similar advantage for his undersea ships of the future. Yet the General Council of British Shipping complains that the Trans-Siberian Railway is taking away the Far East–Europe container trade from oceanic transport.[10] They believe it to be subsidized; but the highly-electrified, efficiently-organized, and intensively-used Soviet rail system is the most profitable part of the economy and needs no subsidy. Pounds (1963), commenting on Malin's

[10] TSR carriage 'is severely affecting the Far Eastern Freight Conference which combines the interests of UK and many other ocean liner companies in Europe/Far East trade'—letter to the author, 16 Dec. 1980.

assertion that, 'Formal statements of philosophies of history may come after the event, and when such limited validity as they possess has already become largely if not altogether obsolete', remarks that 'this is abundantly true of Mackinder's thesis. He wrote at the end of the railway age, not at its beginning' (p. 398)—likewise Mills (1956). But Mackinder is concerned with trans-continental railways, and although there was a line across the United States as early as 1869, the 'age' of the trans-continental came about thirty years later; it is by no means over in Eurasia, as the building of the Baykal–Amur line and the commercial success of the TSR show.

There are some twenty objections to the Heartland theory on historical grounds. There is an underlying assumption that as it is old it must be out of date: 'the factors of time and change must inevitably erode the Heartland theory ... we must be careful not to be caught napping in the nineteenth century' (Weigert *et al.* 1957, pp. 209, 211). Most critics (e.g. Hall 1955, Crone 1962, Blacksell 1977) agree with Learmonth (1971) as to 'the erosion of Mackinder's larger generalizations by seven troublous decades'. However, Mackinder (1904) thought that there was 'a certain persistence of geographical relationship' in 'the broad currents of history', and it must take more than the mere passage of time to prove him wrong.

Spykman (1944) questioned Mackinder's assumption of a long-standing historical duel between sea power and land power, because 'in the three great wars of the nineteenth and twentieth centuries ... the British and Russian empires have lined up together against an intervening rimland power as led by Napoleon, Wilhelm II, and Hitler'. He concluded from this that 'there has never really been a simple land power–sea power opposition'. He had been anticipated in this view by Teggart (1919) and Whittlesey (1943), and was subsequently supported in it by Hall (1955), Weigert (1957), and Muir (1975); but Jones (1964) commented, 'actually Mackinder knew this and said so'. Hall accuses that

in an attempt to prove his point the British geographer twisted the history of the war into false shapes. By concentrating his attention on the last phase of the war, that is, the period after the collapse of Russia and the entrance of the United States, Mackinder attempted to demonstrate that the struggle was one between insular sea powers and continental land powers.[11]

The instances quoted by the critics, with land powers and sea powers combining to oppose other land-power–sea-power alliances did, of course, occur, but the *principal* antagonists were a sea power on one side and a land power on the other; and, in the final analysis, it was sea power that brought victory both to itself and to its land-power allies. As Dugan (1962) has written, 'It is not fair to Mackinder to suggest ... that he regarded previous history as primarily a struggle between sea and land power, when he fairly specifically interpreted the international relations of the nineteenth century as involving British sea power in support of the strongest continental opponent of the strongest power on the continent' (p. 253).

The issue is complicated by the fact that many great powers have been amphibious, yet in any one theatre, because of the unity of the seas, there can be only a single power which has command of the sea; no other power, though amphibious, will be able to exercise its naval force with decisive effect. The sea power can also act as a land power, because it can ferry armies across the seas, while preventing such action in the reverse direction. Another complication is that when international politics and strategy were operating on a continental, i.e. European scale, the centre–periphery antithesis did not coincide with the land-power–sea-power dichotomy; if France or Germany, as a land power, was to be encircled, it had to be to some extent by

[11] The following extracts show that M. (1919, pp. 79–81) deals truthfully with land power and sea power in the 1914–18 war: 'In the very first days of the struggle the British fleet had already taken command of the ocean, enveloping with the assistance of the French fleet, the whole peninsular theatre of the war on land ... On the eastern front ... land-power ... was divided into two contending forces, and the outer of the two, notwithstanding its incongruous Czardom, was allied with the sea-power of the Democratic West. In short, the disposition of forces repeated in a general way that of a century earlier, when British sea-power supported the Portuguese and Spaniards in "the Peninsula," and was allied with the autocracies of the Eastern land-powers ... In 1917, however, came a great change, due to the entry of the United States into the War, the fall of the Russian Czardom ... The world-strategy of the contest was entirely altered ... We should bear in mind the new face of Reality. We have been fighting lately, in the close of the War, a straight duel between land-power and sea-power, and sea-power has been laying siege to land-power.' The passage should be read in full, but the extracts quoted should suffice to demonstrate the falsity of Hall's accusation.

other land powers, but the organizer of the encirclement, the chief source of strength and succour, was the sea power.

The land-power–sea-power antithesis can be traced back to ancient times: it is analysed by Pseudo-Zenophon and Isocrates in the fifth and fourth centuries BC (Toynbee 1924, Monigliano 1944). Aron (1966, p. 193) states that there is every reason to regard as fundamental, throughout history, the opposition of land and sea, of continental and sea-faring power; and Célérier (1955) devotes his attention to 'the continuation of the great struggle between the sea and the land' into modern times. A reminder of the continuing validity of the antithesis is given from *The Strategic Balance 1979*:

In regions such as South-West Asia, where the USSR enjoys the advantages of proximity, how could a Soviet invasion like that of Afghanistan be effectively deterred? The large concentration of U.S. naval forces, assembled in the Arabian Sea in early December to demonstrate American resolve in the Iranian hostage crisis, did not prevent Soviet divisions from marching into Afghanistan. (IISS 1980, p. 9)

The American historian Malin (1959) dealt scathingly with the closed-space concept for which Mackinder has been so widely praised:[12]

human occupation of the globe by primitive man filled all space available to exploitation at the several prevailing and successive cultural levels. Thus ... very early in human history space was closed ... all 'available' global space was occupied continuously ... Successive 'explorations' and 'closures' of space by more complex cultures could have been claimed prior to the one which Mackinder so naively hailed as though it were new—a new phenomenon only to Mackinder and his age, not to the history of man. The lands discovered by Columbus and his successors were not 'vacant lands'. They were occupied by beings just as human as the Western European savage (a relative term) who discovered them. (pp. 350–1)

This is rather like saying a cupboard is not empty because it is full of air. Mackinder was well aware of the varying efficiency of different cultures in the use of space, and knew, of course,

---

[12] e.g. Strausz-Hupé (1942), 'Mackinder, viewing the world as a closed system, arrived at a profounder understanding of modern strategy than any of the leading military experts of his times' (p. 145).

that few lands were 'vacant' in the absolute sense; but he was dealing with power, not culture, and the fact was that the Western European 'savages' had the power, and if they could no longer dissipate it into what were, for them, relatively thinly peopled and poorly exploited lands, they would marshal it against each other.

Some writers claim that in so far as Mackinder's ideas were based on the need of growing nations for more space, the premise was either historically false or has since become so. Yet it was he who drew attention to the fact that the nations of the world were moving from territorial expansion to a struggle for relative efficiency (Mobogunje 1980). The organic view of the state as developed by Ratzel and Kjellen implied that states needed living space or *Lebensraum* from which to feed their growing populations, and Mackinder shared this opinion to some degree. Strausz-Hupé (1942), however, denies that there was really such a link between population growth and imperialism. Malin (1944) pointed out that although 'those who were thinking in terms of space geography' saw a 'closed world order' in which they would have to rob each other for land to support their natural increase, there was an alternative way—that of increasing the yields of their existing lands. According to Aron (1966, p. 200), 'Current opinion ... no longer sees anything but lies and sophisms in the proposition of yesterday's imperialists'; the post-war Germans and Japanese enjoy a much higher standard of living, and yet have greater population and less space than before the war—when it was said they must have more space in order to survive. He adds, however, that this interpretation 'does not entirely convince the historian'; today's Germans and Japanese no longer have the intangible satisfaction of being citizens of independent great powers. This recalls Mackinder's own words (1905, p. 141): 'in a state like Germany defence against French and Russian arms, and against British and American capitalism, is truly greater than opulence, if you once grant the ideal of nationalism'. A similar criticism is that 'population and resource crises' are replacing 'strategic power projection' as the relevant contributions of modern political geography to international affairs (Padelford *et al.* 1976, p. 86); this reflects a widespread modern view that the threat to world stability comes from the gap between the rich North and the poor South, rather than between a capitalist West and socialist East (e.g. Taylor 1980, p. 22). The Soviet intervention in Afghanistan and the resumption of the Cold War have been reminders of the continuing geographical realities.

The Heartland theory has been described as a product of its time (Crone 1951, Dugan 1962, de Blij 1963, Sylvester 1968, Blouet 1973, Muir 1975, Blouet 1977) and therefore too dependent on contemporary thought to be original or too strongly influenced by contemporary events to be of permanent significance. Sylvester wrote: 'On the one hand, the Heartland, to Mackinder, offered a theory for all time ... On the other hand, the theory squarely fixed Mackinder as part of his time ...' (p. 57). Yet he is criticized by Hall (1955) for being out of touch with his time:

... in the perspective of history, Mackinder's first statement of his thesis was untimely. He called attention to a rather remote danger from the great vacant spaces of central Eurasia ... when British statesmen were discovering that the traditional opposition to the possessor of these spaces was no longer suited to the world situation. (pp. 112–13)

Of the same order is de Blij's (1967, p. 134) question, 'if the Pivot area gave so much power to the possessor, why was Russia in 1904 not more of a world power than it was?' Such approaches fail to comprehend that Mackinder was attempting an analysis which would alert people to likely future developments, rather than a recipe for the solution of present difficulties. He was as aware of the dangers of German rearmament as he was of those of applying Darwinian theory to human affairs. Others of his critics, in fact, emphasize how little his basic ideas were products of their time:

The fundamentals of his closed-space concept stand so firmly today that we almost forget how revolutionary the concept was when first formulated forty years ago. The same observation applies to Mackinder's land power thesis which, appearing at what seemed to be the height of the Victorian sea power age, seemed shocking and fantastic to many in the English-speaking world. (Weigert *et al.* 1957, p. 215)

Mackinder's advocacy in 1919 of a tier of states to isolate Russia from Germany has been criticized because it failed, a failure immediately forecast by Teggart (1919, p. 241): 'His proposal in short, is that, having destroyed the old defensive units, we must forthwith proceed to erect a new tier of politico-military organizations between the Baltic and the Black Sea ... To leave the new states between the upper and nether grindstones is to invite destruction.' The English geographer 'seems to have suffered the worst disgrace: he was heeded by statesmen and mocked by events' (Aron 1966, p. 195). Sprout (1964) saw this fiasco as illustrative of the general obsolescence of 'spatial views in the modern world'. 'Geographical space' was 'regarded as a strategic asset' and where it 'was deemed inadequate, a buffer zone of protected states ... might be created to absorb the shock of invasion ... The Peace Conference of 1919 did create such a buffer zone with results that are well known history.' Hall (1955) joins in the criticism. But Dugan (1962) pointed out that Mackinder's scheme had included provisions for the ultimate protection of or succour for the border states which were omitted from the actual settlement: 'They were not created at all in line with Mackinder's suggestions' (p. 252). Others have insisted that the cause of failure was not so much in the idea itself as in the betrayal of it: 'the theories of the Curzons and Mackinders would be discredited only if it could be proven that the solid zone of separation which they had envisaged had actually existed', for it was 'a buffer only on paper' (Strausz-Hupé 1942, pp. 209-10). Strategic needs were sacrificed to ethnic considerations.[13] Yugoslavia did not get the Adriatic port which Mackinder (1919, p. 215) had insisted was essential; Czechoslovakia was abandoned in 1938. In the light of events then—and in 1968—Mackinder's words (ibid., p. 206) are of interest:

Consider the Czechs: have they not stood proof against Bolshevism and asserted their capacity of nationhood under amazing conditions in Russia? Have they not shown the most extraordinary political capacity in creating anew and maintaining Slav Bohemia, though beset on three sides by Germany and on the fourth side by Hungary? Have they not also made Bohemia a hive of modern industry and a seat of modern learning? They, at any rate, will not lack the will to order and independence.

---

[13] M. had said 'I do hope that we shall recognize that a purely racial solution is not necessarily the most stable solution' (1917, p. 11).

The ink was hardly dry on the Treaty of Versailles before Mackinder was asking the House of Commons, in vain, to support the Poles:[14] 'You must not do anything to prevent Poland from supporting the remaining border States, or you must face the fact that you will see restored in Russia, bent on the reconquest of the border States, a new Czardom ... and that Czardom will be a very uncomfortable neighbour for the democracies of the world' (P.D. 1920, cxxix, 1718). After his experiences in Russia and his failure to induce the Cabinet to agree to an alliance of the border states—including the Ukraine,[15] he saw danger as coming from the Russian side. Hitherto his main concern had been to protect Russia—and the Heartland—from a resurrected Germany, and Strausz-Hupé (1942, p. 148) maintains that the 'third tier', imperfect though it was, 'did grant Russia the geographical shelter behind which she developed, within the span of twenty-two years, sufficient political cohesion and economic strength, if not "to cope with the Germans" at least to fight them with a degree of efficiency'.

Hall (1955) criticized the proposal for the third tier from another angle: 'In advocating the creation of the Middle Tier Mackinder overlooked a rule of thumb that had been used by statesmen on many occasions. According to this rule, if you fear your neighbor or covet some of his territory it is advisable to ally yourself to his neighbor on the opposite side' (p. 116). This had, of course, been true particularly of France, who had sought the Turk as a counterweight to Austria, and who had allied herself with Russia against Germany. This is, however, just an aspect of the policy of encirclement of a strong centrally-placed power. Was Hall suggesting that France and Britain should have allied themselves with Bolshevik Russia instead of establishing the 'tier'? Russia would then have overrun the borderlands, which had been promised self-determination and ethnic liberation. Mackinder's 'tier' was intended to safeguard peace, not to further national strategic aims.

[14] Dugan (1962) criticizes M. for backing the Poles rather than the Hungarians: 'He failed to recognize the potentialities of the Hungarians, as a nationality neither German nor Russian and not too favorably disposed towards either' (p. 254).

[15] The practical suggestions for the creation of an effective buffer zone he put so forcibly to the Cabinet in 1920 dispose of another objection of Hall's (1955) that 'no concrete suggestions were made by Mackinder as to how such a system of states could be established'.

Strausz-Hupé (1942, p. 155) asked, 'Is the struggle for the control of the Eurasian Heartland really the one and fundamental issue of world policy as Mackinder and, with him, Haushofer, believed it to be?' A negative answer permeates Hall (1955), and although Strausz-Hupé concludes, 'History does not provide a clearcut answer ...', he continues, 'Spain ruled an empire over which the sun never set, and Britain encircled the globe without any apparent awareness of the sublime strategic importance of the Heartland. Neither ... is there any reference that points to his [Napoleon] having believed that the Eurasian Heartland held the key to universal rule ...' Strausz-Hupé seldom misses the point, but he seems to have done so here. His examples date from the Columbian age when the maritime states had a free hand competing for the margins of the World Promontory and had to worry little about the land power in the Heartland, whereas Mackinder in 1904 was foreshadowing a change in this situation. Even so, as Strausz-Hupé concedes, 'Napoleon's dream of Empire came to grief in Russia', and the British Empire was not entirely unconcerned about the Heartland.

When Pounds (1963, p. 400) writes, 'At no point does Mackinder appear to have envisaged the possibility that the Russians themselves might organize and develop their own vast spaces and resources', he is criticizing not so much the Heartland theory itself, as Mackinder's foresight. Actually Mackinder leaves this open in 1904 and 1919, although obviously believing the Germans more likely to attempt it. By 1920, after he had personally experienced the 'efficiency of the Bolsheviks', he was certainly alive to the other possibility.

A final historical criticism is that Germany was brought to defeat in 1945 by following Mackinder (Hall 1955), but this is not a criticism of the Heartland theory as such. He had not predicted victory for Germany, only that there would be a struggle in eastern Europe between Germany and Russia for access to and exploitation of the Heartland.

A further set of criticisms may be termed philosophical. The American Hartshorne (1964, p. 55) and the East German Heyden (1958, p. 86) both call the Heartland theory pseudo-scientific, the former averring that Mackinder had not attempted 'to provide a conceptual framework for a field of study'. Akin are allegations that it is too simplistic and generalized, relying on too few elements instead of considering all cultural aspects of a nation or region (Hall 1955, de Blij 1967, Sylvester 1968, Muir 1975); but Strausz-Hupé (1942, p. 261) had already commented that 'all great strategic concepts are essentially simple'. Freeman (1961, p. 208) thought 'the perils of generalization' on a global scale such that 'the safest approach to political geography' was through regional study, a typical view amongst the timid geographers who succeeded Mackinder and his co-pioneers. However, Muir (1975) concedes to the geopoliticians a 'valuable demonstration of global unity and interaction, an antidote to the tendency of some geographers to define regions and proceed to study them in isolation' (p. 198). Mackinder (1890) believed there were 'higher flights for the political geographer than the mere mapping of frontiers and detailing of statistics. Humdrum detail is the greater part of every science, but no science can satisfy the mind which does not allow of the building of palaces out of its bricks' (p. 83). On the other hand, although he regarded generalizations as useful and essential tools for making geography an aid to statecraft, he did not overvalue them. Indeed, he wrote: 'Great generalizations may be necessary for purposes of propaganda, for purposes of political discussion in democratic countries, where the sovereign power resides in all the busy adults ... of the nation. But I heed hardly say that generalizations are suspect; they are hardly ever completely true' (1930, p. 254).

Malin (1959) claimed—in relation to Mackinder—that 'a wholeness of view about human culture and the universe is essential', because 'the employment of limited frames of reference for the interpretation of history, and even for policy science, result in distortions that are frequently, if not always, self-defeating'. Muir (1975), in the same vein, speaks of the temptation for geopoliticians 'to interpret past and future history in terms of a perceived master variable and to inflate its importance at the expense of the host of other relevant variables' (p. 198). Such critics fail to see that the Heartland theory is no more than a geostrategic framework or model within which the other factors—technical, economic, social, political, ideological, ethical—operate;[16] but which, such factors being equal, would provide 'a geographical formula into which you could fit any political balance' (1904, p. 443). Indeed, 'other factors being equal' is its overriding condition. For it is by looking to them, so as to ensure that instead of their being equal they are in one's favour, that one may escape a destiny the formula might otherwise indicate. The final paragraph of *Democratic Ideals and Reality* calls for attention to an Ideal in order to combat Reality (p. 267).

A second group of philosophical criticisms claims that the Heartland theory is deterministic, fatalistic, and given to futile prediction of the unpredictable. For East (1950) it was 'both unwise and dangerous to accept, as a predetermined end, the prediction that world hegemony must, on certain assumptions, inevitably pass to the rulers of one specified portion of the earth' (p. 80); for Pounds (1963, p. 404) the theory was 'too rigid' and 'too fatalistic', while for de Blij (1967, p. 134) it was 'a dangerous deterministic prediction'. Similar comments have been made by Mills (1956), Potter and Nimitz (1960), Learmonth (1971), and Muir (1975). Accusations of determinism had, however, already been shown to be unjustified by Strausz-Hupé (1942, p. 141); and Hall (1955), although most critical of the Heartland theory, admits that Mackinder 'was no mere preacher of environmental determinism, for he understood the human motivations and conflicting social forces of the time'. Mackinder (1916, pp. 273-4; 1919, pp. 3-5) had himself condemned the kind of determinism of which he is accused.

Some have regarded this alleged determinism as arising from a Darwinian view of states as organisms. The biologically-trained Mackinder, Ratzel, and Kjellen are said to have

never reached the center of the social sciences, which is man. In the "struggle for areas" corresponding to the "struggle for existence" in the biological evolution, man did not count . . . in the final analysis it is up to man to decide what he will do with nature and its barriers. It is not space that makes history . . . (Neumann 1943, p. 287)

Likewise Bowman (1942) had written 'the *mind* of man is still a more important source of power than a heartland or a dated

---

[16] The attention he gives these other factors has even been seen as negating the Heartland theory itself: 'The only universally valid rule to be derived from his writings is . . . in the long run, the strongest (the most numerous, the richest, the most productive) conquers' (Aron 1966, p. 198).

theory about it' (p. 157). Malin (1959) regarded Mackinder's 'commitment to the doctrine of organism' as 'indefensible and, as a frame of reference, in most hands positively vicious'; Sylvester (1968) takes a similar line. Although there are Darwinian traces in Mackinder's thought and language, he explicitly rejected evolutionary theory as a basis for geostrategy, the whole point of his argument being that man should—and could—rise above such 'fatalism'. But in order to do this he had to be made aware of the geographical realities and historical forces that he would have to contend with.

Most accusations of deterministic prediction arise because the critic has taken the Heartland theory to subsist entirely in the triplet: 'Who rules East Europe commands the Heartland: Who rules the Heartland commands the World-Island: Who rules the World-Island commands the World' (Mackinder 1919, p. 194). Often it seems that this is all he has read of Mackinder. Taken in context this tryptych is clearly a warning of what could happen unless certain steps are taken. Its purpose was to ensure that it did not come true, not to predict that it would do so. But East (1950) refers to the three lines as 'his sweeping prognostications'. He takes them one by one to demonstrate that Mackinder's 'prophecy' contains 'generalizations and assumptions which scarcely withstand close analysis'.

In so far as Mackinder could be said to be 'predicting', i.e. if geographical reality is allowed to take its course, the long time scale is frequently forgotten. The Pre-Columbian Age (land power dominant) and the Columbian Age (sea power dominant) lasted each for centuries. The first century of the Post-Columbian Age (land power dominant) has just begun, and the theory looks to an ultimate, not immediate state of affairs. This ultimate stage may be long in developing, or could be prevented from coming at all. Land power failed to conquer the maritime states of western Europe during the medieval period of its ascendancy. Sea power failed to conquer the Heartland in the Columbian Age. The Heartland may not conquer the Rimland in the Post-Columbian Age. Mackinder repeatedly pointed out the pitfalls of prophecy (e.g. 1900b, p. 153; 1904, p. 443; 1935b, p. 502; 1943, p. 602; 1944, p. 132). Jackson (1962), normally a critic, states that:

Mackinder in 1904 did not prophesy that Russia would one day rule the world; rather, as a geographer who had studied the course of Asian history, he believed that whatever power controlled the pivot, whether Russia allied with Germany, or possibly a conquering China supported by Japan, would enjoy enormous geographical advantages that could lead to world empire . . . ;

and Aron (1966, p. 198) agrees that 'nowhere does Mackinder explicitly answer the question: "in a conflict between a continental empire and a maritime empire, which . . . has the best chance of winning?" ' This is because his analysis is based on more variables than his critics allow. To reject prediction was not, however, to deny the value of informed speculation about the future, nor to deprive his formula of value; because it worked when applied to the past and the present, he thought it might well prove useful in the future. He once concluded a lecture series thus:

Our object . . . has been to endeavour to see the past clearly, to see what consequences have followed from what causes, to look, as best we can, at the causes in action at present, and to anticipate what are the probable consequences, with the small insight we can command. The result can only be a provisional scheme of causes and effects, which must be constantly subjected to the criticism of new events and increasing knowledge, but without some such working scheme, we have no standard by which to measure the events of our own lifetime. (Mackinder 1900b, p. 272)

Hall (1955) rated Mackinder's formula 'unsuccessful', and Weigert *et al.* (1957) maintained that it was not possible 'in terms of geographic realities and of human and natural resources, to construe a balance of power formula which can be applied permanently to the world relationships of one major area, such as the Heartland' (p. 219). Mackinder would probably have agreed with Strausz-Hupé's conclusion:

The geopolitical approach cannot lead to the discovery of immutable principles of statecraft . . . There is no single science, this side of metaphysics, which provides conclusive answers to the whys and wherefores of the rise and fall of nations and empires. There exists, however, an obvious correspondence between the organization of states and the pattern of their natural environment, between political and natural phenomena, that one may justifiably consider historical processes in terms of geopolitical patterns. (1942, pp. 140–1)

The next group of criticisms may be generally termed ethical: Mackinder's global view is from a purely British standpoint and designed to justify and protect British imperialism; it is geography in the service of reaction; it laid the foundations of Nazi militarism, and leads to war. Such opinions range from the mild, 'That he is an Englishman is apparent' (Teggart 1919) or 'Mackinder wrote as a Britisher' (Cressey 1945) or 'Only a Britisher could have written as Mackinder did' (Weigert 1949), through the stronger assertion that he 'enunciated his significant theory of the World Heartland merely to enhance the security of the British Empire' (Pearcy *et al.*, 1948), to extreme and Marxist views of him as an imperialist lackey. Bunge (1973) sees the Heartland theory as advice to make war on Russia: 'Hitler took this advice seriously and did conquer almost all the Heartland.[17] His obsession with geographic space caused him to extend himself into the disaster of Stalingrad.' He continues, 'To conquer the world is to conquer Moscow ... Dulles found the same view toward Moscow as Mackinder and Hitler.' According to Burgess (1976) Mackinder is one of a 'particularly unsavoury bunch'; he 'exceeded the excesses of even Haushofer' by 'helping to organize the British military contribution to assisting counter-revolution'. On the other side of the 'iron curtain' Heyden (1958, pp. 86–7) writes:

Mackinder ... calls for the elimination of Russian rule over the Heartland, i.e. for the conquest of the Russian territory. Immediately after the victory of the Great Socialist October Revolution in 1919 he again put forward his abominable ideas to accompany the intervention of the '14 states' against the infant Soviet power.

None of these statements stands up to serious examination. The 1904 paper was an analysis that could have been written by a German or a Russian or a Spaniard; the 1919 book is a warning to the democracies in general, but the analysis remains neutral, and its conclusions could again be understood in and applied from any part of the world, as indeed they were in Germany, and even in the Soviet Union (Pauly 1974). As for urging the conquest of Russia, he was much more concerned to save Russia from domination by Germany, 'and was by no means the Russophobe he has sometimes been pictured as being' (Dugan

---

[17] In fact, only a relatively small part.

1962). The non-nationalistic, even humanitarian, nature of Mackinder's world view has been observed by Goblet (1956, p. 14):

Mackinder's political geography is the very antithesis of that of Ratzel and his Nazi offspring. Ratzel used his abstractions to claim for the Reich the 'space' demanded by the German 'will to power'. Mackinder's concrete study moves outwards from the region to embrace the whole domain of humanity. Whereas Ratzel's work ends in a map of the Greater Germany, the final outcome of Mackinder's work is a map of the world.

Strausz-Hupé (1942, p. 142) wrote of the 'cool detachment' of Mackinder's book.

Of course, it cannot be denied that Mackinder's Heartland theory contributed to the German decision to dominate Russia, nor that it has been the basis of the American policy of encircling the USSR. It must also be admitted that Mackinder was on the side of the *status quo* as far as Britain, France, and America were concerned, but opposed the building of empires by Germany or Russia. It is easier to justify defence by 'haves' of an existing global system than its upsetting by 'have nots'—one side can be said to be for peace and the other for war. Hence the contrast between the motives of Mackinder and Haushofer should not be overdrawn. Although Mackinder recognized that the varied endowment of territories and peoples led to the unequal growth of nations, and this in turn led to war, he was not prepared to concede anything to the 'ruthless organizers' of ambitious states. Yet his analysis stands unaffected by any one-sided nationalistic or patriotic use of it—it is there for friend and foe alike to learn from. There may be valid Marxist arguments against the abuse of the Heartland theory, but they do not affect the concept itself.

Mackinder's presentation of his thesis has been seen as racialist and Eurocentric (e.g. by Malin 1959) because he uses such phrases as 'war between civilized and half-civilized powers' and 'yellow peril', and because he recognizes peoples as differing in their attributes, and assumes the superiority of the West European culture. Muir (1975, p. 195) comments that his 'value-judgments about non-European cultures will be distasteful to many modern readers', although 'some underlying ideas are striking in their modernity'.

There are some political and ideological criticisms. Jackson (1962) thought that Soviet domination could come from 'factors which do not involve the Heartland', notably its communism; this was 'a faith born of despair' that appealed 'to those who strive for a fuller material life—and demand it immediately', and to those 'with strong anti-Western racist feelings'. Pounds (1963) agrees, while Jones (1964) insists that, 'The great advantages of the Soviet Union have been political, especially its ability to follow a planned strategy persistently.' On the other hand, East (1950) sees ideology as a drawback to the stability of the Soviet bloc, and Hall (1955) thought that, 'The Soviet Union might suffer a relative decline in its influence if the peoples of the earth . . . become convinced of the spuriousness of the Communist philosophy.' There is some substance in these points, and it can only be repeated that the Heartland theory is a geostrategical framework in which other factors may be set, not an exclusive explanatory device. Mackinder was the last person to maintain that geography explained everything,[18] but he did not believe in 1904 that 'any possible social revolution will alter her [Russia's] essential relations to the great geographical limits of her existence'. The communist-capitalist antithesis merely reinforces the land–sea and centre–periphery dichotomies on a global scale, and the operation of one of them does not exclude the working of the others.

Walters (1974, pp. 31-2) observed that, 'Some people . . . have pointed out that it appears that Mackinder later actually rejected his views concerning his Heartland theory', and Hall (1955) wrote that 'only a few years before the cold war began, Mackinder seemed to abandon his 1904 assumption that future power alignments would revolve around his pivot area' (p. 120). This is because in his 1943 paper he hoped for friendly co-operation between an Atlantic alliance and the Soviet Union to prevent a resurrection of German power. This new axis, with its highly developed regions between the Missouri and the Yenisei would 'balance' the densely-populated lands of South East Asia and the Far East. Had he stuck by his 'pivot of history' he would have more accurately represented what was to happen—tension

---

[18] '. . . do not attempt to . . . explain everything human in terms of geography. You cannot and it is well that you should not. The initiative is in the soul of man . . .' (Mackinder 1916, p. 277).

between the Soviet Union in the Heartland and the Atlantic alliance in the Outer Crescent, and competition between them for the Inner Crescent or Rimland, a tension of which his own Heartland theory was to be a major cause. He would have regretted this, just as he had regretted its use by the Nazis. Now at a great age (82), he seems to have been preoccupied with a peaceful world after the war, while still believing that a balance of power was its best safeguard. In seeing that balance as one between the white peoples of North America, Western Europe, and northern Eurasia on the one hand, and the brown and yellow peoples of Monsoon Asia on the other he may have been more far-sighted then most of us. For the alternative might be a great world war in which the Soviet Union was destroyed, or a 'cold' war in which it disintegrated under the strains of the arms race. This would create the situation he had envisaged almost forty years before, enabling 'the Chinese ... organized by the Japanese' to become the Heartland power, but adding 'an oceanic frontage to the resources of the great continent' (Mackinder 1904, p. 437). This world would then no longer be balanced or free.

It seems likely that Weigert (1949) was right in saying 'that Mackinder's new balance of power doctrine, a world divided into two equal, therefore free, hemispheres of one billion human beings each,' was 'a structure built upon shifting sand'. And so the last criticism brings, as with so much in Mackinder's life, a note of failure.

Chapter 9

Conclusion

Mackinder had two careers, one academical and one political. Both lasted about forty years, with the political beginning and ending some fifteen years after the academic. From 1885 to 1925 he was continuously engaged as a university teacher or administrator, the first two years being in university extension. His life as a scholar and geographer was, however, much longer, beginning with a schoolboy's unusual awareness of, and interest in, his environment, and ending with his final words to the Royal Geographical Society in 1945—a period of fertile mental activity stretching over at least seventy years.

In his academic career he excelled both as administrator and as teacher, combining organizing ability of a high order with the gift of translating the thoughts of his active and imaginative mind into clear and forceful language. Because his administrative headships were all of infant institutions struggling to establish themselves, they demanded further qualifications—energy and zeal, courage and conviction, self-confidence and a certain ruthlessness, patience and perseverance, persuasiveness and tact; for he had not only to deal with many difficult and trying situations, including official obstruction and academic resistance to new ideas, but also to lobby for political and financial support.[1] Tributes to his ability as a lecturer abound: his commanding presence, sonorous voice, and fluent articulation without benefit of notes ensured a good and often enthusiastic hearing.[2] His command of the written word was equally assured,

---

[1] See M.'s reports on his early work at Oxford published in the *Proc. RGS* from 1888, and Childs (1933) for his work as the first Principal at Reading. Childs wrote (p. 11), '... he made some opponents, as a leader in stark earnest is bound to do. He sometimes ploughed ahead, leaving a wake of troubled waters, and he certainly gave the rest of us plenty to think and talk about. Masterful, he yet made us his partners.' He was admired by the Webbs as a 'brilliant' Director of the LSE (Mackenzie 1978, vol. ii, p. 316).

[2] Fleure (1953, p. 234) speaks of, 'His handsome presence, with flashing eye and a gift of oratory that has rarely been bettered.' The popularity of his lectures arose too from their being alive with ideas and not weighed down with factual material. 'I do not believe in lectures for the purpose of teaching detail', he once said (1912, p. 204); 'The

and here too a strong and masculine style, simple and direct language, with occasional use of picturesque description or dramatic evocation, held the reader's attention. He was particularly fond of balanced contrasts and comparisons. He addressed his reader personally and directly in the second person, commanded him in the imperative mood, and set his mind to work with rhetorical questions.[3] Hilda Ormsby, his assistant at the LSE, told of his 'testing every sentence over and over again' as he wrote (*The Times*, 17 March 1947). His extraordinarily wide reading into and deep knowledge of so many facets of life and learning enabled him to enrich his writing with a profusion of examples.[4] Occasionally he would employ new words or old words in a new sense, sometimes felicitously, sometimes not. He introduced such terms as 'manpower' and 'nodality'. His use of 'Going Concern' for the momentum of the complex integration of economy, society, and polity was perhaps not so happy but 'Heartland' (the inaccessible fastnesses of northern Eurasia) became a household word in America, and is still the best known and most provocative term in geopolitics.

The origin of or stimulus to his ideas has been ascribed both to the Darwinian principles he imbibed as an undergraduate in Natural Science, and to the nineteenth-century German anthropologists and geographers; but he is too critical of these sources to justify either explanation. Since infancy he had avidly read tales of travel and exploration, and he had shown a precocious interest in international affairs. After taking his

---

sole purpose of a lecture, in my opinion, is to indicate a point of view, and once people have been put into possession of the point of view, then they can very quickly get the facts for themselves.'

[3] e.g. 'Now carry your mind to the "Great Sea", the Mediterranean. You have there essentially the same physical ingredients as in Egypt ... Was it from Crete that the sea-folk settled round the other shores of the Aegean ...?' (1919, pp. 44, 46). Weigert (1949, p. 80) thought his language 'rare and forceful poetry', but Pounds (1963, p. 399) found *Democratic Ideals and Reality* 'somewhat laboured', and Freeman (1980) calls it 'a political monologue not without obscurities' (p. 106); Sylvester (1968, p. 57) complained that 'he overloaded his style with catchy words'. Cantor (1960, p. 326), however, concludes that, 'he was gifted with the ability to project his personality on to the printed page; his strong, salty character stands out clearly on almost every page he wrote. Of him, it may be truly said, "le style, c'est l'homme"'.

[4] It must be apparent to almost any reader of *Democratic Ideals and Reality* that M. was a widely read and deeply learned man, but Sylvester (1968, p. 57) remarks, 'Since he had few footnotes, there was little proof that he had read many sources'!

science degree and before studying the German geographers, he read Modern History, prepared successfully for a geology prize, studied law, and 'got up' economics for university extension work. His keen intellectual curiosity led him along many pathways, and all this gave him a broad but sure foundation on which to build his own integrated geographical philosophy.[5] Of course, many of his ideas had been anticipated by others, and doubtless many of them originated from a familiarity with earlier work. His intellectual achievement was to cement these ideas—whatever their provenance—together into conceptual structures able to stand the test of time. They would be, he hoped, bridges across that growing divide between the sciences and the humanities which he was one of the first to see as a threat to modern civilization.

Besides its bridge-building character he saw geography as 'an aid to statecraft', and his geopolitical fame stemmed from his efforts to give examples. For these to be effective he realized that, in the twentieth century, they would have to give a world view—Eurocentric and other regional approaches would no longer suffice. But to produce a global view into which the actual course of events, past, present, and future, could be fitted without straining his reader's historical sense or political credulity, required the art of generalization in the highest degree. Here Mackinder excelled: from a confused world chaos of intricately inter-related geographical facts and historical events he could pluck simplicity, realizing full well that 'it is always difficult, when called upon to consider and express large ideas in a short time to insert all the necessary limitations and qualifications' (1909a, p. 478).[6] He would most certainly have met Spengler's (1926, p. 41) criterion: 'for me ... the test of value to be applied to a thinker is his eye for the great facts of his own time'.

<hr/>

[5] 'He found British geography at its lowest ebb, at a time when it was not an accepted subject at the higher levels of education, and, by his insistence on a sound intellectual and philosophical basis, coupled with an immense amount of proselytising work, he more than any other single man, won for it a place in the academic sun' (Cantor 1960, p. 327). But Sylvester (1968, p. 57), without adducing any substantial justification, alleged that 'his writing hurt geography'.

[6] H. R. Mill said, 'In all his work Mackinder generalized from the facts of geography regardless of minor details, which to many of us ... have allowed the trees to obscure the outline of the wood. He has always been able to see a subject as a whole' (*Geogrl J.* lxxxvi, p. 13).

It was this rare ability that enabled him to perceive 'the geographical realities' that really mattered and, placing them in the historical context, to beget the concepts of the global closed system, the Heartland, and the land-power–sea-power/centre–periphery antitheses, breath-taking in their sweep, yet sublime in their simplicity. It was his power of generalization that gave him his tremendous influence on world affairs; it explains why 'a brief paper and book, contain all those audacious ideas that Haushofer and his disciples adopted for their world view' (Weigert 1942, p. 119), and why 'the Heartland theory stands as the first premise in Western military thought' (Walters 1974, p. 22). It is perhaps because of their incomprehension of the power of generalization, immersed as they are in detail, that many historians have not recognized the power of Mackinder's ideas, and that so many geographers have cavilled at them.[7]

Mackinder's active political and public career may be said to have begun with his candidature in the 1900 general election, and ended with his resignation from the Imperial Shipping Committee in 1939. Although varied and eventful, it seldom brought him into the limelight, and was unsuccessful in that he never held high office. Yet he achieved much behind the scenes. He was the brain, first of Rosebery's Liberal Imperialist group, and then of the Tariff Reformers.[8] During the 1914–18 war he was responsible for the organization of recruiting in Scotland and the launching of what was to become the National Savings Movement. He served on several committees and royal commissions, and the good will and unanimity of the two imperial committees which he chaired, were practical examples of the kind of harmony and co-operation between the nations of the Empire that he was constantly urging.

He was twelve years (1910–22) a member of the House of Commons, but 'never quite made his mark' there (Amery 1953, vol. i, p. 228). He was neither intellectually nor temperamentally suited to be a politician: his originality of thought and the causes he believed in made it difficult for him to hold to a party line. He took the long view, while the men he was associated with were more concerned with the practical politics of the

---

[7] Few historians of modern times even mention Mackinder.
[8] See Semmell (1958) for an elaboration of this statement.

moment and with electoral advantage: 'practical politicians were not interested in his vision and were bored by his grasp of detail' (Blouet 1975, p. 37). It may be too that his dramatic and didactic style, so effective in the lecture room, was less suited to the atmosphere of the Commons.

He was highly regarded for his intellect and oratory, and it was believed that he was destined for high office in a Liberal administration, and, after his conversion to tariff reform, in a Unionist one.[9] There were four main reasons for his failure in this respect. The first was his poverty. Without the private or business income with which most young and aspiring politicians of the day were blessed, Mackinder had to make ends meet on the small salaries he received from his academic posts, later supplemented by royalties from his schoolbooks, and director-ships of one or two companies. But university administration, lectures, and writing books took time and energy which could otherwise have been devoted to furthering a political career. His second drawback was age, and this followed from the first. Although his interest in politics went back to his schooldays and he had been President of the Oxford Union, he could not afford to stand for Parliament until after 1908. True, he had stood in 1900, but it had put him in debt. Consequently, he was almost fifty when he entered the Commons; then came the war which neutralized politics until he was too old for a political career. A third disadvantage was his integrity and lack of personal ambition. He did not want power for himself but to advance the causes nearest to his heart. He left the Liberal party, when sure of advancement, over the issue of tariffs and empire free trade. He accepted a salary from Lord Milner's Empire group only on condition that he kept his freedom of action. Fourthly, he had bad luck. He joined the Unionists at a time when they were to be out of office for nearly twenty years. Although the 1922 election brought in the first Conservative government for seventeen years, he lost his seat in Glasgow where socialism and anti-imperialism had advanced further than anywhere else in the country. He was sent as High Commissioner to South Russia in 1919, but 'had the ground cut from him by the change of British policy, as well as by the White Russians' own incompet-ence' (Amery 1953, vol. i, p. 228).

[9] For this see Blouet (1975, pp. 18, 43-4).

As Blouet (1975, p. 44) writes:

It was not open to Mackinder, as it was to Sir Edward Grey, to be
sent down from Oxford for gross idleness, devote himself to fly fishing
and nature study, yet take up a local parliamentary seat and with the
passage of time assume the high office which was regarded as the
normal accomplishment of the Greys. Even given his great abilities it
was an achievement for Mackinder to have penetrated, if but for a
short time, the ranks of those who were seriously spoken of as future
Ministers of the Crown. He had to earn a living in a profession
in which it was then easy to be comfortable but difficult to generate
the wealth needed by an aspiring politician. In spite of all the careers,
the books, and the businesses, he left only a few thousand pounds
as he had lived generously and his activities consumed most of his
income.

Mackinder's business career, which began soon after he became an MP and continued into the 1930s, does not seem to
have progressed beyond the chairmanship of a couple of ailing
companies. One was badly hit by an anomaly in the way the
wartime excess profits tax was calculated, while both were
affected by the Great Depression. None the less he remained
convinced that capitalism working in a just society was the best
way to create wealth in the community at large, and although
he had sympathy for the aims of socialism, he did not think it
would work. As Beatrice Webb (1952, p. 158) wrote in 1919,
'He refuses to believe that this drive towards the equalitarian
state is a permanent factor; sooner or later it will be brought to
a standstill, long before it has reached its goal, by the superior
organization of the brain-working capitalist, stimulated by the
love of riches and the delight in adventure.'
On many economic, social, and political issues, it seemed to
Mackinder that attitudes were either too wholly 'idealistic' or
too wholly 'realistic'. Ideals could not be achieved without
taking account of reality, and realism without ideals led to the
harsh rule of 'organizers'. He himself attempted a synthesis, and
it was in his character to do so, for he 'had a way of blending
dreams and hard sense' (Childs 1933, p. 11). He believed in
Empire, not only because it was necessary for the continuance
of Britain's power, but also as the best means of spreading 'the
English tradition', a tradition 'vital to civilization' (1925, p. 3).
He was for tariff reform because it would look after the interests

of ordinary working people rather than those of bankers in London. 'I want', he told the House of Commons, 'to deal with this matter . . . from the point of view of the human beings who constitute the real nation' (P.D. 1910, xiv, 317).

He rejected the claims of *laissez-faire* economists to be the enlightened upholders of a peaceful and moral order, reminding his readers that Carlyle branded open competition as equivalent to "devil take the hindmost" ' (1906, pp. 1–2). Although he believed in efficiency and profitability, he insisted that the free market economy, centralization, and specialization be restrained in the interests of humanity; they led to class warfare and to the impoverishment of the provinces for the benefit of the metropolis. He preferred to see a country divided into provinces and regions, each with a full and balanced economic and social life, and united by 'neighbourliness', rather than divided into classes; he regretted that 'one of the most serious difficulties in the way of the realization of the balanced local community' in Britain lay 'in the difference of dialect spoken by the common people and the upper classes' (1919, pp. 251–2). His balanced regions would avoid the degree of industrial specialization which produced that 'bane of our modern industrial life'—monotony of work. The smaller towns of his autonomous provinces would possess a social cohesiveness denied to the great conurbations produced by *laissez-faire*: 'East-ends and West-ends divide our cities into castes; at whatever sacrifice we must tone away such contrasts' (1919, p. 266).

He was no warmonger, but he did not believe peace and prosperity could be kept without power; and if Britain lost the power to protect her interests, it would be her working classes who would suffer: 'we are apt . . . to forget that the order of the world, and with it the welfare of our teeming population, still rests upon Power' (1906, p. 2). His patriotism was idealistic rather than jingoistic: he was proud of his country and he believed his fellow-countrymen to have special virtues and qualities. To the extent that he thought the white race generally to have distinctive qualities to which it owed its supremacy, he was what would now be called a 'racist'; he sympathized with those in Canada and Australia who were opposed to miscegenation. Such views were almost universally held in his time, but he differed from most of his contemporaries in urging the need for tolerance and understanding of other races, cultures, and religions.

He had intellectual charisma. No one could doubt his mental brilliance akin to genius. His fertile, active, and restless brain seemed always to be throwing out new ideas and original thoughts. These were seldom purely academic concepts, but founded upon present realities or tied to future possibilities. They were ideas for practical application. He may perhaps have been thinking of himself when he wrote (1916, p. 275):

What is the characteristic of the Englishman? Surely almost above all things his refusal to accept the results of a logical conclusion! And why? Because he knows that the most beautiful logic in nine cases out of ten brings you to a result which when tested by experience breaks down. And for that reason he is apt to look askance at academics: he knows that life is so complex that hardly ever have you all your premises expressed in such clear form that you can simply apply either mathematical or logical analysis to them and then safely build on the conclusion that emerges.

He would have explained his gifts as a capacity for 'outlook': an ability to interpret the past, to visualize the present, and to imagine the future. 'Outlook'—backwards, forwards, and all around—made it difficult for him to separate history and geography into 'subjects', since it was the interplay of time and space, of man and place, of historical event and geographical feature that he perceived so clearly. This enabled him to offer remarkable insights into all kinds of situations. By merely contemplating his maps he deduced geological explanations of phenomena which were later demonstrated to be correct, and on the only recorded occasion on which he can be said to have 'blown his own trumpet' a little, he said (1927) that 'several times ... Professor Gregory has given me the very greatest pleasure by writing to me and telling me that now this and now that theory of mine had been substantiated by his detailed work'. His remarks on the geographical position of Britain exemplify his power to interpret the past:

Seen thus in relation to earlier and to later history, Britain is possessed of two geographical qualities, complementary rather than antagonistic: insularity and universality. Before Columbus, the insularity was more evident than the universality. Within closed coasts, impregnable when valiantly held, but in sight of the world and open to stimulus

... her people were able to advance with Europe, and yet, protected from military necessities, to avoid tyranny and to retain the legacy of freedom bequeathed in the German forests. Ordered liberty, fitted to the complex conditions of modern civilization, needed centuries of slow, experimental growth, and was naturally cradled in a land insulated yet not isolated.

After Columbus, value began to attach to the ocean-highway, which is in its nature universal. The unity of the ocean is the simple physical fact underlying the dominant value of sea-power in the modern globe-wide world. Britain—*of* Europe, yet not *in* Europe — was free to devote resources, drawn ultimately from the continent, to the expansion of civilization beyond the ocean. The sea preserved liberty, and allowed of a fertility of private initiative which was incompatible with supreme military organization. The same sea, by reducing the reserve of men and material needed for the protection of the island home, has permitted the devotion of British initiative and energy to trade and rule abroad. (1902, pp. 11–12)

His description of London illustrates his understanding of the present:

The life of the great metropolis at the beginning of the twentieth century exhibits a daily throb as of a huge pulsating heart. Every evening half a million men are sent in quick streams, like corpuscles of blood in the arteries, along the railways and the trunk roads outward to the suburbs. Every morning they return, crowding into the square mile or two wherein the exchanges of the world are finally adjusted ... In a manner all south-eastern England is a single urban community; for steam and electricity are changing our geographical conceptions. A city in an economic sense is no longer an area covered continuously with streets and houses. The wives and children of the merchants, even of the more prosperous of the artisans, live without— beyond the green fields—where the men only sleep and pass the Sabbath. The metropolis in its largest meaning includes all the counties for whose inhabitants London is 'Town', whose men do habitual business there, whose women buy there, whose standard of thought is determined there.[10] (1902, pp. 257–8)

---

[10] R. E. Dickinson (1976) writes: 'His concept of "Metropolitan England", as the area of the south-east that is dominated by association with London, was expressed sixty years ago. It is still one of the dominant realities of our day, one to which we are still seeking means of adjustment in terms of regional and national planning. The thinking of Mackinder was a generation ahead of his time' (p. 37). Even Professor Freeman (1980, p. 172) concedes that 'Mackinder's idea of "metropolitan England" appeared to have more validity than ever before' in the 1960s.

In 1908 he made a remarkably accurate forecast of future political alignment, telling Beatrice Webb 'that eventually the cleavage would be between tariff reform and socialism, the individualist liberal being beaten out of the field[11] (qu. in Blouet 1975, p. 29). However, his most frequent looks into the future cast doubt on the continuing supremacy of Britain and the permanence of the Empire in an age of emerging superpowers.

It was his ability to move from such well-founded speculations about the future to a thorough grasp of immediate practical problems that made him such a good administrator and efficient organizer. It explains why in 1892 he was chosen to head the new college at Reading, where his colleaues found that 'before engaging our chief in argument, it was well to be sure of one's ground' (Childs 1933, p. 11). It was because of his ability to combine vision of the wider issues with a firm grip upon day-to-day affairs that the Tariff Reform League wanted him as their secretary in 1903, that Sidney Webb invited him to take over the London School of Economics in the same year, and that Curzon sent him to Russia in 1919.

Little is known about Mackinder as a private person, and any estimate of his character and personality has to be made from his public life. He became restless after a time in any one occupation and described (1931a) his career as 'a long succession of adventures and resignations'. He had the pioneer spirit, and once said, 'I like beginnings' (Ormsby 1947). He was a romantic, finding it difficult to maintain a coldly scientific attitude to his geographical work, and soon bringing human values to it. His interest in art and music is apparent from frequent analogies in his writing. He insisted that, however necessary scientific and technical education was for survival in the coming age—and he believed it to be vital—humane studies should not be sacrificed; and a concern for humanity and moral values penetrates even his geopolitical work. He warned (1924, p. 286) that, in an increasingly scientific and technological age, 'the happiness of men will depend more than ever on the exercise of moral qualities, for man's power of working evil will have increased equally with his power of good'. His romanticism found expression in his blending of science and

---

[11] After the 1914–18 war the Conservative party stood for tariff reform ('protection') even though its leaders shirked the issue for a time when in office.

art, reason and emotion, the practical and the visionary, the 'military and the missionary', and in a strong sense of history and a belief in tradition. Speaking of the British Constitution, he said (1914a, p. 268):

As a race we owe everything to our sense of history. Nothing is so convenient in practice, because nothing is so nicely fitted to its purpose, as that which has been evolved under the pressure of events. At the same time nothing so easily commands acquiescence as that which comes down from the past, so that 'the memory of man runneth not to the contrary'.

In personal dealings he seems to have been forceful and straightforward, not mincing words and not suffering fools. 'Certainly, he could never be described as a "nice man"—nor would he wish to be so described' (Cantor 1960, p. 326). The eminent human geographer, Fleure, commented that 'if one tolerated his dreams, his was an attractive if formidable personality' (ibid., p. 325). Beatrice Webb, who was an unsparing critic, described him as 'coarse-grained' and her husband called him 'brutal', yet they had 'the highest regard for him' (Blouet 1975, pp. 18, 28). Both Bertrand Russell (1967, p. 176) and Beatrice Webb (1948, p. 399) describe a party given on 8 February 1905 by the Webbs, which included Balfour (the Prime Minister), Wernher ('chief of all the South African millionaires'), Sir Oliver Lodge ('scientist and spiritualist'), Granville Barker ('the young and beautiful actor'), besides Mackinder ('the head Beast of the School of Economics',[12] the Russells, and others. Beatrice notes that, 'There was a subtle antipathy of Balfour to Mackinder and Wernher, mere philistine administrators he would feel ... Mackinder and Wernher chummed up and walked away together.' But Bertrand, who liked Mackinder less than the Webbs, says, 'Poor Mackinder made a bee line for Balfour, but got landed with me, much to my amusement. It was a sore trial to his politeness, from which he extricated himself indifferently.' His successor at Reading tells how, as a young recruit to the staff, he was informed by Mackinder that his work was not good enough, but in such a way as to make a friend:

What he said was unsparing, but not unfeeling. I knew that his criticism was right, but the rightness of things does not always make

[12] The personal descriptions are Russell's.

them palatable. No one had ever talked like that to me before. I felt challenged ... The criticism dealt out to me had braced without wounding ... My unbroken friendship with my chief dated from that hour. (Childs 1933, p. 4)

Mackinder's presence was a formidable one:

Of Halford Mackinder it has been remarked that, when in his presence, one knew one was with 'a great man'. Certainly he was a most impressive man, both physically and mentally. Built on big lines, he was of dignified stature, his appearance enhanced by his handsome leonine head, and, in later years, his silver hair. His physique was matched by his voice which was powerful and sonorous. (Cantor 1960, p. 365)

The story of his life leaves no doubt that he was a man of tremendous energy, and possessed of great physical and moral courage; the former virtue was demonstrated at Mount Kenya in 1899, and in South Russia in 1919–20; the latter when, as a young man of 25, he attacked the views of Major-General Sir Frederick Goldsmid.[13] His honesty and integrity shine forth clearly and have never been questioned, except by Marxists.[14] Yet he was modest, even humble in the face of his own achievements and distinctions; in his descriptions of his Kenya expedition he minimized both the dangers and his own contribution, but gave high praise to other members of the party.

The frantically busy life he led absorbed all his energies and left little time for recreation, though his support of the national theatre idea in Parliament suggests he may have been a theatre-goer; but it is more likely, as Blouet (1975) suggests, that his interest was linked with his moving in a circle that included Shaw and the Granville Barkers. He lived wholly for his country, the Empire, world affairs, education, history, and geography, and for the debate and discussion of the questions these topics threw up. He was, at various times, an active member of three dining and discussion clubs. Geography, to

---

[13] Sir Frederick John Goldsmid (1818–1908), major-general, specialist in oriental languages, and widely travelled.

[14] 'At the pinnacle of his career Mackinder exceeded the excesses of even Haushofer who did at least maintain the pretence of academic distance from his masters. In 1919 he ... helped to organize the British military contribution to assisting counter-revolution. For these services to the advancement of reaction he was knighted in 1920' (Burgess 1976, pp. 12–13).

which he was attached from his schooldays, was undoubtedly his first love; he gave it lifelong service, and it served to unify his other interests in a grand and integrated world view. He showed over many decades an interest in and understanding of Canada, which he visited several times. He saw the Dominion as the foremost member of a future united Empire; he regretted the lack of sympathy for Canadian aspirations which he found widespread in Britain, fearing lest Canada be pushed into the arms of America.

Most of the causes he worked for were betrayed or came to nought, and most of his farsighted warnings went unheeded. Yet in his speeches and writings there is no hint of recrimination or even disappointment. He did permit himself the observation (1931a) that Curzon had advised him to accept the position of High Commissioner to South Russia 'because I should probably enter Moscow beside General Denikin'. He was spared the post-war disintegration of the British Empire. The single great tragedy of his life was the break-up of his marriage early in the century, his wife going to live abroad, first in Italy and later in Switzerland; they were reconciled before he died. Few of his friends and acquaintances even knew he was married, and the usual statement that he was survived by Lady Mackinder failed to appear in his obituary notices. Their only child died in infancy. His last years were afflicted with growing deafness.

Mackinder's abilities were highly thought of by his contemporaries, both by politicians such as Haldane, Curzon, and Amery, and by intellectuals like Wells, the Webbs, and Shaw. Shaw 'had a great admiration for Halford and said that he ought to have been our Ambassador to America. But he quite saw that without a wife he could not have been.'[15] Sir Michael Sadler, the eminent civil servant and educationalist, remembered him as 'a big man—with power and swift insight into the larger problems of world politics ... [For his] ability, strength, courage, he has not been placed as he should have been. *Why?*' (qu. in Blouet 1975, p. 44). On the other hand, in academic life, there was a strange withholding of the recognition due to his gifts and accomplishments. Some British geographers, although they benefited directly or indirectly from his efforts, seemed to resent his eminence, and particularly the fame and influence of

[15] Letter from Mrs Leopold Mackinder to Miss Jean Ritchie, 25 June 1947.

his geostrategic ideas. Freeman (1975, p. 576) writes that 'he did not endear himself to many geographers of his time any more than he endeared himself to Mrs Mackinder.'[16] The Royal Geographical Society failed to honour him until his eighty-fourth year. Cantor (1960, p. 330) writes of his having been 'curiously neglected since his death'.

There was similar lack of recognition from the academic community at large, probably to some extent because he was a geographer and because of the dislike and distrust with which geography was regarded, but also because he did not keep to subject boundaries, ranging often into the preserves of others. According to Howarth (1951, p. 152), 'It was said of Mackinder by historians that he knew no history, by geologists that he knew no geology, by climatologists that he knew no climatology.' Such a contumelious statement is easily refuted from his writings. His Oxford college, Christ Church, failed to elect him to an honorary Studentship,[17] and no honorary degrees came his way, nor any fellowships of learned societies;[18] however, his University did, in 1971, commemorate his name by establishing the Halford Mackinder Professorship of Geography. Despite his achievements and his undoubted influence upon the course of history, he is seldom even mentioned in contemporary general histories and encyclopedias.[19] This is to some degree because he was a man whose ideas worked behind the scenes, not one of those out in the front to whom responsibility is more readily attributed. It may be, however, that 'he will be remembered when others, now more famous, are forgotten' (Cantor 1960, p. 330).

[16] He gives no evidence for this assertion, and there is contrary testimony. There have been exceptions to the subsequent neglect and deprecation of M. among British geographers, notably C. A. Fisher, E. W. Gilbert, J. W. House, R. P. M. Moss, and J. F. Unstead.

[17] A dignity accorded to those who have distinguished themselves in the public service, politics, scholarship, the arts, etc.

[18] He was of course an FRGS, but fellowship of the RGS is gained through interest in geography, not for distinguished scholarship.

[19] He is now in the *Encyclopedia Britannica*, the entry by H. W. Weigert in the 1964 edition (vol. xiv, pp. 590-1) being apparently the first.

Bibliography and List of References

ABDEL-MALEK, A. (1978). 'Geopolitics and national movements: an essay on the dialectics of imperialism', in *Radical geography* (ed. R. Peet), 293-307. Methuen, London (also Chicago, 1977)

ALEXANDER, L. M. (1957). *World political patterns*. Rand McNally, Chicago

AMERY, L. S. (1904). In discussion of Mackinder, H. J., 'The geographical pivot of history', *Geogrl J.* xxiii, 293-307

AMERY, L. S. (1953). *My political life: i, England before the storm, 1896-1914*. Hutchinson, London

ARMYTAGE, W. H. G. (1955). *Civic universities*. Benn, London

ARON, R. (1966). *Peace and war: a theory of international relations*, trans. R. Howard and A. B. Fox. Weidenfeld and Nicolson, London

BAAS (1897). British Association for the Advancement of Science, 'The position of geography in the educational system of the country', in *Report*, 67th meeting (Toronto 1897), 370-409

BAKER, J. N. L. (1963). *The history of geography*. Blackwell, Oxford

BAKER, J. N. L. and GILBERT, E. W. (1944). 'The doctrine of an axial belt of industry in England', *Geogrl J.* ciii, 49-72

BALDWIN, H. N. (1955). 'The Soviet navy', *Foreign Affairs* xxxiii, 587-604

BARKER, E. (1953). *Age and youth*. OUP, London

BARNES, J. and NICHOLSON, D. (1980). *The Leo Amery Diaries, i, 1896-1929*. Hutchinson, London

BARRACLOUGH, G. (1978). *The Times atlas of world history*. Times Books, London

BBC (1980). British Broadcasting Corporation, 'Six continents', Third Programme, 28 May 1980

BENUZZI, F. (1952). *No picnic on Mount Kenya*. Kimber, London

BEVERIDGE, W. (1953). *Power and influence: an autobiography*. Hodder and Stoughton, London

BLACKSELL, M. (1977). *Post-war Europe: a political geography*. Dawson, London

BLOUET, B. W. (1973). 'The maritime origins of Mackinder's heartland thesis', *Great Plains—Rocky Mountain Geogrl J.* iv, 6-11

BLOUET, B. W. (1975). *Sir Halford Mackinder 1861-1947: some new perspectives*. Oxford School of Geography, Research paper 13, Oxford

BLOUET, B. W. (1976). 'Halford Mackinder's heartland thesis', *Great Plains—Rocky Mountain Geogrl J.* v, 2–6

BLOUET, B. W. (1976a). 'Sir Halford Mackinder as British High Commissioner to South Russia, 1919–20', *Geogrl J.* cxiii, 228–36

BLOUET, B. W. (1977). 'H. G. Wells and the evolution of some geographic concepts', *Area* ix, 49–52

BOL. SOV. ENTS. (1952). *Bol'shaya sovetskaya entsiklopediya*, 2nd ed., Gosudarstvennoye nauchnoye izdatel'stvo, Moscow, x, 559–60

BOL. SOV. ENTS. (1971). *Bol' shaya sovetskaya entsiklopediya*, 3rd. ed. vi, 366, Sovetskaya Entsiklopediya, Moscow

BOND, B. J. (1972). *The Victorian army and the Staff College, 1854–1914*, Eyre Methuen, London

BOWMAN, I. (1942). 'Geography versus geopolitics', *Geogrl Rev.* xxxii, 646–58

BOWMAN, I. (1946). 'The strategy of territorial decisions', *Foreign Affairs* xxiv, 177–94

BULLOCK, A. and STALLYBRASS, O. (1977) eds. *The Fontana dictionary of modern thought*, Collins, London

BUNGE, W. W. (1973). 'The geography of human survival', *Annals of the Assoc. of Am. Geog.* lxiii, 275–95

BURGESS, R. (1976). *Marxism and geography*. Dept of Geog., University College, London

BUTTIMER, A. (1974). *Values in geography*. AAG Resource paper no. 24, Washington, DC

CAB. 23/20 (1920). Public Record Office, Cabinet Papers, 'Meeting of the Cabinet, 29 Jan. 1920', Cabinet 6 (20), Cab. 23/20

CAB. 129/25 (1948). Public Record Office, Cabinet Papers, 'The threat to Western civilization', memorandum to the Cabinet from Ernest Bevin, For. Sec., 3 March 1948, Cab. 129/25

CANTOR, L. M. (1960). *Halford Mackinder: his contribution to geography and education*, unpublished MA thesis, University of London (may be seen at University of London Library)

CANTOR, L. M. (1960a). 'Halford Mackinder: pioneer of adult education', *Rewley House Papers* iii (1960–1), 9, 24–9

CANTOR, L. M. (1962). 'The Royal Geographical Society and the projected London Institute of Geography, 1892–1899', *Geogrl J.* cxxviii, 30–5

CARLSON, L. (1958). *Geography and world politics*. Prentice Hall, Englewood Cliffs, NJ

CÉLÉRIER, P. (1955). *Géopolitique et géostratégie*. Presses Universitaires de France, Paris

CHAMBERLAIN, A. (1936). *Politics from inside: an epistolary chronicle*. Cassell, London

CHAMBERS, F. F. (1963). *This age of conflict*. Hart-Davis, London

CHILDS, W. M. (1933). *Making a university: an account of the university movement at Reading*. Dent, London

CHISHOLM, G. C. (1919). 'The geographical prerequisites of a league of nations', *Scot. Geogrl Mag.* xxxv, 248–56

COCHRAN, C. (1972). 'Mackinder's heartland theory: a review', *Assoc. of N. Dakota Geog. Bulletin* xxiv, 29–31

COHEN, P. (1971). 'The erosion of surface naval power', *Foreign Affairs* xlix, 330–41

COHEN, S. B. (1963). *Geography and politics in a divided world*. Methuen, London

COHEN, S. B. (1968). 'The contemporary geopolitical setting', in *Essays in political geography* (ed. C. A. Fisher), 61–72. Methuen, London

COLE, J. P. (1963). *Geography of world affairs*, 2nd. ed. Penguin, Harmondsworth

COLE, M. (1949), ed. *The Webbs and their work*. Muller, London

COOKE, R. U. and ROBSON, B. T. (1976). 'Geography in the United Kingdom, 1972–6: report to the 23rd international geographical congress in Moscow in July 1976', *Geogrl J.* cxlii, 81–100

COONES, P. (1979). 'Manufacture in pre-industrial England: a bibliography', *J. of Hist. Geog.* v, 127–55

CRAWFORD, O. G. S. (1955). *Said and done: the autobiography of an archaeologist*. Weidenfeld and Nicolson, London

CRESSEY, G. B. (1945). *The basis of Soviet strength*. McGraw-Hill, New York

CRONE, G. R. (1948). 'A German view of geopolitics', *Geogrl J.* cxi, 104–8

CRONE, G. R. (1951). *Modern geographers*. RGS, London

CRONE, G. R. (1962). Review of E. W. Gilbert's Mackinder centenary lecture: 'Sir Halford Mackinder, 1861–1947: an appreciation of his life and work', 20 June 1961, *Geography* xlvii, 212

CRONE, G. R. (1967). *Background to political geography*. Museum Press, London

DAVIDSON, I. (1979). 'The flaw in U.S. foreign policy', *Financial Times*, London, 1 Dec. 1979, 21

DEANE JONES, I. (1931). *The English revolution: an introduction to English history, 1603–1714*. Heinemann, London

DE BLIJ, H. J. (1967). *Systematic political geography*. Wiley, New York

DE GAULLE, C. (1970). *Mémoires d'espoir: le renouveau, 1958–62*. Plon, Paris

DENIKINE, A. (1930). *The white army*, trans. C. Zvegintzov. Cape, London

DICKINSON, R. E. (1969). *Makers of modern geography*. Routledge and Kegan Paul, London

DICKINSON, R. E. (1976). *Regional concept: the Anglo-American leaders*. Routledge & Kegan Paul, London

DILLON, E. J. (1919). *The inside story of the peace conference*. Hutchinson, London

DOORNKAMP, J. C. and WARREN, K. (1980). 'Geography in the United Kingdom', report to the 24th Int. Geogrl Congr. (Tokyo, 1980), *Geogrl J.* cxlvi, 94–110

DRYER, C. R. (1920). 'Mackinder's "World Island" and its American "satellite"', *Geogrl Rev.* ix, 205–7

DUGAN, A. B. (1962). 'Mackinder and his critics reconsidered', *J. of Politics* xxiv, 241–57

DUTTON, E. A. T. (1929). *Kenya Mountain*. Cape, London

EARLE, E. M. (1943). *Makers of modern strategy: military thought from Machiavelli to Hitler*. Princeton UP, Princeton, NJ

EAST, W. G. (1950). 'How strong is the heartland?', *Foreign Affairs* xxix, 78–93

EAST, W. G. and MOODIE, A. E. (1956). *The changing world: studies in political geography*. Harrap, London

ENGLISH, J. S. (1974). *Halford J. Mackinder (1861–1947)*. Gainsborough

EUSFTR (1969). *Essential United States foreign trade routes*. US Dept of Commerce, Washington, DC

FAIRGRIEVE, J. (1915). *Geography and world power*. Univ. of London Press, London

FALLS, C. (1948). 'Geography and world strategy', *Geogrl J.* cxii, 4–15

FAWCETT, C. B. (1947). 'Marginal and interior lands of the old world', *Geography* xxxii, 1–12; also in *New Compass of the World* ed. Weigert *et al.* Harrap, London (1949)

FEST, J. C. (1974). *Hitler*, trans. fr. German by R. & C. Winston, Weidenfeld and Nicolson, London

FIRTH, C. R. (1918). *The Oxford School of Geography*. Blackwell, Oxford

FISHER, C. A. (1963). 'The changing significance of the Commonwealth in the political geography of Great Britain', *Geography* xlviii, 113–129

FISHER, C. A. (1965). *The reality of place*. School of Oriental and African Studies, London

FISHER, C. A. (1968) ed. *Essays in political geography*. Methuen, London

FISHER, C. A. (1970). 'Whither regional geography?', *Geography* lv, 373–89

FISHER, C. A. (1971). 'Containing China? II: concepts and applications of containment', *Geogrl J.* cxxxvii, 281–310

FLETCHER, G. (1591). 'Of the Russe Commonwealth' in *Russia at the close of the sixteenth century* (ed. E. H. Bond). Hakluyt Society, London, 1856

FLEURE, H. J. (1953). 'Sixty years of geography and education', *Geography* xxxviii, 231-264

FLEURE, H. J. (1961). 'Chairs of geography in British universities', *Geography* xlvi, 349-53

FO (1920). (1919-20). Public Record Office, Foreign Office 800/251. Russia: private papers of H. J. Mackinder relating to his mission to South Russia

FREEMAN, T. W. (1961). *A hundred years of geography*. Duckworth, London

FREEMAN, T. W. (1975). 'Eminent Edwardians', *Geogrl Mag.* xlvii, 575-7

FREEMAN, T. W. (1980). *A history of modern British geography*. Longman, London

FREEMAN, T. W. (1980a). 'The Royal Geographical Society and the development of geography' in *Geography yesterday and tomorrow* (ed. E. H. Brown). OUP, Oxford

FREEMAN, T. W. and PINCHEMEL, P. (1979). *Geographers: biographical studies*, iii. Mansell, London

FRYER, D. W. (1974). 'A geographer's inhumanity to man', *Annals of Assoc. of Am. Geog.* lxiv, 479-82

GARNETT, A. (1967). 'Some climatological problems in urban geography with reference to air pollution', *Trans. Inst. Brit. Geog.* xlii, 21-2

GILBERT, E. W. (1947). 'The Right Honourable Sir Halford J. Mackinder, P. C., 1861-1947', *Geogrl J.* cx, 94-99

GILBERT, E. W. (1951). 'Seven lamps of geography: an appreciation of the teaching of Sir Halford J. Mackinder', *Geography* xxxvi, 21-41

GILBERT, E. W. (1951a). '*The scope and methods of geography*' and '*The geographical pivot of history*' by Sir Halford J. Mackinder reprinted with an introduction by E. W. Gilbert. RGS, London

GILBERT, E. W. (1955). *Geography as a humane study*, inaugural lecture delivered before the University of Oxford on 12 November 1954. Clarendon Press, Oxford

GILBERT, E. W. (1961). *Sir Halford Mackinder 1861-1947: an appreciation of his life and work*. Bell, London

GILBERT, E. W. (1961a). 'The Rt Honourable Sir Halford J. Mackinder, P. C., 1861-1947', *Geogrl J.* cxxvii, 27-9

GILBERT, E. W. (1968). 'Mackinder, Halford' in *International encyclopedia of the social sciences*. New York, 515-6

GILBERT, E. W. (1971). 'The R.G.S. and geographical education in 1871', *Geogrl J.* cxxxvii, 200-2

GILBERT, E. W. (1972). *British pioneers in geography.* David & Charles, Newton Abbot

GILBERT, E. W. (1975). 'Sir Halford John Mackinder' in *DNB*, (compact ed.), 2772. OUP, Oxford

GILBERT, E. W. and PARKER, W. H. (1969). 'Mackinder's "Democratic ideals and reality" after 50 years' in *Geogrl J.* cxxxv, 228–31

GILBERT, M. (1975) *Winston S. Churchill*, iv: 1916–22. Heinemann, London

GOBLET, Y. M. (1956). *Political geography and the world map.* Philip, London

GOTTMANN, J. (1952). *La politique des états et leur géographie.* Armand Colin, Paris

GOUDIE, A. S. (1980). 'George Nathaniel Curzon—superior geographer', *Geogrl J.* cxlvi, 203–9

GRAHAM, G. S. (1965). *The politics of naval supremacy.* CUP, Cambridge

GREEN, J. R. and A. S. (1879). *A short geography of the British islands.* Macmillan, London

GREGORY, D. (1978). *Ideology, science and human geography.* Hutchinson, London

GYORGY, A. (1944). *Geopolitics: the new German science.* Univ. of California Press, Berkeley and Los Angeles

HACKETT, J. (1978) ed. *The third world war August 1985: a future history.* Sidgwick & Jackson, London

HALL, A. H. (1955). 'Mackinder and the course of events', *Annals of the Am. Assoc. of Geog.* xlv, 109–26

HARRIES, K. D. (1974). *The geography of crime and justice.* McGraw Hill, New York

HARRISON, R. E. and Weigert, H. W. (1943). 'World view and strategy' in *Compass of the world* (ed. H. W. Weigert and V. Stefansson), 74–88. Harrap, London

HART, J. F. (1972) ed. *Annals of the Assoc. of Am. Geog.* lxii, part 2

HARTSHORNE, R. (1939). *The nature of geography: a critical survey of current thought in the light of the past.* Assoc. of Am. Geog., Lancaster, Pa

HARTSHORNE, R. (1954). 'Political geography' in *American geography, inventory and prospect* (ed. P. E. James and C. F. Jones). Assoc. of Am. Geog., Syracuse

HARTSHORNE, R. (1959). *Perspective on the Nature of Geography.* Assoc. of Am. Geog. (also Murray, London, 1960)

HARTSHORNE, R. (1964). 'What is political geography?' in *Political and geographical relationships* (ed. W. A. D. Jackson), 52–60. Prentice Hall, Englewood Cliffs, NJ

HAUSHOFER, K. (1924). *Geopolitik des Pazifischen Ozeans.* Vorwinckel, Berlin

HAUSHOFER, K. (1925). 'Der ost-eurasiatische Zukunftsblock', *Zeitschrift für Geopolitik ii, 81–7*

HAUSHOFER, K. (1936). *Weltpolitik von heute*. Gerlag und Vertriebsgesellschaft, Berlin

HAYEK, F. A. (1946). 'The London School of Economics 1895–1945', *Economica*, NS xiii, 1–31

HENRIKSON, A. K. (1980). 'America's changing place in the world: from "periphery" to "centre" ' in *Spatial variations in politics* (ed. J. Gottmann), 73–100. Sage, London

HEROLD, D. (1974). ' "Political geography" und "geopolitics" ', *Die Erde* cv, 200–13

HEWINS, W. A. S. (1929). *Apologia of an imperialist*. Constable, London

HEYDEN, G. (1958). *Kritik der deutschen Geopolitik*. Dietz, Berlin

HEYLYN, P. (1657). *Cosmographie* (2nd ed.,). Seile, London. (first ed. 1652)

HONEYBONE, R. C. (1954). 'Balance in geography and education', *Geography* xxxix, 91–101

HOOSON, D. J. M. (1962). 'A new Soviet heartland?' *Geogrl J.* cxxviii, 19–29

HOOSON, D. J. M. (1964). *A new Soviet heartland?* Van Nostrand, Princeton, NJ

HOOSON, D. J. M. (1972). Preface to E. W. Gilbert, *British Pioneers in geography*. David & Charles, Newton Abbot

HORSEY, J. (1591). 'Travels' in *Russia at the close of the sixteenth century* (ed. E. H. Bond). Hakluyt Society, London

HOUSE, J. W. (1976). *The geographer in a turbulent age*. Clarendon Press, Oxford

HOWARTH, O. J. R. (1951). 'The centenary of Section E (Geography)', *Advmt Sci.* viii, 151–65

HUGHES, W. (1847). *Remarks on geography as a branch of popular education*. Bell, London

HUGHES, W. (1851). *A manual of British geography*. Black, Edinburgh

HUGHES, W. (1863). *The geography of British history: a geographical description of the British Islands at successive periods from the earliest times to the present day*. Longmans, Green, London

HUGHES, W. (1870). *Geography in its relation to physical science*. Longmans, Green, London

HUNTINGTON, E. (1943). 'The influence of geography and climate upon history', in *Compass of the World* (ed. H. Weigert and V. Stefansson), 174–89. Harrap, London

HUXLEY, T. H. (1877). *Physiography: an introduction to the study of nature*. Macmillan, London

IISS (1979). *Strategic survey 1978.* International Institute for Strategic Studies, London

IISS (1979a). *The military balance 1979-80.* International Institute for Strategic Studies, London

IISS (1980). *Strategic survey, 1979.* International Institute for Strategic Studies, London

IMPERIAL SHIPPING COMMITTEE (1939). *Report of the proceedings of the meeting of the Committee on the 21st April 1939: resignation of the Chairman and election of his successor.* HMSO, London

ISACHENKO, A. G. (1971). *Razvitiye geografícheskikh idey.* Mysl', Moscow

JACKSON, W. A. D. (1962). 'Mackinder and the communist orbit', *Canadian Geographer* vi, 12-21

JACKSON, W. A. D. (1964). *Politics and geographic relationships: readings in the nature of political geography.* Prentice Hall, Englewood Cliffs, NJ

JACOBSEN, H-A. (1979). ' "Kampf und Lebensraum": Karl Haushofers "Geopolitik" und der Nationalsozialismus', *Aus Politik und Zeitgeschichte* (Beilage zur Wochenzeitung das Parlament) 25 August 1979, 17-21

JACOBSEN, H-A. (1979a). *Karl Haushofer, Leben und Werk,* 2 vols. Boldt, Boppard/Rhein

JAMES, P. E. (1972). *All possible worlds: a history of geographical ideas,* Odyssey Press, Indianapolis, NY

JOERG, W. L. G. (1922). 'Recent geographical work in Europe', *Geogrl Rev.* xii, 431-84

JOHNSTON, R. J. (1979). *Geography and geographers: Anglo-American human geography since 1945.* Arnold, London

JONES, E. H. (1974). Review of H. C. Darby, *A new historical geography of England, Annals of the Am. Assoc. of Geog.* lxiv, 460-1

JONES, S. B. (1954). 'Global strategic views', *Geogrl Rev.* xliv, 492-508

JONES, S. B. (1955). 'Views of the political world', *Geogrl Rev.* xlv, 309-26

JONES, S. B. (1964). 'Global strategic views' in *Politics and geographic relationships* (ed. W. A. D. Jackson). Prentice Hall, Englewood Cliffs, NJ

KAISER, K. (1979). 'Die neue Ostpolitik', *Aus Politik und Zeitgeschichte* (Beilage zur Wochenzeitung das Parlament), 27 Oct. 1979, 3-10

KAISER, K. (1980). In *Fortune,* 19 May 1980, 125-8

KAISER, R. (1977). 'The ring of American steel around Russia', *The Guardian,* 14 March 1977, 11

KELTIE, J. S. (1886). *Geographical education.* Murray, London

KELTIE, J. S., MACKINDER, H. J., and RAVENSTEIN, E. G. (1889-92) eds. *The world's great explorers and explorations.* Philip, London

KENDLE, J. E. (1967). *The colonial and imperial conferences 1887-1911: a study in imperial organization.* Longmans, London

KENNAN, G. (1947). 'The sources of Soviet conduct', *Foreign Affairs* xxv, 566-82

KERNER, R. J. (1946). *The urge to the sea: the course of Russian history.* Univ. of California Press, Berkeley and Los Angeles

KRISTOF, L. K. D. (1960). 'The origins and evolution of geopolitics', *J. of Conflict Resolution* iv, 15-51

KRISTOF, L. K. D. (1976). 'Mackinder's concept of heartland and the Russians', preprint, XXIII Int. Geogrl Congr., Symposium K5: History of Geographical Thought (Leningrad, 22-6 July 1976)

KRUSZEWSKI, C. (1940). 'Germany's Lebensraum', *Am. Pol. Sci. Rev.* xxxiv, 964-75

KRUSZEWSKI, C. (1954). 'The pivot of history', *Foreign Affairs* xxxii, 388-401

LATTIMORE, O. (1953). 'The new political geography of Inner Asia', *Geogrl J.* cxix, 17-30

LEARMONTH, A. (1971). *Approaches to political geography,* Open Univ. Press, Bletchley

LUKASHEV, K. I. (1953). 'Geostrategicheskiye konseptsii amerikan-skikh geopolitikov', *Izvestiya vsesoyuznogo geograficheskogo obshchesta* xxxv, 426-7

LYTTELTON, E. (1917). *Alfred Lyttelton: an account of his life.* Longmans, Green, London

MABOGUNJE, N. (1980). 'The dynamics of centre-periphery relations: the need for a new geography of resource development', *Trans. Inst. Brit. Geog.* v, 277-96

MACKENZIE, N. (1978) ed. *The letters of Sidney and Beatrice Webb, ii, Partnership 1892-1912.* CUP, London

MACKINDER, H. J. (1880). 'Geological Epsom', *The Epsomian,* Jan. 1880, March 1880

MACKINDER, H. J. (1885). *Syllabus of a course of eight lectures delivered at Bath by Mr H. J. Mackinder, BA., late Junior Student of Christ Church, on 'Wealth and Wages'.* Oxford University Extension, Oxford

MACKINDER, H. J. (1885a). *Syllabus of a course of lectures on the world— the battlefield of wind, water and rocks.* Oxford University Extension, Oxford

MACKINDER, H. J. (1886). *The new geography,* Oxford University Extension, Oxford

MACKINDER, H. J. (1887). 'The scope and methods of geography', *Proc. RGS NS* ix, 141-60

MACKINDER, H. J. (1887a). 'The teaching of geography at the universities', *Proc. RGS NS* ix, 698-701

MACKINDER, H. J. (1888). *Syllabus of a course of lectures on the history and geography of international politics.* Oxford University Extension, Oxford

MACKINDER, H. J. (1888a). Note on geographical terminology, *Proc. RGS NS* x, 732–3

MACKINDER, H. J. (1888b). *Syllabus of home reading in geography.* Alden, Oxford

MACKINDER, H. J. (1888c). *Syllabus of a course of lectures on physiography.* Oxford University Extension, Oxford

MACKINDER, H. J. (1888d). Report on the year's progress at Oxford, *Proc. RGS NS* x, 531–3

MACKINDER, H. J. (1889). 'Four lectures on the teaching of geography: a summary', *Educational Times and J. of the College of Preceptors* lxii, 504

MACKINDER, H. J. (1889a). Report on the year's progress at Oxford, *Proc. RGS NS* xi, 502–3

MACKINDER, H. J. (1890). 'The physical basis of political geography', *Scot. Geogr, Mag.* vi, 78–84

MACKINDER, H. J. (1890a). 'On the necessity of thorough teaching in general geography as a preliminary to the teaching of commercial geography', *J. of the Manchester Geogrl. Soc.* vi, 1–6

MACKINDER, H. J. (1890b). Report on the year's progress at Oxford, *Proc. RGS NS* xii, 419–21

MACKINDER, H. J. (1890c). Remarks at the presentation of training college prizes, *Proc. RGS NS* xii, 476–8

MACKINDER, H. J. (1891). Report on the year's progress at Oxford, *Proc. RGS NS* xiii, 428–9

MACKINDER, H. J. (1892). 'The education of citizens', *Univ. Extension J.* i, 245–9

Mackinder, H. J. (1892a). Report on the year's progress at Oxford, *Proc. RGS NS* xiv, 398–400

MACKINDER, H. J. (1893), 'Geography at Oxford', *Geogrl J.* ii, 25–6

MACKINDER, H. J. (1894). Review of Reclus's *Universal Geography,* *Geogrl. J.* iv, 158–60

MACKINDER, H. J. (1894a). 'Geography at Oxford', *Geogrl J.* iv, 29–30

MACKINDER, H. J. (1895). 'Modern geography, German and English', presidential address to Section E (Geography), *Report 65th Mtg Brit. Assoc. Adv. Sci.* (Ipswich, 1895), *Trans. Section E,* 1–11. Also, *Geogrl J.* vi, 367–79

MACKINDER, H. J. (1895a). 'A French educational congress', *Univ. Extension J.* i, 24–5

MACKINDER, H. J. (1895b). 'The case for a treasury grant restated', *Univ. Extension J.* i, 6-7

MACKINDER, H. J. (1895c). 'Geography at Oxford', *Geogrl J.* vi, 25-6

MACKINDER, H. J. (1895d). 'The relation between University Extension teaching and secondary education', in *Bryce Commission Report on Secondary Education* v, 302-4

MACKINDER, H. J. (1896). In discussion of H. R. Mill, 'Proposed geographical description of the British Isles based on the Ordnance Survey', *Geogrl J.* vii, 345-56, 357-8

MACKINDER, H. J. (1896a). In discussion of J. E. Marr, 'The waterways of the English Lakeland', *Geogrl J.* vii, 624-5

MACKINDER, H. J. (1896b). In discussion of educational papers, *Report Proc. VIth Int. Geogrl Congr.* (London 1895). Murray, London

MACKINDER, H. J. (1897). 'Geography at Oxford', *Geogrl J.* ix, 653-4

MACKINDER, H. J. (1898). 'Geography at Oxford', *Geogrl J.* xii, 8

MACKINDER, H. J. (1899). 'Geography at Oxford', *Geogrl J.* xiv, 87-8

MACKINDER, H. J. (1900). 'A journey to the summit of Mt Kenya, British East Africa', *Geogrl J.* xv, 453-86

MACKINDER, H. J. (1900a). 'The ascent of Mt Kenya', *Alpine J.* xx, 102-10

MACKINDER, H. J. (1900b). 'The great trade routes', *J. of the Inst. of Bankers* xxi, 137-55, 266-73

MACKINDER, H. J. (1900-8). Stanford's new orographical maps, compiled under the direction of H. J. Mackinder: *the British Isles*, 1900; *Europe*, 1900; *Africa*, 1905; *Palestine*, 1906; *Asia*, 1906; *North America*, 1906; *South America*, 1907; *Australasia*, 1908. Edward Stanford, London

MACKINDER, H. J. (1902). *Britain and the British Seas.* Clarendon Press, Oxford; Heinemann, London

MACKINDER, H. J. (1903). 'Higher education' in *The Nation's Need* (ed. S. Wilkinson), Constable, London

MACKINDER, H. J. (1903a). 'Geography in education', *Geogrl Teacher* ii, 95-101. Also *J. of Geog.* ii, 499-506

MACKINDER, H. J. (1904). 'The geographical pivot of history', *Geogrl J.* xxiii, 421-37

MACKINDER, H. J. (1904a). 'The development of geographical teaching out of nature study', *Geogrl Teacher* ii, 191-7

MACKINDER, H. J. (1905). 'Man-power as a measure of national and imperial strength', *National and English Review* xiv, 136-45

MACKINDER, H. J. (1905a). *Seven lectures on the United Kingdom.* Philip, London

MACKINDER, H. J. (1906). *Money-power and man-power.* Simkin-Marshall, London

MACKINDER, H. J. (1906a). *Our own islands*. Philip, London
MACKINDER, H. J. (1907). *Britain and the British Seas*, 2nd. ed. Clarendon Press, Oxford
MACKINDER, H. J. (1907a). 'On thinking imperially' in *Lectures on Empire* (ed. M. E. Sadler). London
MACKINDER, H. J. (1907b). *Address on the opening of the class for the administrative training of Army Officers*. HMSO, London
MACKINDER, H. J. (1908). *The Rhine: its valley and history*. Chatto and Windus, London
MACKINDER, H. J. (1908a). *Lands beyond the Channel: an elementary study in geography*. Philip, London
MACKINDER, H. J. (1908b). 'The advance of geographical science by local scientific societies', *Naturalist* 614, 70–4
MACKINDER, H. J. (1908c). 'The geographical environment of Great Britain' in *Encyclopedia Americana*
MACKINDER, H. J. (1909). In discussion of W. M. Davis, 'The systematic description of land forms', *Geogrl J*. xxxiv, 320–1
MACKINDER, H. J. (1909a). 'Geographical conditions affecting the British Empire, I: The British Islands', *Geogrl J*. xxxiii, 462–76
MACKINDER, H. J. (1909b). 'The geographical conditions of the defence of the United Kingdom', *National Defence*, iii (July 1909), 89–107
MACKINDER, H. J. (1910). *India: eight lectures prepared for the visual instruction committee of the Colonial Office*. Philip, London
MACKINDER, H. J. (1910a). *Distant lands: an elementary study in geography*. Philip, London
MACKINDER, H. J. (1910b). Introduction to E. Smith, *The Reigate sheet of the One-Inch O.S.: a study in the geography of the Surrey Hills*. Black, London
MACKINDER, H. J. (1911). 'The teaching of geography from an imperial point of view, and the use which should be made of visual instruction', *Geogrl Teacher* vi, 79–86
MACKINDER, H. J. (1911a). *The nations of the modern world: an elementary study in geography*. Philip, London
MACKINDER, H. J. (1911b). In discussion of W. L. Grant, 'Geographical conditions affecting the development of Canada', *Geogrl J*. xxxviii, 377
MACKINDER, H. J. (1912). 'The strategical geography of the Near East', *J. of the Royal Artillery* xxxix, 195–204
MACKINDER, H. J. (1913). 'The teaching of geography and history as a combined subject', *Geogrl Teacher* vii, 4–19
MACKINDER, H. J. (1914). *The teaching of geography and history: a study in method*. Philip, London

MACKINDER, H. J. (1914a). *The modern British state: an introduction to the study of civics*. Philip, London

MACKINDER, H. J. (1914b). *Our island history: an elementary study in history*. Philip, London

MACKINDER, H. J. (1915). In discussion of L. W. Lyde, 'Types of political frontier in Europe', *Geogrl J.* xlv, 142-3

MACKINDER, H. J. (1915a). Obituary of A. J. Herbertson, *Geogrl J.* xlv, 142-3

MACKINDER, H. J. (1916). Presidential address to the Geographical Association, *Geogrl Teacher* viii, 271-7

MACKINDER, H. J. (1916a). In *Constitutional problems: speeches at a conference held between representatives of the Home and Dominion parliaments, 28 July and 2 Aug. 1915*. Empire and Parliamentary Association, London

MACKINDER, H. J. (1917). 'Some geographical aspects of international reconstruction', *Scot. Geogr. Mag.* xxxiii, 1-11

MACKINDER, H. J. (1917a). In discussion of the resolutions of the Five Associations, *Geogrl Teacher* ix, 46-51

MACKINDER, H. J. (1919). *Democratic ideals and reality: a study in the politics of reconstruction*. Constable, London; Holt, New York

MACKINDER, H. J. (1920). 'General report with appendices on the situation in South Russia; recommendations for future policy' in *Documents on British foreign policy, 1919-39*, 1st series, iii, (ed. E. L. Woodward and R. Butler), no. 656, 768-87. HMSO, London, 1949

MACKINDER, H. J. (1921). 'Geography as a pivotal subject in education', *Geogrl J.* lvii, 376-84

MACKINDER, H. J. (1921a). 'L'envoi: a note on the future of Glasgow', *Scot. Geogr. Mag.* xxxvii, 77-9

MACKINDER, H. J. (1922). 'The sub-continent of India', in *The Cambridge History of India, I: Ancient India* (ed. E. J. Rapson), cap. 1, pp. 1-36. CUP, Cambridge

MACKINDER, H. J. (1924). *The nations of the modern world: an elementary study in geography and history*, ii, *After 1914*. Philip, London

MACKINDER, H. J. (1924a). *The world war and after: a concise narrative and some tentative ideas*. Philip, London. The text is the same as MACKINDER (1924)

MACKINDER, H. J. (1925). 'The English tradition and the Empire: some thoughts on Lord Milner's credo and the imperial committees', *United Empire* xvi, 1-8

MACKINDER, H. J. (1927). In discussion of J. W. Gregory, 'The fiords of the Hebrides', *Geogrl J.* lxix, 212-16

MACKINDER, H. J. (1928). 'The content of philosophical geography',

presidential address to Section D (Human geography), *Report Proc.
Int. Geogrl Congr.* (Cambridge, 1928) 305-11, CUP, Cambrige, 1930

MACKINDER, H. J. (1928a). 'Two suggestions for the early historical
geography of England', *Report Proc. Int. Geogrl Congr.* (Cambridge,
1928), 410-1, CUP, Cambridge, 1930

MACKINDER, H. J. (1930). 'Recent economic developments in the
dominions, colonial and mandated territories', *J. of the R. United
Service Inst.* lxxv, 254-65

MACKINDER, H. J. (1930a), 'Mount Kenya in 1899', *Geogrl J.* lxxvi,
529-34

MACKINDER, H. J. (1931). 'The human habitat', *Records of the Brit.
Assoc. Adv. Sci.*, London. Also, *Scot. Geogr. Mag.* xlvii, 321-35

MACKINDER, H. J. (1931a). Speech on his resignation from the Imperial Economic Committee, Mackinder papers, Oxford Univ. Sch.
Geog.

MACKINDER, H. J. (1931b). In discussion of S. W. Woodridge and D.
J. Smetham, 'The glacial drifts of Essex and Hertfordshire, and
their bearing upon the agricultural and historical geography of the
region', *Geogrl J.* lxxviii, 266-9

MACKINDER, H. J. (1932). Speech at the anniversary dinner of the
RGS, *Geogrl J.* lxxx, 189-92

MACKINDER, H. J. (1933). 'The Empire Marketing Board: the attitude
of the Dominions', *United Empire* xxiv, 508-9

MACKINDER, H. J. (1934). 'The Empire and the world', *United Empire*
xxv, 519-22

MACKINDER, H. J. (1935). 'Progress of geography in the field and in
the study during the reign of His Majesty King George the Fifth:
the jubilee address delivered at the evening meeting of 13 May
1935', *Geogrl J.* lxxxvi, 1-12

MACKINDER, H. J. (1935a). Foreward to N. Mikhaylov, *Soviet Geography*, Methuen, London

MACKINDER, H. J. (1935b). 'The Crown', *United Empire* xxvi, 502

MACKINDER, H. J. (1937). 'The music of the spheres', *Proc. R. Philos.
Soc. Glasgow* lxiii, 170-81

MACKINDER, H. J. (1942). 'Geography, an art and a philosophy',
Geography xxvii, 122-30

MACKINDER, H. J. (1943). 'The round world and the winning of the
peace', *Foreign Affairs* xxi, 595-605

MACKINDER, H. J. (1943a). 'The development of geography: global
geography', *Geography* xxviii, 69-71

MACKINDER, H. J. (1944). Speech at the presentation of the medals at
the American Embassy by the American Ambassador, *Geogrl J.* ciii,
132-3

MACKINDER, H. J. (1945). Speech on receiving the Patron's Medal of the RGS, *Geogrl J.* cv, 230-2

MACKINDER, H. J. and SADLER, M. E. (1890). *University extension: has it a future?* Cassell, London

MACKINDER, H. J. and SADLER, M. E. (1891). *University extension, past, present and future.* Cassell, London

MAHAN, A. T. (1900). *The problem of Asia and its effects upon international policies.* Sampson Low, London

MALIN, J. C. (1944). 'Reflections on the closed-space doctrines of Turner and Mackinder and the challenge to their ideas by the air age', *Agricultural History* xviii, 65-74

MALIN, J. C. (1959). 'The contriving brain as the pivot of history. Sea, landmass and air power: some bearings of cultural technology upon the geography of international relations', in *Issues and conflicts* (ed. G. L. Anderson), Univ. of Kansas Press, Lawrence, Kans.

MARCUS, M. G. (1979). 'Coming full circle: physical geography in the twentieth century', *Annals of the Assoc. of Am. Geog.* lxix, 521-532

MARTIN, G. J. (1959). 'Political geography and geopolitics', *J. of Geog.* lviii, 441-4

MATTHEW, H. C. G. (1973). *The Liberal Imperialists: the ideas and politics of a post-Gladstonian* élite. OUP, London

MAZO, E. and HESS, S. (1968). *President Nixon: a political portrait.* Macdonald, London

MEDAWAR, P. B. *Induction and intuition in scientific thought.* American Philosophical Society, Philadelphia.

MEINIG, D. W. (1956). 'Heartland and Rimland in Eurasian history', *Western Political Quarterly* ix, 553-69

MEYER, H. C. (1946). 'Mitteleuropa in German political geography', *Annals of the Am. Assoc. of Geog.* xxxvi, 178-94

MEYER, H. E. (1980). 'Why we should worry about the Soviet energy crunch', *Fortune* 25 Feb. 1980.

MIKHAYLOV, N. (1935). *Soviet geography; the new industrial and economic distributions of the U.S.S.R.*, with a foreword by the Rt Hon. Sir Halford J. Mackinder. Methuen, London

MIKHAYLOV, N. (1967). 'Professor Makkinder i razgovor ob utopiyakh', *Sovetskiy Soyuz* 212, 20-1

MILL, H. R. (1890). 'The vertical relief of the globe', *Scot. Geogr. Mag.* vi, 182-7

MILL, H. R. (1902). Review of H. J. Mackinder, *Britain and the British seas, Geogrl J.* xix, 489-95

MILL, H. R. (1935). In discussion of H. J. Mackinder, 'Progress of geography ...', *Geogrl J.* lxxxvi, 13

MILL, H. R. (1951). *Hugh Robert Mill: an autobiography.* Longman, London

MILLS, D. R. (1956). 'The U.S.S.R.: a re-appraisal of Mackinder's heartland concept', *Scot. Geog. Mag.* lxxii, 144–52

MITCHELL, D. J. (1970). *1919: red mirage.* Cape, London.

MOMIGLIANO, A. (1944). 'Sea power in Greek thought', *Classical Rev.* lviii, 1–7

MOODIE, A. E. (n.d.). *Geography behind politics.* Hutchinson, London

MORGAN, W. B. and Moss, R. P. (1965). 'Geography and ecology: the concept of community and its relationship to environment', *Annals of the Assoc. of Am. Geog.* lv, 339–50

MORRISON, J. A. (1952). 'Russia and warm water', *United States Naval Proceedings*, lxxviii, 1169–70

MOSS, R. P. (1970). 'Authority and charisma: criteria of validity in geographical method', *South African Geographical J.* lii, 13–37

MUIR, R. (1975). *Modern political geography*, Macmillan, London

MULLER-WILLE, W. (1966). Politisch-geographische Leitbilder, reale Lebensräume and globale Spannungsfelder', *Geographische Zeitschrift* liv, 13–38

MURRAY, J. (1942). Inaugural address to the 1942 conference of Geographical Association, *Geography* xxvii, 117–121

NANSEN, F. (1914) *Through Siberia, the land of the future*, trans. A. G. Chater, Heinemann, London

NEUMANN, S. (1943). 'Fashions in space', *Foreign Affairs* xxi, 276–88

NEWBIGIN, M. I. (1925). Review of H. J. Mackinder, *The Nations of the Modern World, vol. ii—After 1914, Geogrl J.* lxvi, 375–6

NOLTE, E. (1965). *Three faces of fascism: action française, Italian fascism, national socialism.* Weidenfeld and Nicolson, London

ORME, A. R. (1980). 'The need for physical geography', *Professional Geographer* xxxii, 141–8

ORMSBY, H. (1947) 'The Rt Hon. Sir Halford J. Mackinder, P.C., 1861–1947 (obituary)', *Geography* xxxii, 136–7

PADELFORD, N. J., LINCOLN, G. A. and OLVEY, L. D. (1976). *The dynamics of international politics*, 3rd ed. Macmillan, New York.

PARKER, W. H. (1960). 'Europe: how far?', *Geogrl J.* cxxvi, 287–97

PARKER, W. H. (1968). *An historical geography of Russia.* Univ. of London Press, London

PARKER, W. H. (1972). *Superpowers: the United States and the Soviet Union compared.* Macmillan, London

PARTSCH, J. (1903). *Central Europe.* Heinemann, London

P.D. (1910–1922). *Parliamentary debates*, 5th series, House of Commons (Hansard)

PAULY, W. F. (1974). 'The writings of Halford Mackinder applied to the evolution of Soviet naval power', *Pennsylvania Geographer* xii, 3-7

PEARCE, A. J. (1962). Introduction to H. J. Mackinder, *Democratic ideals and reality*. Norton, New York

PEARCY, G. E., FIFIELD, R. H. and associates (1948). *World political geography*. Crowell, New York

POPPER, K. R. (1959). *The logic of scientific discovery*. Hutchinson, London

POSTAN, M. M. (1973). *Essays on medieval agriculture*. CUP, Cambridge

POTTER, E. B. and NIMITZ, C. W. (1960) eds. *Sea power*. Prentice Hall, New York

POUNDS, N. J. G. (1963). *Political geography*. McGraw-Hill, New York

PRESCOTT, J. R. V. (1972). *Political geography*. Methuen, London

RATZEL, F. (1897). *Politische Geographie oder die Geographie der Staaten, des Verkehrs und des Krieges*. Oldenbourg, München

RELPH, E. (1976). *Place and placelessness*. Pion, London

RGS (1887). 'Geography at Oxford', Geographical notes, *Proc. RGS NS* ix, 437

RGS (1887a). Oxford University extension lectures for 1887-8, Geographical notes. *Proc. RGS NS* ix, 681-2

RGS (1892). Geographical notes: the new session, *Proc. RGS NS* xiv, 700

RGS (1892a). Presentation of the training college prizes, *Proc. RGS NS* xiv, 489-90

RGS (1893). The monthly record: the Society, *Geogrl J*. i, 157-8

RGS (1893a). Meetings: presentation of the training college prizes, *Geogrl J*. ii, 81-2

RGS (1893b). The monthly record: the Society, *Geogrl J*. ii, 455

RGS (1895). The monthly record: educational lectures, *Geogrl J*. v, 76-7

RGS (1895a). The monthly record: the Society—Mr Mackinder's lectures, *Geogrl J*. v, 165-6

RGS (1895b). The monthly record: educational lectures, *Geogrl J*. vi, 381

RGS (1899). Mr Mackinder's expedition to Mt Kenya, *Geogrl J*. xiv, 93-4

RGS (1942). The monthly record: the Society—Mr Mackinder's lectures, *Geogrl J*. v, 165-6

RGS (1943). The monthly record: medals for British geographers, *Geogrl J*. cii, 273

RGS (1944). The monthly record: presentation of the medals awarded by the American Geographical Society to two British geographers, *Geogrl J.* ciii, 131–4

RGS (1945). The monthly record: medals and awards, *Geogrl J.* cv, 76

RGS (1945a). Meetings: session 1944–5, annual general meeting, 25 June 1945, *Geogrl J.* cv, 230–2

ROBINSON, G. and PATTEN, J. (1980). 'Edmund W. Gilbert and the development of historical geography', *J. of Hist. Geog.* vi, 400–19

ROXBY, P. M. (1914). 'Mr Mackinder's books on the teaching of geography and history', *Geogrl Teacher* vii, 404–7

RUSSELL, B. (1967). *Autobiography 1872–1914.* Unwin, London

SABINE, G. H. (1973). *A history of political theory* 4th ed. (revised by T. L. Thorson). Dryden Press, Hinsdale, Ill.

SAUER, C. O. (1925). *The morphology of landscape.* Univ. of California Press, Berkeley, Calif.

SCARGILL, D. I. (1976). 'The RGS and the foundations of geography at Oxford', *Geogrl J.* cxlii, 438–61

SCHAEFER, F. K. (1953). 'Exceptionalism in Geography: a methodological examination', *Annals of the Assoc. of Am. Geog.* xliii, 226–49

SCHÖLLER, P. (1959). 'Die Geopolitik im Weltbild des historischen Materialismus', *Erdkunde* xiii, 88–98

SEMENOFF, V. G. (1925). 'Das geopolitische Problem des russischen Revolution', *Zeitschrift für Geopolitik* ii, 548–58

SEMJONOV, J. N. (1955). *Die faschistische Geopolitik in Dienste des amerikanischen Imperialismus* (trans. fr. the Russian ed., Moscow, 1952). Berlin

SEMMELL, B. (1958). 'Sir Halford Mackinder: theorist of imperialism', *Can. J. Econ. and Polit. Sci.* xxiv, 554–61

SEVERSKY, A. P. de (1952). *Air power: key to survival.* Herbert Jenkins, London

SINNHUBER, K. A. (1954). 'Central Europe-Mitteleuropa-Europe Centrale: an analysis of a geographical term', *Trans. Inst. Br. Geog.*, Publication No. 20

SLATER, D. (1978). 'The poverty of modern geographical enquiry' in *Radical geography* (ed. R. Peet). Methuen, London

SLESSOR, J. C. (1954). *Strategy for the West.* Cassell, London

SMITH, J. R. (1943). 'Heartland, grassland and farmland' in *Compass of the world* (ed. H. W. Weigert and V. Stefansson). Macmillan, New York

SOMERVILLE, M. (1848). *Physical geography.* Murray, London

SPANIER, J. W. (1972). *American policy since world War II,* 4th ed. Nelson, London

SPATE, O. H. K. (1952). 'Toynbee and Huntington: a study in determinism', *Geogrl J.* cxviii, 406–24

SPENGLER, O. (1926). *The decline of the West*, vol. i: *Form and actuality* (trans. C. F. Atkinson). Allen & Unwin, London

SPENGLER, O. (1928). *The decline of the West*, ii: *Perspectives of world History* (trans. C. F. Atkinson). Allen & Unwin, London

SPINK, P. C. (1945). 'Further notes on the Kibo inner crater and the glaciers of Kilimanjaro and Mount Kenya', *Geogrl J.* cvi, 210–16

SPROUT, H. (1963). 'Geopolitical hypotheses in technological perspective', *World Politics* xv, 187–212

SPROUT, H. & M. (1964). 'Geography and international politics in an era of revolutionary change' in *Politics and geographic relationships* (ed. W. A. D. Jackson). Prentice Hall, Englewood Cliffs, NJ

SPYKMAN, N. J. (1944). *The Geography of the peace.* Harcourt Brace, New York

STAMP, L. D. (1947). Obituary of H. J. Mackinder, *Nature* clix, 530–1

STEPUN, F. (1962). 'Rossiya mezhdu Evropoy i Aziey', *Novyy Zhurnal* lxix, 251–76

STODDART, D. R. (1975). 'The RGS and the foundations of geography at Cambridge', *Geogrl J.* cxli, 1–24

STODDART, D. R. (1976). 'Mackinder: myth and reality in the establishment of British geography', preprint, XXIII Int. Geogrl Union, Symposium K5: History of Geographical Thought (Leningrad, 22–6 July 1976)

STODDART, D. R. (1980). 'The RGS and the "new geography": changing aims and changing roles in nineteenth century science', *Geogrl J.* cxlvi, 190–202

STRAUSZ-HUPÉ, R. (1942). *Geopolitics: the struggle for space and power.* Putnam, New York

SUMNER, B. H. (1951). 'Russia and Europe', *Oxford Slavonic Papers* ii, 1–16

SYLVESTER, J. A. (1968). 'Mackinder lernte von den Deutschen: eine ironische Kritik', *Zeitschrift für Geopolitik* xxxix, 55–9

SYMANSKI, R. (1974). 'Prostitution in Nevada', *Annals of the Am. Assoc. of Geog.* lxiv, 357–77

TAWNEY, R. H. (1926). *Religion and the rise of capitalism.* Pelican, London, 1938 (first published, 1926)

TAYLOR, A. J. P. (1965). *English history: 1914–1945.* Clarendon Press, Oxford

TAYLOR, E. G. R. (1915) *Mackinder's elementary studies in geography. Questions and exercises especially prepared as a companion to Distant Lands, Our Own Island and Lands Beyond the Channel.* Philip, London

TAYLOR, E. G. R. (1947). Remarks at annual general meeting of the RGS, 16 June 1947, *Geogrl J.* cix, 292

TAYLOR, P. J. (1980). *A materialist framework for political geography.* Seminar paper no. 37, Dept of Geography, Univ. of Newcastle

TAYLOR, T. G. (1951). 'Geopolitics and geopacifics' in *Geography in the twentieth century* (ed. T. G. Taylor), 587–608. Methuen, London

TEGGART, E. T. (1919). 'Geography as an aid to statecraft: an appreciation of Mackinder's *Democratic Ideals and Reality*', *Geogrl Rev.* viii, 227–42

TOYNBEE, A. J. (1924). *Greek historical thought from Homer to the age of Heraclitus.* Dent, London

TREVOR-ROPER, H. R. (1953). 'The mind of Adolf Hitler', an introductory essay to *Hitler's Table Talk 1941–1944.* Weidenfeld and Nicolson, London

TROLL, C. (1947). 'Die geografische Wissenschaft in Deutschland in die Jahren 1933 bis 1945', *Erdkunde* i, 3–48

TROLL, C. (1949). 'Geographical science in Germany during the period 1933–45', *Annals of the Am. Assoc. of Geog.* xxxix, 99–137

TROLL, C. (1952). 'Halford J. Mackinder als Geograph und Geopolitiker', *Erdkunde* vi, 177–8

ULLMAN, R. H. (1968). *Britain and the Russian civil war*, Princeton Univ. Press, Princeton, NJ

ULLMAN, R. H. (1972). *The Anglo-Soviet accord.* Princeton Univ. Press, Princeton, NJ

UNSTEAD, J. F. (1949). 'H. J. Mackinder and the new geography', *Geogrl J.* cxiii, 47–57

VNESH. TORG. (annual). *Vneshnaya torgovlya SSSR: statisticheskiy obzor.* Mezhdunarodnyye otnosheniya, Moscow

WALSH, E. A. (1943). 'Geopolitics and international morals' in *Compass of the World* (ed. H. W. Weigert and V. Stefansson), 12–39. Harrap, London

WALTERS, R. E. (1974). *The nuclear trap: an escape route.* Penguin, London

WALTERS, R. E. (1975). *Sea Power and the nuclear fallacy: a re-evaluation of global strategy.* Holmes & Meier, New York (the text is the same as for WALTERS (1974)).

WALTON, K. (1968). 'The unity of the physical environment', *Scot. Geogr. Mag.* lxxxiv, 5–14.

WARD, R. C. (1980). 'Water: a geographical issue' in *Geography to-day and tomorrow* (ed. E. H. Brown). OUP, Oxford

WARREN, C. (1887). Presidential address, Brit. Assoc. Adv. Sci. (Manchester 1887), *J. of the Manchester Geogr. Soc.* iii, 262–73

WARRINGTON, T. C. (1947). 'The autobiography of H. R. Mill', *Geography* xxxii (1947), 166

WARRINGTON, T. C. (1953), 'The beginnings of the Geographical Association', *Geography* xxxviii, 221–30

WEBB, B. (1948). *Our partnership* (ed. B. Drake and M. I. Cole). Longmans, Green, London

WEBB, M. B. (1952). *Diaries 1912–1924* (ed. M. I. Cole, 2 vols). Longmans, Green, London

WEIGERT, H. W. (1942). *Generals and geographers: the twilight of geopolitics*. OUP, New York

WEIGERT, H. W. (1943). 'Asia through Haushofer's glasses' in *Compass of the world* (ed. H. W. Weigert and V. Stefansson), 395–407. Harrap, London

WEIGERT, H. W. (1949). 'Heartland revisited' in *New compass of the world* (ed. H. W. Weigert, V. Stefansson, and R. E. Harrison). Harrap, London

WEIGERT, H. W., BRODIE, H., DOHERTY, E. W., FERNSTROM, J. R., FISCHER, E., and KIRK, D. (1957). *Principles of political geography*. Appleton-Century-Crofts, New York

WELLS, H. G. (1903). *Mankind in the making*. Chapman & Hall, London

WELLS, H. G. (1934). *Experiment in autobiography* (2 vols). Gollancz, London

WHEBELL, C. F. J. (1970). 'Mackinder's heartland theory in practice today', *Geogrl Mag.* xlii, 630–6

WHITTLESEY, D. (1943). 'Haushofer: the geopoliticians' in *Makers of modern strategy; military thought from Machiavelli to Hitler* (ed. E. M. Earle). Princeton Univ. Press, Princeton, NJ

WOODWARD, E. L. (1938). *The age of reform 1815–1870*. Clarendon Press, Oxford

WOODWARD, E. L. and BUTLER, R. (1949) eds. *Documents on British Foreign Policy 1919–1939*, first series, iii (1919). HMSO, London

WOOLDRIDGE, S. W. (1949). 'On taking the ge- out of geography', *Geography* xxxiv, 9–18

WOOLDRIDGE, S. W. and EAST, W. G. (1951), *The spirit and purpose of geography*. Hutchinson, London

WOOLDRIDGE, S. W. and LINTON, D. (1955). *Structure, surface and drainage in south-east England*. Philip, London

Index